THE COMPLETE IDIOT'S GUIDE® TO

The Catholic Catechism

by Mary DeTurris Poust with
Theological Advisor David I. Fulton, STD, JCD

ALPHA

A member of Penguin Group (USA) Inc.

ALPHA BOOKS

Published by the Penguin Group

Penguin Group (USA) Inc., 375 Hudson Street, New York, New York 10014, USA

Penguin Group (Canada), 90 Eglinton Avenue East, Suite 700, Toronto, Ontario M4P 2Y3, Canada (a division of Pearson Penguin Canada Inc.)

Penguin Books Ltd., 80 Strand, London WC2R 0RL, England

Penguin Ireland, 25 St. Stephen's Green, Dublin 2, Ireland (a division of Penguin Books Ltd.)

Penguin Group (Australia), 250 Camberwell Road, Camberwell, Victoria 3124, Australia (a division of Pearson Australia Group Pty. Ltd.)

Penguin Books India Pvt. Ltd., 11 Community Centre, Panchsheel Park, New Delhi—110 017, India

Penguin Group (NZ), 67 Apollo Drive, Rosedale, North Shore, Auckland 1311, New Zealand (a division of Pearson New Zealand Ltd.)

Penguin Books (South Africa) (Pty.) Ltd., 24 Sturdee Avenue, Rosebank, Johannesburg 2196, South Africa

Penguin Books Ltd., Registered Offices: 80 Strand, London WC2R 0RL, England

International Standard Book Number: 978-1-59257-707-1
Library of Congress Catalog Card Number: 2007937308

13   12   11   8   7   6   5

Interpretation of the printing code: The rightmost number of the first series of numbers is the year of the book's printing; the rightmost number of the second series of numbers is the number of the book's printing. For example, a printing code of 08-1 shows that the first printing occurred in 2008.

Printed in the United States of America

Note: This publication contains the opinions and ideas of its author. It is intended to provide helpful and informative material on the subject matter covered. It is sold with the understanding that the author and publisher are not engaged in rendering professional services in the book. If the reader requires personal assistance or advice, a competent professional should be consulted.

The author and publisher specifically disclaim any responsibility for any liability, loss, or risk, personal or otherwise, which is incurred as a consequence, directly or indirectly, of the use and application of any of the contents of this book.

Most Alpha books are available at special quantity discounts for bulk purchases for sales promotions, premiums, fund-raising, or educational use. Special books, or book excerpts, can also be created to fit specific needs.

For details, write: Special Markets, Alpha Books, 375 Hudson Street, New York, NY 10014.

Publisher: *Marie Butler-Knight*
Editorial Director: *Mike Sanders*
Managing Editor: *Billy Fields*
Executive Editor: *Randy Ladenheim-Gil*
Development Editor: *Susan Zingraf*
Production Editor: *Megan Douglass*
Copy Editor: *Jan Zoya*

Cartoonist: *Steve Barr*
Cover Designer: *Bill Thomas*
Book Designer: *Trina Wurst*
Indexer: *Johnna VanHoose Dinse*
Layout: *Chad Dressler*
Proofreader: *John Etchison*

For my husband, Dennis, and our children, Noah, Olivia, and Chiara. —MDP

For my mother, my mother's mother, and for Blessed Mary, the Mother of all Christians. —DIF

Nihil Obstat: Rev. John N. Fell, S.T.D.

Imprimatur: ✠ Paul G. Bootkoski,
Bishop of Metuchen,
September 19, 2007

Contents at a Glance

Contents

Foreword

Any institution with as long and influential a history as the Roman Catholic Church is worth getting to know better, particularly because its teachings have often been the subject of misunderstanding and misinterpretation. Whether you are a Catholic seeking to know more about this faith that believers consider divinely inspired, or simply curious about this church of more than a billion members, I suspect you will be helped, surprised, challenged, and even inspired by the *Catechism of the Catholic Church*, the official text of what the Catholic Church believes and teaches.

But aren't official documents, by their nature, usually not an easy read? Not to worry. This addition to the *Complete Idiot's Guide* series offers a look at the Catechism by a friend and former colleague whose writing combines intelligence and clarity, a respect for what the Church teaches, and an appreciation for the concerns and struggles real people face. Mary DeTurris Poust is a wife, mom, believer, inquirer, and journalist with more than two decades of experience writing about Catholic issues. She is, in my view, just the person to walk you through the Catechism. Your technical advisor, Monsignor David Fulton, is a brother priest and a distinguished theologian with a deep understanding of the faith and fidelity to the Church's teaching.

I hope you will enjoy this approachable and entertaining guide to the riches of the Catholic faith. More important, I hope that, like all good study guides, this one will also stir you to pick up and read the original, thereby adding to your knowledge and enriching your life.

Monsignor William Benwell, J.C.L.

Vicar General, Diocese of Metuchen

Introduction

What exactly is the *Catechism of the Catholic Church?* Is it a rulebook? No. Is it a religious education program? No. Is it a long list of do's and don'ts? No.

Many people—Catholics and non-Catholics alike—really don't know what the Catechism is all about. Its subject matter and hefty size can be a little off-putting to the average reader. But it is well worth the time it takes to study the teachings and beliefs it explores and explains.

This book is going to take all the mystery out of the Catechism and leave you with a solid and easy-to-understand knowledge of everything the Catholic Church teaches. By the time you're done, you'll have an in-depth appreciation of what it means to be a Catholic.

How This Book Is Organized

This book is divided into five sections. Its structure parallels that of the full *Catechism of the Catholic Church* in order to make this book most effective.

Part 1, "Decoding the Catechism," lays the groundwork for studying the Catechism. This is where you'll get the basic background you need to understand why the Catechism exists, who it's for, why it's important, and how to read it. In this part, you'll also find a little pop quiz to test your knowledge of all things Catholic.

Part 2, "A Profession of Faith," takes an in-depth look at the Apostles' Creed, which sums up the beliefs of the Catholic faith in prayer form. We'll take the creed line by line, exploring some of the most difficult-to-understand beliefs of the Catholic Church.

Part 3, "A Mystery Not Meant to Be Solved," focuses on the seven sacraments, which were instituted by Christ and entrusted to the Church. These sacraments fall into three categories: sacraments of initiation, sacraments of healing, and sacraments of commitment or service. In this part, we will also take an in-depth look at liturgy, which is the central action of the Catholic faith.

Part 4, "Living the Good Life," looks at how Catholic beliefs are put into action in everyday life. This is where we look at the Ten Commandments of the Old Testament and reflect on how Jesus expanded and transformed them into laws of love. If any part of the Catechism is like a rulebook, this is it.

Part 5, "Turning Toward Heaven," gets into the practice of prayer answering the questions why do we pray, how do we pray, and where do we pray. This part will give you some pointers on how to have a prayer life and where to go for help. It ends with a line-by-line reflection on the Our Father, the perfect prayer of the Christian faith.

A Little Help on the Side

Throughout each chapter, you will find special messages that provide additional insights or information.

Church Speak

Any words or phrases that might be unfamiliar or hard to understand are defined and explained here.

Teachable Moment

Sometimes we need to take a teaching from the Catechism and put it under the microscope in order to better understand it. These tips will answer some of the most common questions people have about specific Catholic teachings.

You're Absolved If ...

Everyone has some misconceptions about Catholic teaching. This is where you'll get the real scoop on what Catholics believe about some of the more controversial or misunderstood teachings.

True Confessions

You'd be surprised by some of the things the Catholic Church says and does. These tips will give you an insider's view of life in the Catholic Church.

Acknowledgments

I need to start by thanking my friend and colleague Maria Ruiz Scaperlanda, who connected me to this project and set the wheels in motion. Through her I found my agent, Marilyn Allen, whose confidence in me and whose ongoing support have been critical at every stage of this endeavor. I am also grateful to Randy Ladenheim-Gil, executive editor at Alpha; Susan Zingraf, development editor; Megan Douglass, production editor; and Jan Zoya, copy editor, for their encouragement, guidance, and patience. Thanks to everyone at Alpha for working so hard to make this book all that it is.

On the home front, I want to thank my husband and best friend, Dennis, whose knowledge of the Catholic Church and talent as a writer were invaluable to me as I worked on this book. More important, however, was his constant love and his willingness to take on many extra jobs around the house during the months that I was down in the basement or at the local library researching and writing. Our children, Noah, Olivia, and Chiara, also deserve special thanks for being so understanding of my busy schedule and my constant request for "a few more minutes" so I could finish a sentence, a page, a chapter.

Lots of people offered encouragement, prayers, and suggestions along the way, but there are several who deserve a personal thank-you:

Msgr. David Fulton, my theological advisor, has been an absolute treasure. We have never met in person, and yet he threw himself into this work, reviewing chapters in record time, whether he was battling the flu or grading finals or guiding his parish through Holy Week. I am impressed by his brilliance, but even more so by his kindness.

I never would have "found" Msgr. Fulton without the help of my dear friend Msgr. William Benwell, who wrote the foreword to this book. Throughout this project, Bill offered professional and priestly advice, insights, and suggestions, for which I am so grateful, but I am even more thankful for his friendship, encouragement, and sense of humor. I am blessed to have such a friend in my life.

Business colleagues Joyce Duriga and Donna Shelley-Baumler deserve a special note of gratitude for their patience and support. I had to put much of my work for them on hold during this process, and they gladly gave me the time and space I needed to complete this book because they knew how important it was to me.

Finally, I would like to thank my entire family for their unconditional love and for the foundation of faith that they built for me when I was young. This faith that I love, this Church that is not only at the center of my career but at the center of everything I do, began with my family, my mother in particular. There is simply no way I can ever adequately thank them for starting me on this amazing journey toward God.

Special Thanks to the Technical Reviewer

The Complete Idiot's Guide to the Catholic Catechism was reviewed by an expert who double-checked the accuracy of what you'll learn here, to help us ensure that this book gives you everything you need to know about the Catechism of the Catholic Church. Special thanks are extended to Msgr. David I. Fulton.

Trademarks

All terms mentioned in this book that are known to be or are suspected of being trademarks or service marks have been appropriately capitalized. Alpha Books and Penguin Group (USA) Inc. cannot attest to the accuracy of this information. Use of a term in this book should not be regarded as affecting the validity of any trademark or service mark.

Part 1

Decoding the Catechism

Reading the entire "official" Catechism of the Catholic Church from cover to cover would be a monumental project. It's not exactly breezy beach reading, which is why most people don't attempt to undertake it alone. That's where this book comes in.

We're going to dissect the full Catechism piece by piece, clarifying anything that could be confusing, and explaining beliefs that are, at their essence, beautiful, consistent, and grounded in the teachings of Jesus.

In the first two chapters of this book, we'll talk about the basics: what the Catechism is and what it is not, where it comes from, how to use it, and what it can mean for you personally. After that, we will begin at square one and work our way through the entire Catechism, one Church teaching at a time.

1

Not Your Grandmother's Catechism

In This Chapter

◆ The *Catechism of the Catholic Church* defined

◆ How to use the Catechism to further your understanding of Catholic faith and morals

◆ The Catechism of today as compared to the early days

◆ What the Catechism can mean for you

At first glance, just the concept of Catholic Catechism can seem overwhelming. It's not just the sheer volume of material involved, because there is a load of it, but it's also the subject matter. We're talking about some pretty heavy-duty *Church* teachings that can at times be confusing, controversial, or simply over the heads of those who don't have theology degrees.

Church Speak

The term **Church** in this book refers specifically to the Catholic Church.

But there's one more important aspect of the Catechism that people too often overlook: the beauty of the teachings it contains. That's right. The Catechism is a complete and beautiful explanation of Church teachings that many of us first learned about as children. By delving more deeply into these Catholic beliefs contained in the Catechism, you can come to a fuller adult understanding of what you've likely been professing, and living, for years.

If you're not Catholic, some of the Catechism's teachings may seem mysterious to you or the beliefs might seem unbelievable. So I can promise you this journey through the Catechism will certainly be enlightening. It will let you explore the depths of the Catholic faith and emerge with a deeper understanding of it and, hopefully, an appreciation for its beauty and breadth, whether you were raised Catholic or not.

What Catechism Is, and Is Not

Let's begin with an understanding of what the term *catechism* means. The word catechism refers to any manual used to instruct others in faith. When it is used in the specific context of the Catholic Church, as will be the case throughout this book, it means, simply, the instruction manual for followers of the Catholic faith. The *Catechism* refers to the specific book used by Catholics that contains all the teachings of the Catholic faith.

The Catechism is so chock-full of the do's and don'ts of life, it's easy to think of it as the official Catholic rulebook, but it's not. While there are some pretty specific do's and don'ts set forth in the Catechism, it goes much deeper and is about so much more than rules. It is about the most basic and meaningful teachings of the Catholic faith.

It's not about fire and brimstone. It's not about judgment. It's not about checking off where you hit or miss the mark in your life and thoughts. It's about faith, hope, love, and the teachings that bring these things to life in the world around you. It's about opening up the Christian faith in Catholicism in a way that invites all people to explore more deeply some of life's most basic questions.

When I think of the Catechism, I think of it as operating instructions for Catholics. Sure, there are plenty of rules spelled out in detail, but there are also entire sections explaining Catholic beliefs about everything from the creation of the universe to the coming of Jesus to the rhythm of prayer in our daily lives.

Church Speak

The word **catechism** refers to a summary or compendium of Catholic teaching that is used for instruction of the faith. **Catechism**, capitalized, refers to the most recently published volume, *The Catechism of the Catholic Church*, which contains all Catholic teachings.

In his Apostolic Constitution at the beginning of the Catechism, Pope John Paul II wrote that the Catechism is "a statement of the Church's faith and of Catholic doctrine, attested to or illumined by sacred Scripture, Apostolic Tradition, and the Church's *magisterium*." He then declared it a "sure norm for teaching the faith" and called on all of the faithful to use it to "deepen their knowledge of the unfathomable riches of salvation."

In other words, what Pope John Paul II is saying is that the Catechism puts together in one nifty volume all the Church teachings and moral guidance you need to live a spiritual life, a righteous life, a life worthy of eternal salvation.

If you want to know what it means to be a Catholic and how to live a Catholic life, then the Catechism is the book for you.

Church Speak

Magisterium is the term that refers to the Church's teaching authority, which rests with the pope, who is the successor of St. Peter and the head of the college of bishops (who are the successors of the apostles), and with the bishops, who are united with one another and with the pope in a unity of faith.

A New Approach

For some people there's just no getting around the immediate—and sometimes visceral—response they have to anything related to cat-echism. All too often, particularly for those raised Catholic, the subject may conjure up images of the old *Baltimore Catechism* of pre-Vatican II days, or maybe boring religion classes once known as C.C.D. (Con-fraternity of Christian Doctrine). I was born too late to be formally educated with the *Baltimore Catechism*, but my grandfather made sure I had my own copy of this book. To this day, the first things that come to mind when I think of that catechism are the many illustrations featur-ing a stereotypical red-horned devil. It was not exactly a warm and fuzzy introduction to the faith, even if it was accurate in its theology.

The reality is that the *Catechism of the Catholic Church*, as the current book is referred to, is not a rehash of the *Baltimore Catechism*. It is not a question-and-answer, take-no-prisoners method of imparting the faith, but rather an expansive, in-depth discussion of beliefs and teachings.

The current Catechism presents a whole new way of looking at the Church, reflecting the work of the Second Vatican Council in the 1960s.

True Confessions

The *Baltimore Catechism* was commissioned at a meeting of the U.S. bishops in Baltimore in 1829, although the first edition did not appear until 1885. It became the standard religion text in the United States from the late 1880s until the 1960s, when the Church moved away from a strict catechism-based style of religious instruction. There is, however, a revised edition of the *Baltimore Catechism* in cir-culation today that is a perennial favorite of more traditional Catholics, who prefer the old-time religion.

Understanding Catechesis

Before we can get into the specifics of the Catechism, we need to take a step back to something called "catechesis" (pronounced cat-eh-KEY-sis), which is the education of children and adults in the faith. It's more than catechetical instruction, or religion classes.

Catechesis is the "totality of the Church's efforts to make disciples," meaning that it doesn't encompass only classroom education but every aspect of faith-building that helps others believe more fully in Jesus Christ and strengthens his Church on earth. (4)

The word *catechesis* comes from the Greek word *katechizo*, which means to teach orally.

You're Absolved If ...

You think catechesis is the equivalent of those religion classes you used to attend once a week in the parish auditorium. While those classes—and their modern-day faith-formation counterparts—are certainly one aspect of catechesis, the Church strives for a much more well-rounded and long-term approach to learning about the faith today. Adult faith formation, intergenerational faith formation, and many other styles of ongoing religious education are part of the wonderful world of catechesis.

What's in It for You?

No stone was left unturned when this Catechism was written, and anyone who reads it cannot help but come away with a better understanding of the Catholic Church and the Catholic faith. In addition, the Catechism gets into a plethora of teachings that sometimes get a bad rap in society today because they are often taken out of their faith context.

If you go ahead and give the Catechism a chance, you are likely to find out things about the Catholic faith that you never imagined, or things that you thought you knew but maybe didn't fully understand. There's a reason the Catechism has been a bestseller since it was released, not only among Catholics but among the broader public as well.

Here are three off-the-cuff reasons for jumping into the Catechism with both feet:

◆ Where else can you read about adultery, angels, and environmentalism all in one place?

- If you are going to read only one book this month, why not make it a book that gets you thinking about the big stuff—heaven and hell, life and death, love and murder?

- The next time you're at a party and someone starts talking about those crazy Catholics, you'll be armed with answers to questions about the Body of Christ, virginity of Mary, and authority of the pope.

True Confessions

The second edition of the *Catechism of the Catholic Church* clocks in at a hefty 904 pages, including more than 200 pages dedicated to an extensive glossary, index of citations, and index by subject.

Just for kicks, I'll pick a few random but consecutive entries from the index of the full Catechism, and I'd be surprised if you're not intrigued:

- lust, lying, magic

- order, organ transplants, original sin

- tenderness, terrorism, and tests

The subjects may seem odd or disconnected at first, but the wonder of the Catechism is that everything is put into a faith perspective, and everything is connected to Scripture and Tradition.

Just about any question you could possibly ask about the Catholic faith is answered in the Catechism. And if you decide you want to go even deeper into the subject than what's provided in the main text, there are references to documents that can help you trace the belief or teaching back to its source.

It's Not as Scary as It Looks

If you've seen the actual Catechism, then you know that it contains more than 900 pages of teachings grounded in the Bible, Church documents, canon law, and encyclical upon encyclical. It can be overwhelming and intimidating taken as a whole, but it doesn't have to be.

The Catechism is divided into logical and easy-to-follow sections once you get the hang of it. We're going to follow that basic structure in this book as well.

This is how the full Catechism breaks down:

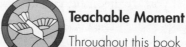

Teachable Moment

Throughout this book you will see numbers in parentheses. These numbers correspond to numbers throughout the full Catechism. If you want to know about a particular teaching, just look up the same number in the *Catechism of the Catholic Church* and you will find more than you ever imagined.

- Part I: *The Profession of Faith*, which covers basic Catholic beliefs about God, Jesus, the Holy Spirit, Mary, and lots of other major topics.

- Part II: *The Celebration of the Christian Mystery*, which focuses on liturgy and the seven sacraments.

- Part III: *Life in Christ*, which covers human dignity, morality, and the Ten Commandments.

- Part IV: *Christian Prayer*, which includes a discussion of prayer in general and a detailed explanation of the Our Father.

We are going to work our way through the Catechism part by part, topic by topic, and break it down into smaller pieces that remain theologically accurate while being easy to understand and fun to read.

You don't have to start at the beginning and work your way through to the end. You can begin with any subject you like or jump around from one chapter to another, depending on what piques your interest.

We'll get more into the specifics of how to use the Catechism in the next chapter. For now all you need to do is keep an open mind and an open heart. If you can do that, everything else will be easy.

Pop Quiz

Whether you sat through 12 years of Catholic school or never darkened the doorstep of a Catholic Church, you probably have a strong idea or two about Catholics. Before we get to the heart of the matter, let's take a little True-False quiz to see just how much you know about Church beliefs and teachings. Keep track of your answers and then take the quiz again after you've finished this book, and see all you have learned.

1. If you are divorced, you cannot receive Communion in the Catholic Church.

2. Angels are the spirits of those who have died and gone to heaven.

3. Respecting and caring for animals is part of the seventh commandment against stealing.

4. When the bread and wine are consecrated at Mass, they become the body and blood of Jesus Christ.

5. The Immaculate Conception refers to the moment when Jesus was conceived by the power of the Holy Spirit in Mary's womb.

6. Catholics cannot hold that evolution is true, only the literal interpretation of the Genesis story of Adam and Eve.

7. Anointing of the sick, one of the seven sacraments, can be received only one time when someone is on the verge of death.

8. Chastity is expected of all people, even married couples.

9. Meditation is a Catholic form of prayer.

10. The Virgin Mary is sometimes called the "new Eve."

11. A creed is a profession of faith.

12. The Holy Trinity is made up of God, Jesus, and Mary.

13. A deacon can baptize babies, bless marriages, and preside over funerals.

14. The "greatest commandment" is number five: You shall not kill.

15. Amen means, "So be it."

So how do you think you did? Maybe you breezed right through these questions and feel pretty confident about your knowledge of all things Catholic, or perhaps you struggled with a few and hedged your bets with an educated guess or two.

Fortunately, it doesn't matter how you did now because by the time you're done with this book you'll be able to answer these and just about any Catholic question someone throws at you. Even if you did answer all or most of these questions correctly, you can learn all the reasons behind these answers, and many, many others. We'll get to all of them in due time and in great detail, but in the meantime, if you'd like to see how you did, here are the correct answers.

Survey Says ...

Pat yourself on the back for being brave enough to take a pop quiz *before* you had a chance to study! Here are the answers to the quiz, with references to the chapters that will cover each topic in detail.

1. False (Chapter 20) Divorce alone does not prevent you from receiving the Sacraments.

2. False (Chapter 5) Angels are spiritual, noncorporeal beings.

3. True (Chapter 21)

4. True (Chapter 12)

5. False (Chapter 6) The Immaculate Conception refers the conception of the Virgin Mary without original sin.

6. False (Chapter 4) Catholics are allowed to hold that evolution is true as long as they also recognize God as the divine author of all creation and everything that evolved from it.

7. False (Chapter 13) Anointing of the sick can be received any time someone is seriously ill, preparing to undergo surgery, or near death because of old age.

8. True (Chapter 20)

9. True (Chapter 24)

10. True (Chapter 23)

11. True (Chapter 3)

12. False (Chapter 4) The Holy Trinity is God the Father, Jesus the Son, and the Holy Spirit.

13. True (Chapter 14)

14. False (Chapter 16) The "greatest commandment," as specified by Jesus, is to "love the Lord your God with all your heart, and with all your soul, and with all your mind." Jesus adds that there is a second commandment that is like it: "Love your neighbor as yourself." (Matthew 22:34)

15. True (Chapter 25)

The Least You Need to Know

- The Catechism is not a question-and-answer rulebook but a complete and expansive discussion of Catholic beliefs and teachings.

- Just about any question you have about the Catholic faith can be answered by the Catechism.

- The Catechism is broken down into four distinct parts: Profession of Faith, Celebration of the Christian Mystery, Life in Christ, and Christian Prayer.

- This book is designed to help you understand difficult theological concepts of the Catholic faith and be able to see and gain appreciation for the beauty of the teachings within it.

2

A Little History, Please

In This Chapter

◆ The origin and evolution of Catholic catechism

◆ Why we need the Catechism and how to study it

◆ God's connection to the Catechism

◆ Resources and tips for breaking open the Catechism

Now that you know a little about the Catechism in general, we need to put everything into proper perspective. Clearly this is not the first catechism ever written, so let's go back and explore how the earliest catechisms in the Church were formed and how they grew into the Catechism we are about to study.

For many people, the Catechism may seem like something that should be left to the professionals, as if there is a flashing sign on the cover that says, "Don't try this at home." The reality is that the Catechism, although directed specifically toward bishops as a teaching tool, was written for every person who has an interest in faith. It is not reserved only for those who work for the Church, are ordained to the priesthood, or have advanced theology degrees. Of course, sometimes the language used makes it *seem* as if it's written for theologians, but this book is going to help you get past all of that.

In this chapter, we are going to fill in background information you may need in order to put everything into context as you move through the Catechism. Particularly, we'll make the connection between the Catechism and God—because there is one. Before you're finished with this chapter, you will have the tools you need to make this trip through the Catechism as enjoyable and informative as possible.

Catechism 101

Catechisms are not unique to the Catholic Church, and, in fact, have been part of the transmission of the Christian faith since the earliest disciples began spreading the message of Jesus Christ. Some even consider the four Gospels—Matthew, Mark, Luke, and John—to be like a first catechism of sorts because they transmit the teachings Jesus preached in his lifetime. Until the invention of the printing press, catechism texts were none too common. One we do know of is the *Doctrine of the Apostles*, or *Didache*, which dates back to first-century Syria and was used to prepare people for baptism. In the fifth century, St. Augustine wrote the *Enchiridion*, which was a treatise on faith, hope, and love, for use in educating others in the faith.

The first universal Catholic catechism was not published until 1566, when the *Catechism of the Council of Trent* was written. Designed mainly to help parish priests teach the faithful, this *Roman Catechism*, as it was commonly called, became a model for future catechisms. Like the current Catechism, the *Roman Catechism* was divided into four sections: creed, sacraments, Decalogue (or Ten Commandments), and prayer.

In later centuries, numerous minor catechisms popped up, such as the *Baltimore Catechism* in the United States and the *Penny Catechism* in Great Britain, which used the simple question-and-answer format that most people associate with catechisms.

In 1986, under the direction of Pope John Paul II, a commission of 12 cardinals and bishops was appointed to produce the first complete rewrite of the *Catechism of the Council of Trent*. The president of that commission was Cardinal Joseph Ratzinger, who later became Pope Benedict XVI.

True Confessions

Some credit Martin Luther with producing the first catechism, at least according to our modern understanding of a catechism text. Published in 1529, Luther's little catechism used materials from his sermons to guide teachers and parents. It is still a mainstay in Lutheran churches. He later wrote a second catechism specifically for children. The Calvinists got their own catechism in 1563, when John Calvin published the *Heidelberg Catechism*.

It took six years to complete the revised version, called *Catechism of the Catholic Church*, which was published in French in 1992. The English version was released in 1994, and the Latin version, which is now the official text, in 1997.

Teachable Moment

There are two classes of catechisms: major and minor. A major catechism, such as the current *Catechism of the Catholic Church*, is one that would be used as a teaching tool from which any minor catechisms, such as the *Baltimore Catechism*, would be written. The *Catechism of the Catholic Church* is also known as a *universal* catechism, meaning that it is written for the worldwide, universal Church.

Theology Degree Not Required

Because major catechisms are so comprehensive in content, they tend to be written in a style that is less than engaging for the average person. So we are going to take the complicated passages of the Catechism and hammer them down into prose, heavy on meaning but light on what I like to call Church-speak—that long-winded, lingo-laden academic writing that can make anyone's eyes glaze over.

You don't need an advanced degree in theology or philosophy or anything else to benefit from a study of the Catechism. Sure, if you were working straight from the original text with no study guide, you might start to feel a little woozy from all those footnotes and long citations, so that's why you have this book.

In fact, this is going to be fun because we hit all of the highlights of the Catechism and every core teaching, but don't dwell on the more minute details that are unnecessary for a basic understanding of Catholicism. Everything you read in the coming chapters is what's key to understanding the Catholic faith.

True Confessions

The *Catechism of the Catholic Church* became an immediate bestseller when it was released. However, it did not rise to the top of *The New York Times*, or any other, bestseller list because sales figures from each of the 15 individual publishing houses that produced it were counted separately instead of as one total, despite the fact that the editions were identical. To date, the Catechism has sold more than three million copies in nine languages.

In the Beginning

You might be thinking that the Catechism sounds like something that is written by bishops for bishops, but you'll be happy to know that the Catechism starts with God. This is not saying God penned the Catechism, because he didn't. What it means is the text of the Catechism grows out of God's love for humankind and his desire that all people seek him out and learn to love him.

Church Speak

Good News refers to the central teachings of Christianity, which spring from the words and deeds of Jesus, as found in Scripture, especially the four Gospels—Matthew, Mark, Luke, and John. In fact, the word *gospel* means *good tiding* or *good news*.

God sent his Son, Jesus Christ, to give us the *Good News*, and his Son picked the Twelve Apostles to carry on the traditions of the faith. From that original group, over the course of centuries, millions of Christians have continued to spread the Gospel. Every man and woman who believes in Jesus is called to share his message with others, whether through formal classes or casual conversations or quiet actions.

The Catechism simply takes that love of God, that call to action, that challenge of faith, and puts it into a single manual that can serve as a lifelong guide to living the Catholic faith in a meaningful and authentic way.

Getting Started

Well, we're just about ready to begin the real thing. Hopefully at this point you feel comfortable with what's ahead and confident it won't be difficult. It's almost guaranteed at some point during this learning process, you will sit back and marvel at the scope of the Catechism. It really is something to behold.

How to Use It

Before you begin, I want to recommend ways to approach the Catechism and how to use this book. You could simply read through this book and stop right there. The teachings and explanations are complete and provide everything you really need to understand the Catholic faith.

However, if you wish to gain a deeper and more comprehensive study of the Catechism, this book is a true study guide for it, too, a complement to the full Catechism, to be used in conjunction with it. Reference numbers for specific Catechism passages are included throughout this book, meaning whenever you see a number in parentheses, all you need to do is look for that same number in the full Catechism to find the unabridged version of that teaching.

The Catechism is very simple to use because of its number system. Every paragraph is numbered and cross-referenced. You can pretty much find any subject you can imagine ... and a few you probably can't!

You can read through this book and the Catechism itself section by section, in order, or you can take a chapter by itself and just read that. There is no right or wrong way to read the Catechism. In fact, you don't have to read it at

True Confessions

One of the drafts of the Catechism submitted to the bishops of the world for their consideration resulted in 24,000 suggested changes.

all. You can use it as a reference guide, for simply looking up specific subjects of interest to you or to answer questions you may have. It is designed to help you understand the faith, in whatever way makes you most comfortable.

Extra Resources

If you want to use this book as a guide to assist you in studying the larger Catechism, there are several resources you'll find handy to have within your reach:

◆ *Catechism of the Catholic Church*, Second Edition, published by the Libreria Editrice Vaticana.

◆ A Bible. This book uses the New American Bible translation, but you may use whatever Bible you have available.

◆ A notebook. This will be helpful for jotting down questions or taking notes on things you might want to explore further.

◆ Internet access. You may want to be able to quickly locate Church documents or other references, which are typically available online.

The Next Step

Before you turn the page and jump in, it might be nice to take a moment of quiet—or a moment of prayer, if you're comfortable with that—to focus on opening your heart and mind. Put aside any preconceived ideas you have about Catholic teaching, and let the Catechism speak to you.

Teachable Moment

Catholic Bibles differ from Protestant versions. The Catholic Church takes as "inspired" seven books in the Old Testament that are not accepted by Protestants. Catholics consider the following books, known as the deuterocanonical texts, to be part of the canon of Scripture: Tobit, Judith, Wisdom, Sirach, Baruch, and 1 and 2 Maccabees.

The Least You Need to Know

◆ A catechism is any manual used to instruct others in the faith and has existed in various forms since the early Christian Church.

◆ The current *Catechism of the Catholic Church*, which is a universal catechism, was the first complete rewrite of the *Catechism of the Council of Trent*, originally published in 1566.

◆ Although the Catechism was directed toward bishops when it was written, it is meant to be read by any person interested in learning more about the Catholic faith.

◆ Studying the Catechism requires little more than an open mind and an open heart. Having on hand a Bible and the full text of the Catechism along with some type of study guide for it can help make the process more effective and complete.

Part 2

A Profession of Faith

For Catholics, standing up and professing their belief in God is as basic as breathing. At every Sunday Mass, Catholics make the *profession of faith*, which begins with the words: "We believe …."

If you break down the profession of faith—also known as a creed—line by line, you will discover the entirety of the Catholic faith summarized for you in prayer form. There is nothing incidental or superfluous about it.

In the coming chapters, we will study and reflect on the words of the Apostles' Creed, one of two pivotal professions of faith in the Catholic Church, so that you will know exactly what Catholics mean when they say, "We believe …."

3

Why We Believe

In This Chapter

- ◆ Why humans hunger for a relationship with God
- ◆ How God reveals his plan for humankind
- ◆ The connection between the Bible and Church teaching
- ◆ The meaning of faith

Before we get into Part One of the Catechism and the actual profession of faith, it's important to look at faith in general. What is faith? Why do we have any need or hunger for faith? And if we have faith, what is its connection to reason, logic, and the world around us?

These are some of the big, deep questions we face in life. It comes down to what degree of importance we put on God and how significant a role we want him and faith in him to play in our lives.

For some people, faith is like a life soundtrack—always playing, always present, always influencing their decisions or the ways they respond to events in their lives. For others, faith is more like a one-hit wonder—something that's great in small doses and pulled out on certain occasions, but never consistently takes center stage. And then there are those that fall somewhere in between.

No matter where you fall on the spectrum of faith, it's almost inevitable that at some point in your life you will have questions about what your faith means. Crises, turning points, celebrations, and sorrows tend to make us ask the question, "Why?"

The only way to find the answer to *that* question is to start at the beginning. And I mean the very beginning.

The Desire to Know God

The Bible tells us God made man and woman in his own image and out of love. Because of that there is an invisible but lasting bond between humankind and its creator. The Catechism says that the "desire for God is written in the human heart" and that the truth and happiness people seek can be found only in God. (27)

You have to admit, most of us are on a pretty constant quest for happiness. So, as the Catechism states, if God is the only answer, then how do we get to the point where saying the words "I believe …" is no longer just words or habit but living, breathing faith?

True Confessions

The English translation of the Catechism was held up for more than a year when some U.S. bishops objected to the use of "man" and "men" to represent both men and women. In the end, the U.S. bishops lost the fight for inclusive language, and the Church opted to keep the original generic male-centered language. So when you see man or men, it is meant to refer to men and women, or humanity as a whole.

The Catechism says that humans are religious beings from the start, and that we express our hunger for God through prayers we say, sacrifices we make, and meditations and rituals we incorporate into our lives. That may be so, but it's still a long road from ritual to redemption.

Redemption is, after all, the ultimate goal, although it's certainly not any easy journey to get there. We'll get into the concept of redemption in more detail later on. For now, let's just remember that redemption was the point of Jesus' life and death. He came to redeem humankind from sin and to open the door to eternal salvation.

What can explain, then, why many of us who are supposedly naturally drawn to God so willingly and actively leave God out of our life equation? Why do we become indifferent or focused on other things, like money and material wealth, self-righteousness and selfishness, or all of the above and more? (29)

Well, we are, after all, only human, and being mere mortals, we're not always able to fathom God's God-ness. We can never really grasp what God is or express it fully in words, but we can give it our best shot. (43)

The Catechism says that people who seek out God and make him a regular part of their lives tend to see his presence in both the extraordinary and ordinary aspects of the world around them—from the natural beauty of the earth and the mystery of the universe, to the truth, beauty, moral goodness, and spiritual longing of the human person. (31)

Teachable Moment

Human reason enables men and women to come to recognize God as the beginning and end of all things. But it is only through divine revelation that humans are able to attain a deeper understanding of God and his plans, that God is personal, not just powerful.

God Meets Man—and Woman

So if human beings are so limited in their ability to truly know God, how do we go from interested to enlightened, from finite faith to burning belief?

The truth is, we can't do it on our own. We need a little help from above, or maybe a lot of help. God sent us the ultimate kind of help in the form of his Son, Jesus Christ. Remember, Christian teaching doesn't start with Jesus but with the beginning of time, the universe. So we have to trace our family tree through the Old Testament, which begins with the beginning of time, to watch God's plan for us slowly unfold.

First God revealed himself slowly over time to the people of Israel, as recorded in Jewish Scripture. This was followed by the *piece de resistance* of his plan: His Son.

God's Plan Revealed!

When we talk about God revealing his plan, we're talking about God wanting us to understand him better. He doesn't want us just stumbling along in spiritual darkness. He wants to light the way for us. So while God may seem mysterious, rest assured he makes his plan for us known to us one way or another, even if we sometimes don't catch on until after the fact.

Church Speak

Revelation in the Church sense means something communicated by God and of God. In the Old Testament, we see this communication through the law and the prophets. In the New Testament, God reveals himself in the person of Jesus Christ and through the Holy Spirit.

Before he sent Jesus, God set about shining his light on humankind through Adam and Eve, Noah, Abraham, and the Israelites.

It all started with God manifesting himself to Adam and Eve, whom God invited into "intimate communion" with himself (54). Even after they disobeyed him and were banished from paradise, God still stood behind his offer of salvation for them and for their descendants.

Then along came Noah, the flood, the rainbow, and God's promise. God makes a *covenant* between himself and all living creatures, saying that he will never again destroy his creation because of the rebellion of his creatures. This is all part of the plan.

Church Speak

Covenant is a solemn agreement that contains promises but also imposes obligations. In the Old Testament, we find covenants between God and Noah, God and Abraham, God and Moses, God and King David, God and the Israelites. In the New Testament, we see a "new" covenant—the promise of eternal life—forged by Christ's death and resurrection.

Now enters Abraham, whom God proclaims "the father of a multitude of nations." (Gen 12:3) Abraham's descendants—the Israelites—will be the chosen ones, with whom God establishes a covenant, which includes the Ten Commandments given to Moses on Mount Sinai.

Then we have God's covenant with King David, by which God promises the people of Israel a "messiah," the anointed king of the House of David.

Finally we come to last part of God's plan revealed: Jesus Christ, who is given to humanity as God's promised Messiah, God's Word made flesh, God's revelation of a new and final covenant. And this is the end of his plan. There will be no further "public revelations" from God. (66)

So how do we fit into this plan if it was over and done with before any of us arrived on the scene? Well, this story is our story. We are not separate from the plan; we are extensions of the plan, living out what God set into motion at the beginning of time. The covenant God made with humankind through his Son is a covenant for all time and for all people.

Teachable Moment

Jesus is known as the "Word made flesh." How is Jesus a Word? Well, in Jewish tradition, the "word" or *dabar*, is at once a creative force and a moral force. When we speak of Jesus as the Word, we are not referring to a spoken word as we understand it but to God's Word spoken from the consciousness of divinity in a timeless and eternal way. Jesus is God's Word—the link between humanity on earth and God in heaven. In the Gospel of John, Jesus described this: "In the beginning was the Word, and the Word was with God, and the Word was God. He was in the beginning with God. All things came to be through him, and without him nothing came to be." (John 1:1-3)

Isn't That Divine?

Okay, the average person does not receive shazam-thundered divine messages and revelations on a regular basis. So how exactly does God's plan get passed on to those of us who are not hearing God's voice, building arks, or receiving tablets of stone? Well, we have the Bible, of course, and we also have something called *Apostolic Tradition*.

Church Speak

Tradition, with a capital "T," refers to the living faith that is not necessarily contained in Scripture but is handed down from generation to generation, first by the apostles and now by their successors in the college of bishops.

Jesus told the apostles to go out and spread the Gospel message, which would lead men and women to salvation. The apostles did this by preaching. The preaching they began in those early years after Jesus' death and resurrection continues today uninterrupted through Scripture and Tradition. (76)

Is All This in the Bible?

The Catechism says very clearly that the Church's Tradition and Scripture, while distinct from each other, are "bound closely together and communicate one with the other." (80)

Think of Jesus Christ as the main source of revelation, from which flows two bubbling springs: Scripture and Tradition. Scripture is the word of God spoken through the Holy Spirit, and Tradition is the word of God come to life, living faith, in the form of Jesus Christ.

So how does everything that is in the Bible and everything that Jesus taught to his apostles and earliest disciples fit into what the Catholic Church teaches today? Well, the college of bishops, headed by the pope, is the continuation of the Twelve Apostles in the Church today.

Teachable Moment

The Catholic Church accepts the 46 books of the Old Testament and the 27 books of the New Testament as divinely inspired. The Old and New Testaments are connected in that the Old Testament foretold what would happen in the New Testament, and the New Testament fulfilled the messages of the Old Testament.

The magisterium (remember, that's the Church's teaching authority, as discussed in Chapter 1) teaches "only what has been handed on to it" either through "divine command" or the Holy Spirit. It is not superior to the word of God, but rather interprets the word of God. (86)

The Catechism says that Tradition, Scripture, and the magisterium are so closely intertwined that one cannot stand without the other. Together they "contribute effectively to the salvation of souls." (95)

That means that the Bible (or Scripture) and Tradition passed on through the apostles, and the Church's authentic interpretation of both, combine to give us all of the teachings you will find in the Catechism.

Responding to Transcendent Love

We're just about ready to dive into the profession of faith, if you can believe it. I know it's been a while since we started this discussion, but, as you can see, there's a lot to understand about faith in general before we can put faith under a microscope and study the little intricacies that make specific beliefs so beautiful.

Maybe you think of faith as something beyond explanation or human comprehension. The Catechism gets into a very detailed explanation of faith, which it calls "a *grace*." Faith, the Catechism says, is a "supernatural *virtue*" that is a cooperation between human intellect and divine grace. (155)

Although faith is often beyond reason, it can never be completely contradicted by reason because "the things of the world and the things of faith derive from the same God." (159) In other words, faith can happily coexist with something like science.

Church Speak

Grace is a supernatural gift that God bestows upon men and women to help them live as children of God and to achieve eternal salvation. A **virtue** is an attitude or disposition that enables a person to act in a righteous way.

Finally, faith, the Catechism says, is a personal act that humans can freely choose to accept or reject, but faith is necessary for salvation. (161)

The Least You Need to Know

- Human beings are naturally drawn to their creator God, who wants them to know him and love him.
- God revealed his plan through the Israelites, the Old Testament patriarchs and prophets, and, finally, Jesus Christ.

◆ Since most of us are not getting messages directly from God, we need divine revelation, which comes to us from Jesus Christ through Scripture, Tradition, and Tradition's fine-tuning by the Church's teaching authority, called the magisterium.

◆ Faith is a grace and virtue that is freely chosen and necessary for salvation.

4

God the Father

In This Chapter

- ◆ How the Apostles' Creed sums up Catholic beliefs
- ◆ Believing in God as Father
- ◆ Understanding the Holy Trinity
- ◆ How Father, Son, and Spirit work together

This is where we finally get into the nitty-gritty of Catholic beliefs. Everything you need to know about the most basic tenets of the Catholic faith is summed up quite concisely in either of two *creeds* that are central to Catholicism—the Apostles' Creed, which is recited at baptism, and the Nicene (pronounced NI-seen) Creed, which is recited at Mass.

Two Creeds, One Message

The creeds are divided first into two main parts, the first focusing on God and the second focusing on God's works. The first part of each creed—the part about God—is then divided into three main parts, in reference to the nature and work of the three persons of the Holy Trinity: the Father, Son, and Holy Spirit.

Church Speak _____

A **creed** is a statement of a community's belief. It comes from the Latin *credo*, which means "I believe." A creed is also known as a symbol of faith.

If you break down the creeds, which are called "professions of faith," you will find that each line contains an important belief, from the creation of the universe to the virgin birth to the resurrection of Jesus to the Church and its saints.

The Catechism breaks down the Apostles' Creed line by line, making constant reference to the Nicene Creed along the way:

Apostles' Creed

I believe in God,

the Father almighty,

creator of heaven and earth.

I believe in Jesus Christ,

his only Son, our Lord.

He was conceived by the

power of the Holy Spirit

and born of the Virgin Mary.

He suffered under Pontius Pilate,

was crucified, died, and was buried.

He descended into hell.

On the third day he rose again.

He ascended into heaven

and is seated at the right hand

of the Father.

He will come again to judge

the living and the dead.

I believe in the Holy Spirit,

the holy catholic Church,

the communion of saints,

the forgiveness of sins,

the resurrection of the body,

and life everlasting.

Amen.

The Nicene Creed, which probably rolls off the tongues of most practicing Catholics without hesitation, is a more detailed creed:

Nicene Creed

We believe in one God,

the Father, the Almighty,

maker of heaven and earth,

of all that is seen and unseen.

We believe in one Lord, Jesus Christ,

the only Son of God,

eternally begotten of the Father,

God from God, Light from Light,

true God from true God,

begotten, not made, one in

Being with the Father.

Through him all things were made.

For us men and for our salvation

he came down from heaven:

By the power of the Holy Spirit

he was born of the Virgin Mary,

and became man.

For our sake he was crucified

under Pontius Pilate;

he suffered, died, and was buried.

On the third day he rose again

in fulfillment of the Scriptures;

He ascended into heaven

and is seated at the right

hand of the Father.

He will come again in glory to judge

the living and the dead,

and his kingdom will have no end.

We believe in the Holy Spirit,

the Lord, the giver of life,

who proceeds from

the Father and the Son.

With the Father and the Son

he is worshipped and glorified.

He has spoken through the Prophets.

We believe in one holy catholic

and apostolic Church.

We acknowledge one baptism

for the forgiveness of sins.

We look for the resurrection of the dead,

and the life of the world to come.

Amen.

The Apostles' Creed begins: "I believe in God ..."

Pretty straightforward, isn't it? This is the foundation. Everything else flows from this statement. The full line is actually, "I believe in God, the Father almighty, creator of heaven and earth."

Basically, if you don't believe in God, the rest of this creed will not make any sense.

In the Nicene Creed, the word "one" is added. "We believe in one God ..." Why is "one" so important? Because in professing God's oneness, the creed emphasizes that believing in the Trinity and in Jesus Christ as Lord does not in any way divide God. (202)

What's in a Name?

The Catechism's next section on the subject of God the Father is titled, "God Reveals His Name." That's quite a headline. But what does that mean? Well, the Catechism says that God revealed himself to the people of Israel, and in doing so made it possible for them to have a more intimate relationship with him. He was no longer "an anonymous force." (203)

God tells Moses, "I am Who am" (Ex 3:14). How are we supposed to wrap our minds around *that* statement? This is how the Catechism explains it: "The divine name is mysterious just as God is mystery. It is at once a name revealed and something like the refusal of a name ...." (206)

A name revealed and the refusal of a name—that does make sense, in a weird philosophical sort of way. This is God, the Alpha and Omega, the omnipresent but invisible. I guess you could say that the creed doesn't tell us so much about *what* God is but rather about *how* God is.

So, we have this God who is the beginning and end of everything, and with whom we have this intimate relationship. And yet, many of us view him as vengeful, or, at the very least, as a really tough taskmaster. I guess all the floods, destruction, and plagues that dot the many pages of the Old Testament didn't help his image. But when God tells Moses his name, he also tells him that he is merciful and forgiving and steadfast in love. (211)

Catholics believe that God *is* love and God *is* truth. That God simply *is*. (214) The first part of the profession of faith is at once a statement of God's greatness and a proclamation of the believer's willingness to put God before all other things and to have faith in him alone.

Understanding the Trinity

Every Mass, every Catholic prayer for that matter, begins with the Sign of the Cross and the words: "In the name of the Father and of the Son and of the Holy Spirit." This is the Trinity, and it is the central belief of the Christian faith.

The doctrine of the Trinity is a distinctively Christian doctrine of God, something that separates Christians from other religious traditions. The Trinity is not just one teaching among many. It is *the* Christian teaching of God. Everything a Christian does flows from this teaching, is centered upon this teaching, and leads back to this teaching.

Trinity is the belief in three in one. God is one God, but in his oneness, he is comprised of three persons: Father, Son, Holy Spirit. It is a mystery, and a good part of the time that is the explanation you will get if you ask someone to tell you how this can be.

True Confessions _____

Legend has it that back in fifth-century Ireland, St. Patrick used the shamrock to explain the Trinity to pagans. He would hold up a shamrock, asking if it had one leaf or three. It has both one leaf and three, he would explain, stating that so, too, the Trinity is one God in three persons.

Let's go back over the reason for discussing the Trinity at this point. Remember, the creed is divided into three parts, and although it covers many, many aspects of Catholic faith, it is grounded in the Trinity. The first part of the creed focuses on God the Father, the second on God the Son, and the third on God the Holy Spirit.

Although it is incredibly difficult to comprehend, the Trinity is absolutely the core belief of the faith that Catholics profess. From the moment of baptism and over and over again throughout their lives, Catholics continually rededicate themselves to the Trinity. It pervades liturgies, home prayers, and even the baseball diamond whenever a player blesses himself as he steps into the batter's box.

Father and Son

It's not so unusual to hear a person of faith—any faith—speak of God as "Father." We see God as creator, and so view him as the ultimate parent, protector, head of our family of faith. Despite the male moniker, however, God is neither man nor woman. He is beyond such distinctions. (239)

Although God revealed himself to us slowly over time—remember the covenants we discussed in the previous chapter—it was Jesus himself who revealed God's true nature, saying that he should be called Father not simply because he is the creator. Jesus reveals that God the Father is "eternally Father in relation to his only Son, who is eternally Son only in relation to his Father," the Catechism explains. (240)

This dovetails with the belief that Jesus is the Word, which we also covered in the previous chapter, because Jesus comes to earth as the image or "word" of an invisible God.

"The Father and I are one," Jesus says, which almost gets him stoned by an angry crowd that sees him as a blasphemer. (John 10:30) Trinity has never been an easy belief.

Everlasting Spirit

So where does the Holy Spirit fit in? Well, in the Gospel of John, at the Last Supper, Jesus comforted his apostles by telling them that he would not leave them "orphans." A careful reading of the Spirit texts in chapters 14 and 16 of the Gospel of John indicate that sometimes Jesus is sending the Holy Spirit, and other times the Father is sending the Spirit in Jesus' name.

"He will teach you everything and remind you of all that I told you," Jesus tells his disciples (John 14:26). Jesus personalizes the Spirit, reminding his followers that the Spirit is not just a power or presence but a person, too.

The Holy Spirit, then, is personal, not just "the force." He does for us now what Jesus had done for his disciples while he was living among them.

Later on, we will discuss in further detail the specifics of the Holy Spirit. For now we'll just focus on the Holy Spirit's role in the Trinity, keeping in mind that the Spirit did not just come into being at the Last Supper or with Jesus' birth. The Holy Spirit, as one person in the Trinity, has existed since before time began, as have the Son and the Father.

Spirit of Controversy

The Holy Spirit is "one and equal" with the Father and the Son despite the fact that he "proceeds" from them. This is a doctrine that is not without controversy. Between the eighth and ninth centuries, the dogma that the Holy Spirit "proceeds from the Father and the Son" was added to the Latin version of the *Nicene Creed*. The Eastern Orthodox Church objected to this, saying that the Spirit proceeds from the Father *through* the Son, which goes to show that when it comes to theology, one little word can make a big difference. (245)

I know, it can make your head hurt after a while. Let's sum it up as easily as we can possibly sum up a mystery beyond human comprehension:

The Roman Catholic Church says—and the Catechism quotes the Second Council of Lyons from the year 1274 to explain—that although the Father is the first origin of the Spirit, his communion with the Son makes them a "single principle" from which the Holy Spirit proceeds. (248)

The Trio of One

In order to be sufficiently grounded in our understanding of the Trinity, we need to go over a few more ground rules about what is sometimes referred to as the "triune Godhead."

The dogma of the Trinity was present, although not fully developed, from the very beginning of Christianity. St. Paul, for example, concludes his Second Letter to the Corinthians with this blessing: "The grace of the Lord Jesus Christ and the love of God and the fellowship of the Holy Spirit be with all of you." (2 Cor 13:13). That same word-for-word line is one of the introductory rites that is sometimes used at Catholic Mass. In fact, any practicing Catholic who just read that line probably silently responded, "And also with you," out of force of habit.

That's not to say that trinitarian belief wasn't debated at length during the first centuries of Christianity. In those earlier years, the Church had to articulate the teachings on the Trinity that came from Jesus' own words and the apostles early preaching.

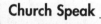

Church Speak

Consubstantial means that the Father, the Son, and Spirit are of one and the same substance or being—no divisions of divinity.

"The Trinity is one." That is how the Catechism states it (253), and that sounds simple enough on the surface but it's pretty deep. It means that although there are three persons in the Trinity, there are not three separate Gods but one God in three persons. They do not *share* divinity between them, but are each fully divine and distinct from one another but related to one another.

So, according to Catholic teaching, the Father is wholly present in the Son and Spirit, as are the Son and Spirit wholly present in the Father and in one another. (255)

Teachable Moment

Sometimes you will hear the term *divine economy* used in reference to the Trinity. This has nothing to do with heavenly finances, and has everything to do with what is considered the "common work" of the three persons of the Trinity. Also known as the *economy of salvation*, these terms mean, in effect, that the three persons of the Trinity work together to help humankind achieve eternal salvation.

Although they are all for one and one for all, so to speak, the three persons of the Trinity also have individual jobs they perform to further the common work of the economy of salvation. They do this in accordance with their "unique personal property," as the Catechism explains. According to the Council of Constantinople II, which was held in 553, and based on the New Testament, this means that there is "one God and Father from whom all things are, and one Lord Jesus Christ, through whom all things are, and one Holy Spirit in whom all things are." (258)

And even though it may seem like a lofty proposition, all Christians are called to be a dwelling place for the Trinity, entering into a kind of participation in the life of the Father, Son, and Spirit. (260) The Catechism quotes from John 14:23: "Jesus answered and said to him, 'Whoever loves me will keep my word, and my Father will love him, and we will come to him and make our dwelling with him.'"

The Least You Need to Know

- ◆ The two creeds crucial to Catholicism are the Apostles' Creed and Nicene Creed. Each is divided into two basic parts, first about God and second about God's works. The first part of each creed is then divided into three parts in reference to the Holy Trinity.

- ◆ Catholics believe that God is love and truth in all things, and that God revealed himself to Moses by telling him, "I am Who am."

- ◆ The Holy Trinity, the core Christian belief about God, is the belief that God the Father, God the Son, and God the Holy Spirit are three persons in one God.

- ◆ Trinitarian belief can be found in Scripture, in the words of Jesus and the apostles, although it was further articulated by the Church fathers in the early centuries of Christianity.

Chapter 5

Opposing Forces

In This Chapter

- ◆ The Catholic interpretation of evolution
- ◆ Why evil exists in God's own creation
- ◆ Understanding angels and their role in our world
- ◆ Tracing man and woman back to the beginning
- ◆ The fall of humanity through the original sin

Now that we've covered the basic belief in God and the Trinity, we can move on to the rest of the first line of the creed. Yes, we're still on the first line. You'll be amazed by how much ground we're going to cover with this one sentence. God has many attributes—we covered kind and merciful and steadfast in love in the previous chapter—but none of those are mentioned by name in the creeds. The only one of God's qualities that is singled out for emphasis is "almighty," as in "I believe in God, the Father almighty …."

Well, that's a big one, sort of all-encompassing, don't you think? Being almighty means that God not only created everything out of nothing but also rules everything and can do anything and everything. (268)

The almightiness of God often leads humans to question a lot of things about their creator and about the world. What is an almighty God worth to us down here if he can't make the world a perfect place? Ah, well, perfection may be the ultimate goal, but our world is a work in progress, and in imperfect places there are going to be imperfect realities—like evil and sin and sorrow. God wanted it to be perfect—a garden of paradise—but humanity got in the way, and humanity is still getting in the way.

How Did We End Up Here?

As we said at the beginning of the previous chapter on the creed, the first line of the Apostles' Creed includes the words, "I believe in God, the Father almighty, creator of heaven and earth." In the Nicene Creed, the words "of all that is seen and unseen" are added at the end of that line. So, what is the significance of these lines in the creeds and in the Catholic faith?

Catholics believe that God created everything, and they mean everything. The universe was not created by some random explosion or bang. They're not saying there couldn't have been a bang, but not a random bang. Nothing can be entirely random when God's fingerprints are on the whole universal mix.

Before he ever created humankind, God began his plan for the salvation of humankind with the creation of the heavens and the earth, a plan that finds its ultimate completion in Jesus Christ. So out of his wisdom and love, God created the universe, including humankind, whom he made in his own image and invites to share in his being and goodness. (295)

What does this mean for those who side with science and the theory of evolution? Do these not conflict with the belief that God created everything out of nothing? Nope. Catholics can believe that humans evolved over time into the beings we are today. However, Catholics cannot believe that human evolution occurred devoid of divine inspiration.

When it comes to creation, there is no blind chance. You've seen it printed on tacky T-shirts, "God doesn't make mistakes." Well, that's sort of the point here. God created everything that led to everything, and God makes humans unique by giving us souls.

Most of the time when we think of creation, we think of God the Father as *the* creator, but because the three persons of the Trinity cannot be divided in their work of creation and salvation (as we discussed at length in Chapter 4), it means that creation is the work of the Trinity as a whole. So the Son and Spirit are also responsible with the Father for all of creation. Once again, when it comes to the Catholic faith, there is a consistency and an interconnectedness that always brings you back around to the core beliefs.

Good, Bad, and Evil

If God is so good, why is evil so bad? There's a loaded question if ever there was one. You know you've heard it. Maybe you've asked it. It's hard to look at all the sorrow and tragedy and outright wickedness in the world and not wonder how God could possibly be so distracted that he's missing all of this, or think he's causing it or allowing it to happen. The Church teaches that he hasn't missed, and isn't missing, a thing, and he hasn't *caused*, or isn't causing, a thing when it comes to evil.

When bad things happen to good people, we can sometimes get to thinking that God is either good or powerful but not both. If he's good but not powerful, then he's a doddering old uncle. If he's powerful but not good, then he's no better than the gods of Greek tragedies. So where do Christians find the answer to the "problem" of evil? They find it in Jesus Christ, who did not come to fix the world's problems but to live amidst all the world's problems. Jesus came not only to suffer *for* us but to suffer *with* us.

Here's how the Catechism explains the presence of evil in the world: God created humankind, and through something called "divine providence" tries to guide humans ever closer to the ultimate goal of perfection and eternity with him. But, and this is a significant "but," God allows his creation to cooperate with him in this effort. How does this happen? Because God has given humanity free will, and although he hopes we will choose right and avoid wrong, he will not force our hands. (307)

Teachable Moment

The Catechism says God created a world that is "journeying" toward perfection, meaning that the world is not yet perfect.
Physical good and physical evil must co-exist in an imperfect world. "In God's plan this process of becoming involves the appearance of certain beings and the disappearance of others, the existence of the more perfect alongside the less perfect, both constructive and destructive forces of nature." (310)

So God does not *will* evil; he permits evil out of respect for the freedom he has given all of his creation, and somehow, in ways we typically don't understand until much later on, he finds ways to bring good from the bad. (311)

What Are Angels?

When Catholics profess that they believe in a God who is the creator of "all that is seen and unseen," what exactly are they professing? The "seen" part is easy. Look around. But what about the "unseen" part? I'll give you a clue: think wings.

Angels are the "unseen" creations. Mortals seem to be especially intrigued by the idea of angels, as evidenced by the little cherubic, winged statues that are so commonly found in flower gardens and any shop that sells crystals and incense. Angels are interesting, maybe because they are so mysterious.

What exactly is an angel? Often you hear people talk about how a dead relative is now an angel. Wrong. Catholics believe people who die do not become angels, but that angels are spiritual beings who never had bodies like us, and never will.

The Catechism goes back to St. Augustine for an explanation of angels. It turns out that "angel" is just a job description. The Greek word *angelos* means "messenger." Angels, as we observe them in Scripture, are sent from God with a message for us. Think about the angel Gabriel announcing the Good News to Mary; think about the choirs of angels announcing the Good News of Jesus' birth to the shepherds. We often use the word "spirit" to describe these ethereal attributes we observe or feel about beings we think of as angels.

Angels are free creatures, intelligent creatures, who are perfect in ways their earthly counterparts are not. "With their whole beings the angels are servants and messengers of God," the Catechism explains. (329)

According to Catholic teaching, Christ is the center of the angelic world, which has existed since the beginning of the rest of creation and is central to the completion of the God's divine plan. Angels are ever-present in the pivotal events of the journey toward salvation, from the Garden of Eden to the announcement that Mary would bear the Son of God to Jesus' own death and resurrection. (332)

True Confessions

Satan is a "fallen" angel. Once on the side of God, who created him, he rejected God and became evil by his own doing. Satan is pure spirit, like all other angels. (391)

Oftentimes Catholics talk about their "guardian angels." The Church teaches—and the Catechism quotes St. Basil the Great as saying—that every believer has an angel who serves as protector and guide throughout a person's life from the beginning to end. (336)

Why Me?

Many of us wonder on a fairly regular basis why we're here. We want to know our purpose, the point of our existence. That's not easy to figure out because so much of it is beyond our human comprehension.

Things happen on our paths through life—sometimes terrible things—and yet somehow, years later, we often find a glimmer of good came out of the bad. Life is funny that way. It seems to have a mind of its own.

Bingo. It does have a mind of its own, and it's the result of God's will. God created order out of nothingness and gave us everything we see before us. Then he loved us into being. Each of God's creations has within it a "particular goodness and perfection," reflecting God's goodness. (339)

Although human beings are the "summit" of God's visible creation, we are expected to live in harmony with the rest of creation. Our rank in the hierarchy of creation does not give us the right to do anything that would destroy the order and balance that God gave to the universe. We are called to live in "solidarity" with the whole of creation. (344)

So humankind was created by God and in God's image. But of all the creatures on earth, only humans have the capacity to know and love their creator—which sets us apart from the rest of creation. We are not some*things* but some*ones*, able to freely give ourselves to God if we so choose. (357)

You're Absolved If ...

You can see how you inherited many of your amazing qualities from your biological parents. While you may get your brown eyes or blond hair from your earthly mother or father, your soul comes directly from God. No genetics necessary there.

Human beings have the benefit of being both physical and spiritual, meaning that we get to enjoy both a body and a soul. The Catechism explains that it is because of our soul that our human bodies come to life. In other words, the body could not take living form without the soul. (365)

Our soul is the part of us that lives on after we die, and what will eventually be reunited with our bodies at the final resurrection at the end of all time, which we will discuss in further detail in Chapter 10.

Original Sin

So God gave us all these cool things—goodness, freedom, bodies, souls, and, at the outset, a nice little starter home in a neighborhood called paradise. He made man and woman with equal dignity to complement each other. He offered them friendship and the promise of eternal life. Who could ask for more?

Apparently humankind can always ask for more. Suddenly paradise started feeling a little cramped. The suburbs started looking better and better, and before you know it, Satan, in the form of a serpent, sold Eve a bill of goods and "original sin" was born. But before we get into the specifics of original sin, let's talk about how humankind, if we are made in God's image, is capable of sinning at all.

How Is Sin Possible?

Sin is here. There's no getting around it. And it's been here almost since the beginning of time. To some, what the Church calls sin might seem like nothing more than plain old human weakness or maybe just character flaws gone awry. But sin has to be viewed in relationship to God. The Church teaches that when we look at God's plan and our place in that plan, then we are able to grasp that sin is a turning away from God's plan and an abuse of the freedom he gave us. (387)

Let's go back to the "fall" of Adam and Eve. They were given life and had every opportunity to do the right thing to honor God. But they wanted the one thing God said they couldn't have: to be like God, but on *their* terms. So the very first humans disobeyed God, and the rest, as they say is history. Paradise, as God had originally created it, was no more. Eternal life was now a distant promise, and, for God knows how long, humanity wandered through the annals of history searching for a sliver of paradise lost and wondering when God would step in to save them.

Original sin, the Catechism says, is the "reverse side" of the Good News Jesus came to preach. Adam is the original sinner, and Jesus, the new Adam, is the one and only redeemer sent to fix what started with the fall in Eden. (389)

Whether or not you believe in a literal Adam and Eve, it is obvious there exists in our world a kind of evil that pulls humans away from good and pushes them toward a self-centeredness harmful to others, and ultimately themselves. Unfortunately, as the Church teaches, an actual Eden is not necessary for evil to come into existence in our world.

Teachable Moment

Catholics don't believe in the literal interpretation of the Genesis story of Adam and Eve with magic trees and talking snakes. The Catechism explains belief in original sin as Genesis giving a figurative account of a "primeval event" that occurred at the beginning of humankind's existence. Our first parents—regardless of what names they had—sinned. And their sin was bigger than them. Its roots were in the kind of evil that exists in opposition to God. So as a Catholic you don't have to believe in Adam and Eve as specific historic persons, but you do have to believe in the original sin of humanity, a sin that leaves a mark on every human since the very first.

Satan's Legacy

Satan, who represents all that is in opposition to God, is called the "father of lies." He seduced humanity's first parents, and countless generations since, into sin. Jesus, on the other hand, came to defeat Satan. (394) He conquered death and evil, proving that although Satan is powerful, he has his limits. Satan cannot stop God, no matter how much harm or destruction or mindless evil he causes on earth. God allows Satan to exist, but continues to help humanity push away the choice of evil and live by the wisdom and goodness of its creator. (395)

Church Speak

Concupiscence means that humankind is inclined to sin, even if we are baptized, because of the original sin we inherited from our first parents' decision to reject God and choose evil. (1264)

So why is it Catholics believe that all people carry the burden of the first humans' original sin? We weren't there; we shouldn't share the blame, right? This is how original sin works: Adam and Eve chose evil over good. "They wanted to be like gods," and so they listened to the devil's empty promises instead of God's promises. Satan convinced them that disobedience would result in omnipotence. By eating from the Tree of Knowledge they would have powers that rivaled God's power. That was quite a temptation, and one they could not resist.

Once that first sin occurred and humankind was put in tension with its creator and the rest of creation, the floodgates of sin were opened. Cain kills his brother Abel, and that's just the tip of the iceberg. Throughout the Old Testament, we see humanity turning away from God in hopes of finding power or glory or something better than what they already have, or are.

And so the Church teaches that we are guilty because of our inherited tendency to sin—our solidarity, so to speak, with our first parents. The Church finds the proof of such guilt in the way humans continue to fall prey to the same original temptation of trying to become God on our own terms.

Simply stated, the bottom line is that our first earthly parents screwed up. And all these years later, we're still paying for our parents' mistakes, and repeating them ourselves. (Tell *that* to your therapist next week!)

The Church teaches that the misery in our world and humanity's "inclination toward evil and death" must be understood in connection to Adam's sin. Because we are united to Adam through the human race, we share in his sin. Jesus Christ, who is called the "new Adam" in Church tradition, offers us the flip side of that, allowing us to share in his justice. We have to take the bad with the good.

Catholics believe that the way they erase the sin of our first parents is through the healing waters of baptism, which we will discuss at length in Chapter 12.

Basically original sin comes down to this: By our first parents' sin, all that is opposed to God gets a modicum of control over humanity, and the world is left in "a sinful condition." (408)

And while that sounds sort of hopeless, Catholics believe that all is not lost because God did not abandon humankind after the fall. They believe he will not abandon anyone who falls and seeks his mercy. God sent his Son as a man, like us, in everything *except* sin, and, in doing so, saved humanity from itself.

The Least You Need to Know

◆ Catholics can believe in the big bang or evolution but not that creation came about because of a completely random act independent of God's creative will.

◆ God does not cause evil in the world. He allows all of his creations to work in cooperation with him, giving them the free will to choose good or evil.

◆ Angels are spiritual beings who are servants and messengers of God and who protect and guide humans on earth.

◆ God created man and woman in his image, giving them body and soul, and goodness and freedom.

◆ Original sin dates back to the beginning of human existence, when the power of evil turned the first humans away from God. All people carry this burden of Adam and Eve's sin.

◆ Jesus came to defeat death and evil and redeem humankind from sin and from sin's control.

Chapter 6

Son of God Is Born

In This Chapter

- Who is Jesus, the Son of God, the Christ, the Messiah?
- The meaning of the Incarnation
- The Virgin Mary's role in salvation history
- The Immaculate Conception, Mary's virginity, and Mary's predestination as Mother of God

The next part of the creed focuses on Jesus, the Son of God. Not surprisingly, this is a pretty substantial part of both the Apostles' Creed and the Nicene Creed. This portion of the creed is not just about professing a basic belief in Jesus; it is about professing a profound belief in the many aspects of Jesus' birth, life, death, and resurrection that make him the keystone of Christianity.

By delving more deeply into this section of the creed, we will get a closer look not only at Jesus the man and Jesus the Messiah, but also at Mary his mother, and at the particular events of Jesus' life that led up to his victory over death and sin. The Nicene Creed once again expounds on some of the simpler language of the Apostles' Creed giving us, in this case, a prayer that is filled with poetry and imagery.

For many people, this part of the creed will feel the most familiar and, despite its extremely heavy subject matter, will be the easiest to understand. And that is precisely the point. By becoming a man, God made it possible for us to know him better and to grasp his existence in a way that makes sense to us.

God Becomes Man

The second part of the Apostles' Creed states: "I believe in Jesus Christ, his only Son, our Lord." The Nicene Creed, on the other hand, says the same thing like this: "We believe in one Lord, Jesus Christ, the only Son of God eternally begotten of the Father, God from God, Light from Light, true God from true God, begotten, not made, one in Being with the Father. Through him all things were made. For us men and for our salvation he came down from heaven ...."

As you can see, there's quite a difference. In the Nicene version we need to wrangle not only with the idea of God having a Son but also with the more esoteric ideas of "light from light" and "eternally *begotten*."

Church Speak

Begotten means to generate through procreation. However, repeatedly in the New Testament Jesus is referred to as the "only begotten," a term that comes from the Greek *monogenes*, meaning "only" (*mono*) and "birth" (*genes*). This sets Jesus apart from any other believer who is considered a son of God. In the creed, Jesus is referred to as "begotten, not made," meaning that he is not a work from God's creation, nor is he just a thought that pops into God's mind. Jesus' relationship to the Father is unique in that he is not an adopted child of God, as are the rest of us, but the one and only Son of God. By taking on human form in the person of Jesus Christ, God became human like us in every respect except sin.

Let's begin with the basics: Who is Jesus of Nazareth? There are certain aspects of Jesus' life we can understand from a strictly human perspective. He was born in the time of King Herod in a town called Bethlehem to a young woman named Mary and a carpenter named Joseph. As an adult, Jesus healed the sick and preached by parables to crowds who flocked after him. At first they wondered who this man from Nazareth could be, then they praised him, and finally they crucified him.

He inspired many people with his invitation to leave everything behind and follow him. He scared some people with his radical message of love and forgiveness and mercy. He scandalized other people with his willingness to sit down to dinner with sinners or let an adulteress walk away from a stoning unharmed.

Those are the seemingly more human aspects of Jesus. To truly know him, however, we must recognize he is not simply just one more holy man. The Gospel of John and the first seven councils of the Catholic Church tell us he is God made man, a distinction that is at once startling and comforting.

The Catechism says the Good News we often talk about or hear about can be summed up in one sentence: God has sent us his Son. This message is at the core of the Catechism. Jesus is the "heart of catechesis," the Catechism explains, reminding us that the Christian faith is about bringing people to Jesus, about spreading his word,

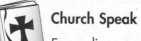

Church Speak

Evangelize comes from the Greek word *euag-gelein*, which means "announcing good news." When you evangelize, you bring others to Jesus Christ by spreading the Gospel through both your words and actions.

and about helping people understand Jesus is God, who alone can bring us into communion with the Trinity and who will live with us forever. (426)

He Is the Christ, and the Messiah

When the angel Gabriel appears to Mary in Luke's Gospel and tells her that she is to bear the Son of God, he also tells her this child will be named Jesus, Y šûa' or its shortened form Y šû in Hebrew, which means "God saves." So Luke gives us not only the name of God's Son but "his identity and his mission." He has come to save people from their sins, God's greatest gesture on behalf of the people he created in his image. (430)

Jesus is also known as the Christ and the Messiah. The words—*Christ* is from the Greek and *Messiah* is from the Hebrew—mean "anointed" and refer to Jesus as the anointed king of the House of David, long awaited by Israel, who was sent to bring the rule of God into the world in a definitive way. He is consecrated by God and anointed by the Spirit not only as king, but also as prophet and priest. (436)

At the time of Jesus, "messiah" was not a strictly religious term; it had political connotations. Jesus accepted the title of Messiah, but did not use the term to describe himself. He had to constantly remind his followers he was not going to be an earthly king of any old run-of-the-mill kingdom. (439) That was a hard one for people of the times to grasp. They expected a political revolution, not a spiritual revolution.

When Jesus' own disciples argue over who is going to have the greater power in Jesus' kingdom, Jesus has to break it to them that those who want to be the greatest among them will be the servants. "Just so, the Son of Man came not to be served but to serve, and to give his life as a ransom for many." (Matthew 20:28)

Son of God

Jesus Christ, the long-awaited Messiah, is first and foremost the Son of God. In the early "symbols" or creeds, Jesus is known as the "only begotten Son of the Father" and the "eternally begotten Son," reminding us, once again, of his presence since before time began and his role as second person of the Holy Trinity.

The Catechism explains that in the Old Testament, the title "son of God" (with a lowercase "s") was given to "angels, the Chosen People, the children of Israel, and their kings." This was not a title that would have shocked people who heard it used in reference to Jesus, because it referred to an adopted-child relationship with God. So saying Jesus is the "son of God" would not have necessarily implied he was more than human. (441)

However, in Jesus' case, we have come to understand we use Son with an uppercase "S," meaning this title takes on a very different and unique meaning, much more than what everyone expected. Even among Jesus' own followers, many could not recognize him for who he really was—*the* Son of God.

When Jesus asks his disciples who the people say he is, Simon Peter responds: "You are the Messiah, the Son of the Living God." (Matthew 16:16) And Jesus tells him only his Father could have revealed this to him, a truth that will become the cornerstone of the faith. (442)

Teachable Moment

Twice in Scripture God speaks directly of his "beloved Son." When Jesus was baptized by John in the Jordan River, the heavens opened, and the Spirit of God descended on him like a dove. A voice from the heavens said, "This is my beloved Son, with whom I am well pleased." (Matthew 3:16) Later on, Jesus took the apostles Peter, James, and John up a mountain and was transfigured before them with Moses and Elijah on either side, and a voice from heaven once again said, "This is my beloved Son, with whom I am well pleased; listen to him." (Matthew 17:5) In these cases, Jesus is not only the Son with a capital "S," but he is also the son child and servant of God, as written about by the Old Testament prophet Isaiah.

Lord of Lords

In the last chapter, we talked about how God revealed himself to Moses in the Old Testament, calling himself "I Am Who Am," or the Hebrew word YHWH. Pious Jews, unwilling even to speak the name of God, used another term: *Adonai*, which is translated in Greek as *Kyrios* and in English as *Lord*. Now, in the New Testament, "Lord" is used not only as a name for God the Father but also for Jesus the Son. Jesus refers to himself in this way to his apostles, and then demonstrates his "divine sovereignty" through his power over nature, sickness, demons, and death. (447)

The Catechism explains that the earliest Christian creeds professed that the same "power, honor, and glory due to God the Father are due also to Jesus." (449) By calling Jesus Lord, believers—with the assistance of the Holy Spirit—recognize Jesus' divinity and his place of prominence in the world, in history, and in their own individual lives.

The Incarnation

Jesus is often referred to as the "Incarnation" or as "God Incarnate." That's really just an impressive way to say Jesus is God in the form of a human being. It comes from the Latin meaning "in flesh."

Why did God choose to become flesh? Couldn't he have done whatever he needed to do from above? The Catechism explains God took human form for several important purposes:

◆ To save us by "reconciling us with God" (457)

◆ To help us "know God's love" (458)

◆ To be "our model of holiness" (459)

◆ To make us "partakers of the divine nature" (460)

Teachable Moment

Going back to the idea of Jesus as the Word, we now take that a step further: Jesus is known as the "Word made flesh." This is how it is stated in the poetic prologue of the Gospel of John (John 1:14) and is the same as the Incarnation: God's one true Word was Jesus, who was God in the flesh of a fully human man.

The Catechism says belief in "the true Incarnation of the Son of God is the distinctive sign of Christian faith." (463) To be Christian, you must first believe in this singular event: that God, being fully God, became a man, who was fully man. Jesus was not part God and part man, and God was not watered down by taking on human form. Even more, Jesus is not a third thing, distinct from God and man, like the color green you get by mixing blue and yellow.

As we discussed in Chapter 3, God the Father and God the Son are each fully God, and yet Jesus is also fully human. As the Nicene Creed reminds us with its poetic language: "God from God, Light from Light, True God from True God."

It's interesting, but the Catechism notes the first heresies in the Church did not necessarily deny that Christ was divine, but instead took issue with the idea of him being truly human. I guess we humans have a hard time believing that our God would want to take our form. (465–469)

He Is Body and Soul

So if Jesus is fully God, is it really possible for him to be human just like the rest of us? The Church teaches the Son of God had a "rational, human soul" along with his human body. Jesus even had to learn many things through experience just like we do. (471)

The Catechism refers to the Third Council of Constantinople in the year 681, which affirmed that Jesus "possesses two wills and two natural operations, divine and human," which do not contradict or oppose each other but cooperate as the Father willed it to be. (475) So, yes, Jesus really is human just like the rest of us.

True Confessions

Because Jesus had a true human body, just like you and me, his image can be recreated and venerated. He is the unseen God made visible to us. Put in modern terms, if Jesus were alive today, we could take an actual photograph of him, unlike God the Father or God the Spirit—whose image cannot be captured.

Hail Mary, Full of Grace

In the next line of the creed, the Virgin Mary enters the scene. The Apostles' Creed, when referring to Jesus' birth, says, "Who was conceived by the power of the Holy Spirit, born of the Virgin Mary ...." The Nicene Creed says, "By the power of the Holy Spirit he was born of the Virgin Mary, and became Man."

When we talk about Jesus being "conceived by the power of the Holy Spirit," we are talking about the Spirit of God allowing Mary to conceive Jesus in her womb sans sex. So Jesus, who is God's Son and is God, will be born of an earthly woman, who was "invited" to bear the Christ child. As always, God allows his creation to exercise free will. Mary freely chose to do as God wished, which is known as Mary's *fiat*.

Church Speak

Fiat refers to Mary's statement of choice to conceive the Son of God: "Behold, I am the handmaid of the Lord. May it be done to me according to your word." (Luke 1:38)

"The Holy Spirit will come upon you," the angel of God says to her. (Luke 1:34) The Catechism explains the Holy Spirit "is sent to sanctify the womb" of Mary and "divinely fecundate it," meaning God conceives the child within her. (485)

Now, God didn't choose just *any* woman to bear his Son. The Church teaches that Mary was predestined to be the mother of God. For all time, God had handpicked this "daughter of Israel" to be the mother of the Messiah. (488)

The Catechism explains that throughout the Old Testament we come to know the holy women who prepared the way for Mary: Eve, Sarah, Ruth, and Esther, among others. Quoting from *Lumen Gentium*, which is the Dogmatic Constitution on the Church written at Vatican II, the Catechism states Mary "stands out among the poor and humble of the Lord" and that in her the "new plan of salvation is established." (489)

> **Teachable Moment**
>
> The Feast of the Annunciation is celebrated March 25 and commemorates Luke's narrative of the announcement by the Angel Gabriel that Mary would conceive and bear the Son of God. Note it is 9 months before the celebration of Christ's birth on December 25.

The Immaculate Conception

So how did God prepare Mary to be mother of the Son of God? Well, when the Angel Gabriel appears to her, he says she is "full of grace."

> **You're Absolved If ...**
>
> You may think the Immaculate Conception refers to Jesus' conception in Mary's womb, but actually it does not. The Immaculate Conception refers to Mary's conception without the stain of original sin in preparation for her role as the mother of Jesus and, therefore, the Mother of God.

Over the years the Church has come to understand that from the moment of her conception, Mary is filled with God's Spirit and is free from the original sin that the rest of us carry with us into this life. (490–491)

What did Mary say when presented with this most unusual request? Well, after the initial shock of being told she would bear a child without the assistance of a man, she agrees without hesitation to take the job.

Pretty impressive! Imagine how incredibly frightening this must have been for her. Remember, Mary would have been very young, a young teenager in fact, and she had to know telling her neighbors she was pregnant by the Holy Spirit was not going to go over well with them, or with Joseph, her betrothed.

Mary could have said no, but she was "full of grace" and, therefore, capable and willing to do what would have been too overwhelming for those of us walking around with the baggage of original sin. Her now-famous line, the *fiat* that we spoke of earlier, is this: "Behold, I am the handmaid of the Lord. May it be done to me according to your word." (Luke 1:38) And with that, Mary became the "new Eve," giving human-kind the opportunity to be redeemed. She says "Yes," where Eve said "No." She obeys God's wishes where Eve disobeyed. (494)

A Virgin Birth

As if the Immaculate Conception of Mary is not hard enough to grasp, we now have to try to understand the virgin birth. As the creed reminds us, Jesus was "born of the Virgin Mary."

Mary was young and unmarried; she did not "know man" in the biblical sense. The Spirit of God conceived a child within her womb who would be both true God and true man. Doesn't it make sense that Jesus would be born of a woman and yet also begotten by God? Jesus could not sim-ply be an ordinary child born of two ordinary human beings. He was God made flesh. If Jesus is divine, and that's pretty much the heart of the matter if you are a Christian, it would stand to reason his concep-tion and birth would occur in an extraordinary way.

Matthew's account of Jesus' infancy tells us how when Joseph learned of Mary's news, he was not exactly overjoyed. He planned to divorce her. But an angel appeared to him in a dream and told him that the Holy Spirit had conceived the child she was to bear. Apparently this was one convincing angel because Joseph reversed course, married Mary, and went on to become Jesus' foster father, as he is known in the Church.

True Confessions

Mary's virginity is not an easy thing for many people to accept. The Catechism goes back to the writings by St. Ignatius of Antioch, a bishop and martyr in the first century. He addressed the fact that some early Christians were "troubled by the silence of St. Mark's Gospel and the New Testament epistles about Jesus' virginal conception." He wrote that faith in the virgin birth was met with mockery and opposition from people of all stripes—Jews, non-Jews, and pagans—which flies in the face of claims that belief in the virgin birth was motivated by a nod to paganism. The virgin birth is "accessible only to faith," meaning that like so many other aspects of faith, it is a mystery that cannot be fully understood in human terms and must be accepted as part of the larger mystery of God's divine plan. (498)

Mother to Us All

Okay, so Jesus was conceived and born of the Virgin Mary, but it doesn't end there. The Church teaches that Mary remained "ever virgin." Once again quoting from *Lumen Gentium*, the Catechism explains the birth of the Christ child did not "diminish his mother's virginal integrity but sanctified it." (499)

Why all the fuss about virginity? Well, first of all, if Jesus had been born of two human parents like everyone else, where would the divinity be? The Church teaches that in being conceived by the Spirit and born of the Virgin, the Son of God was never separated from his heavenly father. Jesus, the "new Adam," inaugurates a "new creation." (504)

Mary, the new Eve, through her perpetual virginity, remains an "undivided gift" to God and the spiritual mother of all of us. (506) She is the symbol of the Church. So we can call on Mary our heavenly mother in much the same way that we might call on our earthly mothers for help. She may not be available to watch the kids or fold the laundry, but through prayer she can be a comfort, guide, and support.

You're Absolved If ...

You may think Catholics worship Mary, but they do not. Mary accepted Jesus into her life in the most profound way. She is known as the first disciple and is a model for those trying to accept Jesus into their own lives. Catholics turn to Mary in prayer, not because they see her on an equal plane with God but because they see her as a way to God.

The Least You Need to Know

◆ Jesus is also called Christ, Messiah, Son of God, Lord, and the Incarnation.

◆ Jesus Christ is true God and true man, the physical, visible sign of an invisible God.

◆ God's Spirit allowed Mary to conceive Jesus in her womb, making him truly human but also truly divine.

◆ Although Mary was predestined since the beginning of time to be the mother of God, she had the freedom to accept or reject God's request.

◆ The Immaculate Conception refers to Mary's conception without the stain of original sin, in anticipation of her role in salvation history.

◆ The Virgin Mary is the spiritual mother of all Catholics and a symbol of the Church.

Chapter 7

The Journey of Jesus Christ

In This Chapter

- ◆ Jesus' life from birth through Ascension
- ◆ The role of Jesus' miracles
- ◆ When Jesus is tempted by Satan
- ◆ Understanding why the Crucifixion occurred
- ◆ The hope and grace of the Resurrection

Now we come to actual events of Jesus' life, the events recorded in Scripture that give us a picture of who Jesus is, what he said, and how he lived. For many Christians, some of these stories are as familiar as the stories of their own families' lives. For others, hearing about the many ways in which Jesus helped, healed, and saved will be refreshingly "good news."

Jesus saved humankind through his death on the cross and his Resurrection. However, it was the individual events of his entire life that led up to this culmination of his mission on earth. We cannot possibly understand what Jesus did for us if we don't go back and look at the life that he lived.

The Meaning of His Life

The creed breaks down the events surrounding the Incarnation—Jesus' conception and birth—and the events surrounding what the Church calls the "paschal mystery"—his *Passion*, Crucifixion, death, burial, descent into hell, Resurrection, and Ascension. (512)

> ### Church Speak
>
> **Passion** comes from the Latin word *patior*, meaning "to endure, to undergo, or to suffer." We get the noun "patient" as well as "passion" from this Latin root. In the Church, the Passion of Christ refers to the suffering and death Jesus endured. Palm Sunday is also known as Passion Sunday. Twice during Lent—on Palm Sunday and Good Friday—Catholics hear the Passion, which is the Gospel account of Christ's final hours, from the Last Supper to his Crucifixion.

The Catechism explains that Christ's entire earthly life—from the things he said and did to the events of his "hidden life" (something we'll explain further in a minute) and the sufferings he endured—is a revelation, bringing us ever closer to God the Father. His life was a "mystery of redemption." (517)

His life is also called a "mystery of recapitulation." Sounds bad, but it's not—at least not for us. What that means is everything Jesus had to go through in his life occurred in order to return us to our original vocation, so that what we had lost in Adam we might recover in Jesus. (518)

We have to start off by recognizing that Jesus Christ did not enter into life on earth so he could buy a nice house in a suburb of Nazareth and become CEO of God, Inc. He came to earth not to achieve anything for himself but to achieve everything for us. As the Nicene Creed says, "For us men and our salvation, he came down from heaven."

Birth and Baptism

It all begins on Christmas, which, of course, wasn't called Christmas back then. As Luke tells the story that we hear at each Christmas Midnight Mass, Joseph and Mary made a long, arduous trip to Bethlehem because of a government census, and, as most of us have probably experienced in our own lives with things like this, it couldn't have come at a worse time. Mary was large with child. There was no room at the inn. But it turns out that this is exactly how it was supposed to be.

In Luke's account, Jesus was not meant to come in palatial glory but in humility. He arrived in a filthy stable, surrounded by hay and barnyard animals.

There is a series of events in Jesus' infancy, recounted by Matthew and Luke, that hold great importance in the life of the Church and the faith. They may seem fairly common on the surface, but the Catechism explains that they signify much more than meets the eye:

◆ Luke's account of the circumcision of Jesus when he was 8 days old is not simply a Jewish tradition that Jesus' family was bound to uphold. Instead it's a sign of Jesus' connection to the covenant people of Israel, whose laws he would observe and whose rituals he would celebrate throughout his life. It is also a foreshadowing of the baptism that would one day be the pivotal event that would usher all Catholics into the family of faith. (527)

◆ Matthew's story of the Epiphany—when the wise men, or magi, came from the East to pay homage to the child Jesus—is not about Mary and Joseph doing that whole new-parent thing and insisting, "You have to come see the baby." The Epiphany is what the Catechism calls a "manifestation of Jesus as Messiah of Israel, Son of God, and Savior of the world." In other words, the Epiphany demonstrates that people of all nations and backgrounds can come to Jesus, as the wise men did when they sought out the "king of nations." (528)

◆ Luke's account of the presentation of Jesus in the temple is another ordinary event with extraordinary significance. When Jesus was brought before Simeon and Anna, he was recognized as the Messiah. This event signified the anticipation among the people of Israel for the long-awaited Messiah. This was also where the sorrow in Jesus' life was predicted, and Mary was told that a sword would pierce her heart. (529)

◆ Matthew's account of the flight into Egypt and the massacre of the innocents by King Herod's soldiers signifies that Jesus' entire life would be lived "under the sign of persecution." His departure from Egypt was reminiscent of the Exodus of the Jewish people from Egypt and set Jesus up as the new Moses and "definitive liberator" of humankind. (530)

◆ The finding in the temple is a later event in Jesus' childhood, recounted by Luke, that gives us a rare glimpse of Jesus during a time that is otherwise absent from the Gospels. In this episode, we see Jesus step out of his "hidden life" to show us his complete commitment to the mission of his Father.

Mary and Joseph took Jesus to Jerusalem every year for the feast of Passover. When he was 12 years old, he did not join his parents' caravan home but remained in the temple, listening to the rabbis and asking questions. More than a day had gone by before Mary and Joseph realized he was not with them and several more days had passed before they found him. When they finally did catch up with him in the temple, he said simply, "Did you not know that I had to be in my Father's house?" (Luke 2:49) Even as a child, Jesus was called to a special role in his Father's plan, although Mary and Joseph often could not fully understand it.

After Luke's account of the finding in the temple, the Gospels all jump from the earliest days of Jesus' infancy to his adult life in the public eye. What we miss are the many years he spent being a normal person—living a simple life amid regular people, working, praying, and being obedient to his family and Jewish law. The part of Jesus' life we don't hear much about in Scripture is called the "hidden life" of Jesus, and is the part that is probably most like ours.

With his baptism by John in the Jordan, Jesus came into public view once again. You may wonder why Jesus would need to be baptized if he was the Son of God. The Catechism explains that by being baptized, Jesus accepted his mission as the suffering servant of God (as prefigured in Isaiah 42–53) who would suffer for the sake of the people of Israel at the hands of the people of Israel.

By his baptism, Jesus, though sinless, "allow[ed] himself to be numbered among sinners" and anticipated the "baptism" of his bloody death. With his death and resurrection, the heavens that were closed by Adam were reopened, and Jesus took on the role as the *Lamb of God*, who would take away the sins of the world. (536)

Church Speak

Jesus is known as the **Lamb of God,** a title referring to his sacrifice for humanity in a new Passover, just as a lamb is sacrificed in Jewish tradition to mark the start of the Passover of the Hebrews under Moses.

Temptation in the Desert

Now we come to Jesus' temptation in the desert, which might seem odd at first to think Jesus could be tempted. If Jesus is God, how can he be tempted, and what was he doing in a desert for 40 days? Wasn't he pure enough? Remember, he's God but he's also man in all things, except sin. This desert experience presented an opportunity for Jesus to take everything Adam did and turn it on its head.

When Jesus was in the desert, hungry and alone and probably a little worn out, Satan decided to test his mettle. He tempted Jesus three times, suggesting he should be a flashy Messiah, a showy Savior. Satan, who is the symbol of all that is opposed to God, told him to turn stones to bread, to jump off the top of the temple to see if God would save him, and to bow down to Satan and receive power beyond his wildest dreams. These temptations by Satan remind us of how he tempted Adam in Paradise and the Israelites while they wandered in the desert for 40 years. The similarities end there, however, as Jesus rebuffed all of Satan's temptations. And Satan "departed from him for a time," meaning that he had every intention of coming back when things are looking bleak and Jesus is looking weak. (Luke 4:13)

The Catechism explains that in the desert Jesus "is the devil's conqueror," giving us a glimpse of what was to happen during the Passion when Jesus submits himself in complete obedience to the will of his Father. (539)

Teachable Moment

The Church season of Lent connects Catholics to Jesus' 40-day fast in the desert. During Lent, Catholics journey through a spiritual desert, fasting and praying for 40 days in preparation for Holy Week and Easter.

Signs and Wonders

After Jesus was baptized, things started to happen quickly. Before you know it, John the Baptist was arrested and beheaded. Meanwhile, Jesus was in Galilee preaching and selecting the men who were to become his apostles. Throughout all of this, Jesus' main message was as the Son of Man, he has come for *all* people, not just the children of Israel but every single human being. And it doesn't matter if you are a sinner; as long as you repent and follow Jesus, then you, too, can enter the kingdom of God.

The Catechism reminds us that Jesus "shares the life of the poor" and he reached out to the poor in a special way, telling his followers they must love and care for those in need if they hope to have a share in God's kingdom. He also reached out to the sinners, those who were the outcasts and pariahs of society. He "invites them to conversion" and shows them the Father's mercy. (544–545)

> **Church Speak**
>
> In his preaching, Jesus used **parables,** which are stories that teach people lessons about God through comparisons to real-life experiences. The Good Samaritan, the Prodigal Son, and the Lost Sheep are a few of the better-known parables that Jesus used to teach deep doctrine in easy-to-understand ways.

Jesus, of course, didn't just preach the Good News. He had the miracles to back up the words. His signs of wonder were not performed to satisfy curiosity but to bear witness to who he was and what his mission was. He fed the hungry, cured the lame, and cast out demons as visible signs of his invisible connection to God the Father. Through his miracles, Jesus gave everyone a glimpse of his victory over Satan once and for all. (550)

To help him in his mission on earth, Jesus chose the Twelve Apostles, giving them a "share in his authority" and sending them out to preach the Good News. Simon Peter, whom Jesus called the "rock" on whom he will build his Church, recognized Jesus early on as the "Messiah and Son of the living God" (Matthew 16:16–18). Peter was promised the keys to the kingdom of heaven and eventually took the "first place" among the Twelve. (552)

After his Resurrection, Jesus made their mission even more specific. He gave Peter the "power of the keys," indicating the authority to govern the house of God, which is the Church. Even more, he gave the apostles power to "bind and loose," which means to absolve sins, and to pronounce "doctrinal judgments," which are authoritative interpretations of the teachings of Jesus. (553) This mandate continues to this day, carried out by the college of bishops with the pope functioning like Peter before him.

Transfiguration

As we get toward the end of Jesus' public preaching life and move toward his Passion and death, there are two important events that must be discussed: the Transfiguration and Jesus' entry into Jerusalem.

During the Transfiguration, Jesus took Peter, James, and John up a mountain where he was "transfigured" before them. His face and clothes became dazzling with light. Moses and Elijah appeared on either side of him. A cloud came and cast a shadow over them and then a voice said, "This is my chosen Son; listen to him." (Luke 9:35)

Jesus revealed his true nature during the Transfiguration, and, according to St. Thomas Aquinas in his *Summa Theologica*, also revealed the Holy Trinity: "the Father in the voice; the Son in the man; the Spirit in the shining cloud." (555)

The Gospel account is clearly about the Lord's Transfiguration, and it is also about the suffering he was to endure. It is about his glory, and it is also about his impending death. It is about his status with the greatest of the lawmakers and the greatest of the prophets, and it is also about his status as the suffering servant of God, who, though innocent, would suffer and die for Israel.

The Transfiguration gave the three apostles who were privy to it something to hold on to when things turned increasingly more desperate and dangerous as Jesus' Passion and death neared. For Catholics today, the Transfiguration remains a promise of things to come, something to hold on to as we journey toward heaven.

Teachable Moment

In the Catholic Mass, at the beginning of the Liturgy of the Eucharist, the people sing **Holy, Holy,** and **Hosanna,** echoing the shouts of the eager crowds in Jerusalem all those years ago.

When Jesus entered Jerusalem so triumphantly less than one week before his Crucifixion, it was hard to imagine things would turn out so badly. But as he headed toward the holy city, Jesus knew he would die there. He told his apostles he would die there. Riding on a donkey, he entered Jerusalem to a crowd waving palm branches and shouts of *Hosanna,* which means "save us."

Agony and Death

The Apostles' Creed says Jesus "suffered under Pontius Pilate, was crucified, died, and was buried. He descended into hell; the third day he rose again from the dead; he ascended into heaven, and sits at the right hand of God the Father almighty; from thence he shall come to judge the living and the dead."

The Nicene Creed skips the part about hell and adds a few bonus phrases about Jesus doing everything for our sakes, fulfilling Scripture, coming in glory, and opening up to us a kingdom with no end.

Before we get to the glory, however, there is much, much agony. The Church calls going from agony to glory the "paschal mystery," which refers to Jesus' suffering, death, and Resurrection. This is the apex of Jesus' mission on earth, and this is the heart of the Good News that every follower of Jesus Christ is challenged to proclaim: Jesus, the Savior of the world, has set us free through his cross and Resurrection.

Let's talk about why anyone wanted Jesus dead in the first place. Wasn't he a good guy? He was curing people, getting rid of demons, turning water into wine. Who wouldn't love that? Well, some of the things we find so incredibly amazing and comforting are the very things that got Jesus into trouble with the Pharisees, the Sadducees, and the government.

For instance, he healed on the Sabbath—a no-no according to Jewish law. He ate with public sinners. He was accused of demonic possession, blasphemy, and all sorts of religious crimes that set him up as an enemy of Israel. And when he said he was the Son of God, one with God, well, that was the last straw for the people in power.

You're Absolved If ...

Some may think the Catholic Church blames the Jews for Jesus' death. While there is a scriptural reference where the people in the crowd condemning Jesus shout, "Let his blood be on us and on our children" (Matthew 27:25), the Church today teaches that Jews cannot be held accountable for crimes committed during the Passion.

As we approach Jesus' Passion, his final suffering, the one question that most likely comes to mind is why Jesus had to die at all. If he is God, couldn't he have found another way to save humankind? The Church teaches that Jesus' death was not an accident, a coincidence, or bad timing on his part, but that his death was God's plan from the beginning of time.

Of course, that makes it sound as if Jesus did not have free will or as if the people responsible were not acting of their own accord. But that's not true. You have to remember God, who exists from before time began in his own sort of timeless universe, not only knows the plan but also knows how everyone will eventually react to the plan. So although he set the plan in motion, he does not choose the end results. People do that. (600)

In other words, Jesus freely offered himself up to death to free us from sins, as it was written in Scripture and in his Father's divine plan. (601)

Christ's final days begin with the Last Supper, when he sat down with the apostles to share the Passover meal and transformed it—what the Church would remember and continue to celebrate as the Eucharist. "This is my body, which will be given for you; do this in memory of me." (Luke 22:19) We will explore the Eucharist further in Chapter 13, so for now let's simply understand that Jesus offered himself to his disciples. Then he invited his apostles to "perpetuate" that offering, which is what happens every time a priest celebrates Mass. (611)

From the Last Supper we move to the Agony in the Garden of Gethsemane, where Jesus asked God to take away the suffering he was about to endure, but freely accepted whatever the Father willed. This was where Jesus was arrested after his betrayal by the apostle Judas Iscariot.

The Catechism explains just as Adam's disobedience brought sin upon all of us, Jesus' obedience to the Father brought us redemption. Jesus, the "suffering servant," made an offering of himself for us—all of us, for all time. He substituted his obedience for Adam's disobedience. (615)

Just because Jesus atoned for our sins doesn't mean we don't have some work to do. Jesus called on all of his disciples to "take up his cross and follow me" (Matthew 16:24), reminding us that we are not immune from suffering. Not that we have to die on a literal cross, but we must be willing to bear the crosses that are placed on our shoulders in the forms of suffering, pain, and sorrow, and to die to our own weaknesses and failings. (618)

After Jesus' death on the cross, he was placed in a borrowed tomb. He died and was buried like every other human, but, unlike the rest of us who are fully mortal, Jesus' body was kept from corruption. (627)

Resurrection and Ascension

Now we get to the part where Jesus descended into hell, which is only in the Apostles' Creed and not in the Nicene Creed. You're probably wondering why Jesus would go to hell. If he, of all people, didn't go straight to heaven, then who would? Well, it's not exactly hell in the sense we might imagine, the one reserved for those playing fast and loose with the big commandments.

Jesus died a human death, and therefore descended into the "realm of the dead," where he brought the Gospel message of salvation to complete fulfillment. (634) According to Church teaching, everyone—good or bad—must await salvation, which they cannot achieve on their own. They need Jesus. So Jesus, when he died, did not descend into the place of eternal damnation and hellfire, but to a realm where there were souls awaiting their redeemer. (633)

The Catechism explains that by dying a human death and descending to the realm of the dead, Jesus conquered death and the devil, and that he opened the gates of heaven for those souls who had descended to the dead. (635)

The Apostles' Creed links Jesus' Resurrection to his descent into hell almost into the same breath. "On the third day he rose again," it says. This is it, the crowing glory. Jesus' death was not in vain. Just as he promised, he rose from the dead and, in doing so, gave every person reason to hope, to know that death cannot own them.

The Church teaches that Jesus' Resurrection is not merely a figurative event or a literary device. It is a real and actual event, although we do not and cannot fully comprehend it in human terms.

True Confessions

After Jesus' Resurrection, the apostle Thomas would not believe the news and said until he put his finger into the nail marks and his hand into the side of Jesus, he would not believe. (Matthew 20:24–29) So at first, Jesus' Resurrection was met with disbelief not only by his enemies but also by many of his followers.

The Catechism explains that by his death Jesus freed humankind from sin and by his Resurrection he opened a new way of life for all people. Through his death and Resurrection, Jesus gave all humanity a share in his grace, making all men and women his adopted brothers and sisters. (654)

After his Resurrection, Jesus remained on earth, walking among humans and revealing himself to his apostles in various ways, often in the breaking of the bread. After this period, he ascended, body and soul, to his Father in heaven.

We end this section of the creed with the words, "From thence he shall come to judge the living and the dead," meaning Jesus will return, at which point he will be the judge of those who have lived righteous lives and those who have lived lives filled with sin and evil.

The Church teaches that before Jesus comes again, his followers will have to stand a "final trial." Jesus, however, will triumph in the end of time, at which point he will reveal the secrets within the heart of each person. (679)

The Least You Need to Know

◆ Jesus came for all people and performed miracles to bear witness to God's power and to his own mission of redemption.

◆ The Transfiguration, which was a pivotal moment during Jesus' ministry on earth, revealed his true nature to the apostles Peter, James, and John.

◆ By freely accepting the Crucifixion, Jesus opened the gates of heaven for all humanity.

◆ Jesus redeemed humankind from the sin of Adam through his death on the cross and Resurrection.

◆ Having ascended into heaven, Jesus now sits at the right hand of his Father, his humanity forever linked with the Trinity.

◆ At the end of the world, Jesus will come again and will judge both the living and the dead.

Chapter 8

Spirit of God

In This Chapter

- ◆ Understanding the Holy Spirit and his role
- ◆ The names and symbols for the Spirit
- ◆ Learning what Pentecost was all about
- ◆ The Spirit at work in the Catholic Church today

Now we get to what I consider the most elusive aspect of the Trinity, the Holy Spirit. To me, God the Father feels more concrete even though he is invisible. God the Son is very concrete in Jesus. The Spirit, on the other hand, is literally like trying to catch the wind.

We're going to talk about where the Holy Spirit comes from, how he got here, and why we need him. The key thing to remember through all of this is that the Holy Spirit is no less God than the Father and Son. He is equal to them and has existed as one with them since before time began.

This part of the Apostles' Creed is short and sweet: "I believe in the Holy Spirit." Nothing more, nothing less.

As always, the Nicene Creed goes a little further, saying, "We believe in the Holy Spirit, the Lord, the Giver of life, who proceeds from the Father and the Son. With the Father and the Son he is worshipped and glorified. He has spoken through the prophets." Well, that seems like a whole other story, doesn't it? Suddenly a much clearer picture of this third person of the Trinity begins to emerge, and that is where we will begin.

Who Is the Holy Spirit?

Jesus told his apostles at the Last Supper (in John 14 and 16) that "another Advocate" or *Paraclete*, a Greek term meaning advocate, would be sent to them. This Advocate is the "Spirit of truth," who was to be sent by either the Father at the request of Jesus (John 14) or by Jesus himself when he went to the Father (John 16). This Paraclete-Advocate-Spirit was sent to dwell among the disciples in order to guide them and remind them of what Jesus told them when he was with them. So after Jesus had gone to the Father, the Spirit remained on earth, and the Spirit still lives among us today. We cannot see the Spirit or hear the Spirit in a physical way, but he is alive within us, around us, in Scripture, and in the works of the Church.

The early creeds of the Church proclaimed first and foremost that the Holy Spirit is one of the three persons in the Holy Trinity, and this sets the stage for everything else. It means the Holy Spirit is coequal and coeternal with the Father and Son. He didn't begin with Jesus or with the Resurrection. The Spirit was, since before time began, fully in cooperation with the Father and Son, although he is the last person of the Trinity to be revealed to us.

The Catechism explains that for Catholic believers the Spirit is "the first to awaken faith in us and to communicate to us the new life." (684) So it is the Spirit that brings faith to life and allows the faithful to know God and Jesus in a personal way.

You're Absolved If ...

Some still use the name "Holy Ghost" when referring to the Holy Spirit. This was the name for the third person of the Trinity used until the 1960s when parts of the Mass began being celebrated in English rather than Latin. Because Scripture translations used "Holy Spirit" instead of "Holy Ghost," it was thought that using the Holy Spirit reference throughout all worship and prayer would be more consistent with Scripture. Also, there was a feeling that "Ghost" conjured up haunting images from modern English and didn't accurately symbolize the third person of the Trinity in the same way the word "Spirit" does, which symbolizes the wind or breath of God.

Signs of the Spirit

The Holy Spirit goes by a few different names in Scripture and in Church teaching, although Holy Spirit is the most common. He is also known as the Paraclete, as we mentioned earlier, which the Catechism explains as "he who is called to one's side," or the Advocate. He is also known as consoler, sanctifier, and Spirit of truth, among other lesser-known titles found in the Acts of the Apostles and the Epistles of St. Paul. (692)

You may also know the Holy Spirit by the symbols that represent his presence and action in the life and hearts of believers, and there are quite a few:

◆ **Water,** the sign of new birth, is symbolic of the Holy Spirit and the cleansing actions that occur through him during the sacrament of baptism, which we will discuss at length in Chapter 12. The Catechism explains that in the Spirit we are "born into the divine life." (694)

◆ **Anointing** with oil, the sign of the sacrament of confirmation, verges on being a synonym for the Holy Spirit, according to the Catechism. Jesus was anointed by the Spirit, which he now pours out for the rest of us. (695)

◆ **Fire** symbolizes the Spirit's "transforming energy," which is seen throughout the Old and New Testaments. John the Baptist tells his followers: "I am baptizing you with water, but one mightier than I is coming. I am not worthy to loosen the thongs of his sandals. He will baptize you with the Holy Spirit and with fire." (Luke 3:16) Just as fire transforms whatever it touches, so does the Spirit. (696)

◆ **Cloud and light,** the former signifying darkness or obscurity and the other luminescence or revelation, are "manifestations" of the Spirit. In both the Old and New Testaments these manifestations reveal God to his people—Moses on Mount Sinai, Mary at the Annunciation, the three apostles present at the Transfiguration, and so on. (697)

◆ The **seal** is a symbol of anointing, indicating that the believer now bears an "indelible" or permanent mark of the Holy Spirit. The seal is a critical part of the sacraments of baptism, confirmation, and holy orders, as will be discussed in later chapters.

◆ The **hand** represents the Spirit, in that Jesus would heal the sick and bless children by laying hands on them. The apostles later did the same in his name. Even more pointedly, it is by the apostles' laying on of hands that the Holy Spirit was given to others. (699)

◆ The **finger** of God's outstretched hand is seen as a symbol of the Spirit. In the Old Testament, God uses his finger to write the Ten Commandments on stone tablets. In the New Testament, Jesus is said to "write" on human hearts. (700)

◆ The **dove** is one of the more common symbols of the Spirit. When Jesus came up from the water after his baptism, the Holy Spirit came upon him in the form of a dove. Christian iconography traditionally uses a dove to connote the Spirit. (701)

The Spirit at Work

We have looked at who the Spirit is and how he is symbolized. Now let's consider more specifically what the Spirit does.

The Catechism explains that we can see the work of the Holy Spirit in a variety of important ways: In the Scripture he has inspired; in the Tradition of the Church; in the Church's magisterium, which the Spirit assists; in the words and symbols of the liturgy; in prayer where the

Spirit intercedes for us; in the ministries of the Church on earth; in the signs of apostolic and missionary life; and in the witness of the saints who exhibit the Spirit's holiness. (688)

The Spirit, who is united with the Father and the Son, never works independent of them. He is on a joint mission with the Son in the work of salvation, and he brings that mission to life in the lives of the adopted children of the Father, meaning all of us. (689–690)

Clearly, based on everything we've discussed so far, the Holy Spirit plays a pretty big role in seeing God's divine plan to its fulfillment. He was there from day one. He spoke to humankind through the words of the *prophets* of the Old Testament. He came upon Mary and allowed her to conceive the Son of God. He was with Jesus throughout his life and death, and he remained with the apostles and remains with all of us for all time. That's some resumé.

> ### Church Speak
>
> A **prophet** is someone sent by God to proclaim his word, to speak in God's name. Although prophets did not principally predict the future, sometimes they did, yet sometimes their predictions were wrong. Oftentimes they chastised Israel; other times they consoled Israel and offered hope for the future. The Old Testament includes 18 prophetic books. John the Baptist, in the New Testament, completed the work of the old-school prophets.

I think sometimes the Holy Spirit doesn't get his due because he seems like he's a Johnny-come-lately in terms of divine revelation and intervention. Nothing could be further from the truth. The Holy Spirit is the "breath" of God. At the beginning of creation, it is the Spirit that breathes life into all living things. Certainly that's nothing to shrug off. (703)

Later on, it is the Spirit that reveals, through various manifestations, great truths to the patriarchs of the Old Testament, from the Ten Commandments to the Psalms. (707–708)

Scripture tells us John the Baptist was "filled with the Holy Spirit" from the moment of his conception in his mother's womb. And, of course, we know it was the Holy Spirit who came upon Mary at the Annunciation and allowed God to become one of us.

The Catechism says that when the pregnant Mary visited her cousin, Elizabeth, who was pregnant with John the Baptist, it was a "visit from God to his people." Even before his birth, God made man was reaching out to the rest of humankind. (717)

John the Baptist was the prelude to Jesus, and the Church teaches that through John, the Holy Spirit "concluded his speaking through the prophets." (719)

Now let's backtrack just a bit to revisit Mary and the role of the Spirit in her life and her decision. The Catechism explains that Mary was "the masterwork of the mission of the Son and the Spirit in the fullness of time." (721) Wow, Mary was the "masterwork." She became God's dwelling place, and the Holy Spirit made it happen.

The Holy Spirit "prepared" Mary by his grace, "fulfilled" the Father's plan in her, "manifested" in her the Son of God, and through her brought all people "into communion" with Jesus Christ. (722-725) *That* is the work of the Holy Spirit.

According to the Catechism, we must read the entire second section of the creed—the section on Jesus Christ—in light of the role of the Holy Spirit. They were on a "joint mission," which Jesus revealed slowly throughout his preaching life and completely after his death and Resurrection. (727)

After his Resurrection, when Jesus appeared to his disciples, he said, "Peace be with you. As the Father has sent me, so I send you." (John 20:21) He then "breathed" the Holy Spirit on them, giving them the mission—which is the mission of the Church to this day—to continue the work he began.

Pentecost

Fifty days after the Resurrection, on what is known as *Pentecost*, after Jesus had already ascended into heaven, the Spirit of the Lord came upon the apostles and the Holy Trinity was fully revealed. (732)

"... Suddenly there came from the sky a noise like a strong driving wind, and it filled the entire house in which they were. Then there appeared to them tongues as of fire, which parted and came to rest on each one of them. And they were filled with the Holy Spirit and began to speak in different tongues, as the Spirit enabled them to proclaim." (Acts 2:1–4)

Church Speak

Pentecost comes from the Greek word *pentekoste*, meaning "fiftieth day," and in the Catholic Church commemorates the day when the Holy Spirit descended upon the apostles, which was about 50 days after Easter. For Jews, it was the "feast of weeks," which fell on the fiftieth day after Passover, when the first fruits of the grain harvest were presented to the Lord (Deut 16:9).

Okay, so once Pentecost was over and the apostles accepted the fact that now they could be understood by people who spoke languages the apostles had never spoken, what happened to the Holy Spirit? Well, the Spirit is present today just as he was present in the room with the apostles all those years ago. Maybe we're not hearing rushing winds or seeing fire descend from the heavens, but the Spirit is alive and well, nonetheless.

The Church teaches it is by the gift of the Holy Spirit that God's love is given to each of us, and that through the Spirit each of us can be restored to the "divine likeness" we lost through sin. (734)

The Catechism explains—and quotes St. Paul's Letter to the Galatians (5:22–23)—that by the "power of the Spirit," we can bear the "fruit of the Spirit," which are love, joy, peace, patience, kindness, goodness, faithfulness, gentleness, and self-control. (736)

Teachable Moment

The Church teaches that there are seven "gifts" of the Holy Spirit: wisdom, understanding, knowledge, counsel, piety, fortitude, and fear of the Lord. These gifts are spelled out in Isaiah 11:1–3 as characteristics of the Spirit of the Lord that will rest upon the Messiah. They are an explicit part of the prayer that is said when the minister of the sacrament of confirmation extends his hands prior to anointing the believer.

The Spirit in the Church Today

So how is the Holy Spirit evident in the Church today? The Catechism explains that the joint mission of Christ and the Spirit is "brought to completion" in the Church (737), and that the Spirit "builds, animates, and sanctifies" the Church on earth (747). And what does all of that mean? The Church's mission is not separate from or in addition to the mission of Jesus and the Spirit but is "its sacrament," meaning that the Church makes Jesus' mission present in the world today. (738)

Through the seven sacraments of the Church (which we will discuss in the next section of this book), Christ sends his Spirit to the faithful. Quoting from St. Paul's Letter to the Romans, the Catechism explains that the Spirit, who helps believers face their weaknesses and is the "master of prayer," intercedes in the lives of the faithful "with sighs too deep for words" (Romans 8:26), giving us a poetic and somewhat concrete picture of a being that is in many ways beyond description. (741)

The Least You Need to Know

- ◆ The Holy Spirit is the third person of the Holy Trinity who was fully revealed to humanity on Pentecost. He is equal with Father and Son and, like them, has existed since before time began.

- ◆ There are numerous names for the Spirit and a series of symbols—like water, fire, anointing, and the dove—that represent our human attempts to capture the Spirit's essence and activity.

- ◆ Jesus and the Holy Spirit are on a "joint mission" to save humanity, which was inaugurated with Jesus' death and Resurrection and brought into a final but not-yet-over stage through the outpouring of the Spirit.

- ◆ The Spirit sanctifies and animates the Church today so it can continue the mission of Jesus.

- ◆ The power of the Holy Spirit offers believers "fruit" in the form of love, joy, and patience, as well as many "gifts," such as wisdom, fortitude, and piety.

Chapter 9

The Holy Catholic Church

In This Chapter

- ◆ What it means to profess a belief in "one, holy, catholic and apostolic Church"
- ◆ The People of God, non-Catholics, and non-Christians
- ◆ Understanding the role of the pope and bishops
- ◆ The consecrated life of poverty, chastity, and obedience

From the Father, Son, and Spirit, we now move to a profession of belief in the Church itself. On the surface it may seem like an odd jump, but if you look a little closer you quickly see this belief flows directly out of the preceding sections of the creeds.

The Apostles' Creed says simply, "I believe in … the holy Catholic Church." The Nicene Creed says, "I believe in one, holy, catholic, and apostolic Church." In this chapter, we will start with the basics of the Apostles' Creed on profession of belief and move into the specifics of the Nicene Creed.

We will get into not only the Church as a whole, but the individual parts that make up that whole, from the pope, bishops, and priests to religious sisters, brothers, and lay men and women. This chapter is a primer on the structure of the Church and the roles of its members.

Mission Possible

At the beginning of this section on the creed, the Catechism includes a striking description of how the Catholic Church depends on Jesus Christ and the light he came to bring to the world. "... the Church is like the moon, all its light reflected from the sun." (748) Doesn't that put the Church in a whole new light, so to speak?

The Church does not exist for its own edification but for the glorification of Jesus Christ and to continue his mission on earth. The full sentence of the Apostles' Creed says, "I believe in the Holy Spirit, the holy Catholic Church ..." They are uttered in one breath because the Church flows from the Spirit. The Catechism explains that the Church is where the Holy Spirit "flourishes." (749)

Church Speak

Catholic and **catholic** (with a lowercase "c") mean two different things. The first refers to someone who is a particular type of Christian who adheres to three basic things: (1) the tenets of a faith started by Jesus and continued by the apostles and their successors in the college of bishops, (2) forms of worship that date from the apostolic age, and (3) a particular system of governance. The second definition, the one used in the Nicene Creed, refers to "universality." The Church is "catholic" in that it is on a mission from Christ to bring salvation to all of humanity. The Eastern Orthodox Church, in its nearly identical creed, also uses the term "catholic," even though members are not in communion with the Catholic Church, and Protestants who pray the creeds also understand "catholic" with a small "c."

Regardless of how we describe it, this Church was, according to the Catechism, planned from the world's beginning. That means from the beginning of time God planned that the world would be brought into communion with the Trinity through a "convocation" of people, which we know as the Church. (760–761)

The Church, as the Catechism explains, is born of Christ's total self-giving and is anticipated in Christ's institution of the Eucharist and fulfilled through his death on the cross. (766)

Through the power of the Holy Spirit, the Church began its mission, which is to spread the Gospel of Jesus Christ and make disciples of all nations. (768)

Teachable Moment

The Church is said to be a "sacrament," or a sign and instrument, of humanity's communion with God and of the unity of the whole human race. The Church becomes then the "visible plan" of the love God poured out for all humanity. (775)

People of God

The Catholic Church is made up of the "People of God," headed by Jesus Christ. You are not born into the People of God. Rather, you choose it through the spiritual rebirth of baptism, or, in the case of infant baptism, your parents and the community of the Church choose it for you and then nurture you in the faith.

The People of God share in Christ's work as priest, prophet, and king. Every individual, in accordance with the circumstances of their own lives, is called to take on these roles. The priestly role is shared with those who are baptized and become part of the "holy priesthood" of the faith; the prophetic role relates to teaching, which believers demonstrate by proclaiming the Gospel and witnessing to it in the world; and the kingly role relates to governing and shepherding, which means that Catholics are challenged to become like Christ the King, who is the servant of all. (783)

Let's put these roles in real people terms: parents, in the "domestic church" of their families, have their children baptized or "Christened" and pass along the faith to their children (priestly), teach them by word and example (prophetic), and oversee or "govern" them not only through rules but through an unconditional love that requires them to put the lives of their children first (kingly).

The Church's Role

The Church is known as the "Body of Christ" and as the "Bride of Christ," titles that refer to the Church's intimate relationship with Jesus. The Catechism explains that through the sacraments, especially baptism, confirmation, and the Eucharist, and with the aid of the Holy Spirit, believers become members of Christ's body, meaning they are united with him and with one another in him. (790)

And the Church is known as the "Temple of the Holy Spirit," the Spirit being the soul and the life force of the Church. So the Spirit is to the Body of Christ what the soul is to a human being. (797)

What About Everyone Else?

When Catholics say in the Nicene Creed they believe in "one holy, catholic, and apostolic Church," what exactly are they professing? Well, let's break that down word by word.

The Church is "one" because of its "source," which is the unity of one God in the Trinity; the Church is one because of its "founder," Jesus Christ, who reconciled all men and women to God by the cross; and finally the Church is one because of its "soul," which is the Holy Spirit, who brings about a communion of the faithful with Christ and with one another.

Once again, the prominence of the oneness of the Holy Trinity in the life of the Church can be found in even the most basic language of its prayers. (813)

The Catechism explains that this oneness joins all the faithful together in a unity held together by charity. We also see this unity of the Church present in the profession of faith received from the apostles, the common celebration of divine worship especially in the sacraments, and the succession that continues from the time of the apostles to this day. (815)

True Confessions

From the beginning, the Church has had to deal with disputes, heresies, and schisms, and yet there is an ongoing desire and effort to reunite all Christians. The Catechism explains that for this unification to occur, certain things are necessary, including common prayer, a deeper knowledge of one another, ongoing dialogue, and collaboration in service to humankind. (821)

The Church is "holy" because Jesus sanctified the Church through his death and Resurrection and endowed it with the Holy Spirit, making the Church not only sanctified but also sanctifying. The goal of the Church and its members is perfect holiness, and charity is "the soul" of that holiness. (823–826) The Church has models of this holiness in the Blessed Virgin Mary and the many saints—extraordinary men and women who are officially recognized by the Church for their faithfulness and virtues. We will discuss the saints further in the next chapter.

When professing the Church is "catholic" (remember that's with a lowercase "c," meaning "universal" or "in keeping with the whole"), believers are saying two things: the Church is catholic because the "fullness of Christ's body" exists within it, and the Church is catholic because it is on a mission to bring Jesus Christ to the entire human race. (830–831)

Up until now we have been talking about the universal Catholic Church, meaning the worldwide Catholic Church. But this idea of a catholic-with-a-small-"c" Church also extends to the individual churches that make up the larger Church.

The universal Church is found within geographical regions and within countries as "local churches," more commonly known as "dioceses," each one headed by a bishop. The dioceses are divided into "parishes," which are smaller worshipping communities typically divided by geographic location. These smaller local churches together make up the one, holy, catholic, and apostolic Church.

Other Christians

The Catechism teaches that all people are called to be members of the People of God, although only those who profess the Catholic faith and receive its sacraments are properly called Catholic. Still, the Church recognizes that many people who do not profess the Catholic faith will still be baptized Christians. These non-Catholic Christians, according to the Catechism, have an imperfect but certain communion with the Catholic Church. Quoting Pope Paul VI, the Catechism acknowledges that Orthodox Churches are so closely linked to the Roman Catholic Church that there is very little preventing the two Christian faiths from sharing a common celebration of the Eucharist. (838)

Non-Christians

Those who do not believe in Jesus Christ and have not received the Gospel are still connected to the Catholic faith in various ways. The Jewish faith, unlike any other non-Christian faith, shares a deep bond with the Catholic faith. (840)

Teachable Moment

For Catholics, there is a deep and lasting connection to the Jewish faith. Jesus was a devout Jew raised by devout Jewish parents.

One of the only key moments of Jesus' older childhood recorded in Scripture is when he was found in the temple in Jerusalem, where his parents had journeyed as part of the Passover custom. The first Eucharist occurred at a Passover meal. Hebrew Scripture and the rituals of the people of the Old Covenant play an integral part in the Catholic faith and the rituals of the Church to this day.

The Church recognizes that other non-Christian religions are on a search for God, a search that is good and true. The Catechism explains that the Church views these religions as a "preparation for the Gospel" and says they are given "by him who enlightens all men," meaning God. (843)

Are Only Catholics Saved?

So here's the big question: Do you have to be Catholic to be saved? Most precisely, the answer is, No! But the Church is very specific about this and teaches that those who know Christ yet still refuse him cannot be saved. On the other hand, those who do not know Christ and the Church but are making a sincere effort to know God can achieve salvation.

Related to that, there are some who wonder why it is that Catholics need to spread the Gospel and send out missionaries to bring Jesus to others. Can't they just believe and be done with it? Well, no. The Church's mission, as given by Jesus, is to bring his message to others and to "make disciples of all nations, baptizing them in the name of the Father and of the Son and of the Holy Spirit." (Matthew 28:19)

The Pope and Bishops

Finally we get to the last adjective in that line of the Nicene Creed: "apostolic." What does it mean that the Catholic Church is apostolic? It's very simple. The Catechism explains the Church is apostolic because it was "founded on the apostles" in three distinct ways:

◆ The Church is built on the "foundation of the apostles," who were chosen and sent by Jesus.

◆ Through the Holy Spirit, the Church hands on the teachings of the apostles.

◆ The Church continues to be guided by the apostles through their successors in the college of bishops, assisted by priests and headed by the pope. (857)

The Church teaches that the Twelve Apostles, chosen by Jesus, were a form of a "permanent assembly," headed by Peter, just as today the college of bishops serves as the permanent assembly, headed by the pope. (880)

Church Speak

Apostolic succession refers to the fact that the work of the apostles—both their preaching and their teaching authority—is handed on to their successors today, the bishops.

Jesus himself chose Peter and declared he was the "rock" on whom he would build his Church. "I will give you the keys to the kingdom of heaven. Whatever you bind on earth shall be bound in heaven; and whatever you loose on earth shall be loosed in heaven." (Matthew 16:19)

The pope, also known as the bishop of Rome, is the successor to St. Peter. He is Christ's representative on earth, is the shepherd of the entire Catholic Church, and has the ultimate power over it. However, he must work in communion with the college of bishops, of which he is a member and head. The college of bishops cannot act on its own but only in collaboration with the pope.

The bishops participate in Christ's tasks of teaching, ruling, and sanctifying in their roles as heads of their dioceses and shepherds of the People of God in their care. Because of this, diocesan bishops—and the pope, as their head—are known as "vicars of Christ," meaning they represent Christ on earth.

Teachable Moment

People often misunderstand the Church's teaching on **papal infallibility**. It does not mean the pope cannot sin or ever be wrong on any matter. This infallibility refers to those rare occasions when the pope formally proclaims that a **doctrine of the Church** on faith or morals is without error. An example of this occurred in 1950, when Pope Pius XII declared Mary's Assumption into heaven to be an article of faith.

Calling All Faithful

The Church is, of course, made up of many, many people, both those who are ordained as priests, deacons, or bishops and those who are not. While the ordained are called "clergy," all the nonordained members are called "laity." Among both clergy and laity there are men and women who have consecrated their lives to God in a special way.

Lay Men and Women

We talked about the Catholic Church being made up of the People of God. Well, the majority of those people are the laity, or lay men and women. These are regular people—married or single, young or old—who profess the Catholic faith and bear witness to it out in the world.

The Catechism explains that lay men and women have a *vocation* to "seek the kingdom of God" and to give glory to God through the everyday words and actions of their earthly lives. (898)

Church Speak

Vocation is a term used to signify whatever calling we may have in life. Oftentimes people assume vocation refers only to a specific religious profession, such as a priest or a religious sister or brother. But the Church recognizes that every person is called by God to fulfill a particular vocation, or destiny, to glorify him.

Consecrated Life

To live a *consecrated life* means to publicly profess vows of poverty, chastity, and obedience, which are called the three "evangelical counsels." The consecrated life is open to any Catholic who wants to be committed to God in a more profound way. However, men and women who profess these vows most often do so as part of a vocation to a particular community as a religious priest, a *religious sister* (often popularly referred to as a "nun") or a *religious brother.*

Church Speak

Consecrated life refers to a permanent state of life chosen by a Catholic—clergy or laity—who publicly professes vows of poverty, chastity, and obedience, which are known as the three evangelical counsels.

Through these evangelical counsels, the Catechism explains, the consecrated man or woman works toward the "perfection of charity," which all people are challenged to achieve. Consecrated men and women do this, however, within a permanent state of life that is recognized by the Church. (915) Poverty seems pretty easy to understand on the surface, but how it translates into day-to-day consecrated life is somewhat complex. Those who profess a vow of poverty as a religious priest, sister, or brother do not have personal possessions. Everything they have is held in common with the religious community.

Some religious communities take this vow a step further and voluntarily live extremely austere lives in solidarity with the poor people they serve. Those who live consecrated lives out in the world, of course, do "own" things but must make a conscious effort to live simple lives.

Church Speak

Religious sisters and religious brothers are women and men who profess vows of poverty, chastity, and obedience as members of particular religious communities. They hold property in common, worship in common, work toward a common mission, and often live together in community. Brothers are not ordained and cannot celebrate the sacraments as ordained clergy can. (We will discuss these types of vocations in more detail in a just little bit.)

Chastity is lived, in a consecrated life, through celibacy. Those who profess a vow of chastity refrain from sexual relations for the rest of their lives.

Teachable Moment

Some priests are "religious" priests and some are known as "diocesan" priests. The difference is that a religious priest belongs to a specific "order," such as Franciscan or Dominican or Jesuit, or to a secular institute or society of apostolic life. These religious priests follow a certain type of spirituality that shapes their prayer life and ministry. A diocesan priest, on the other hand, is educated for and serves in a specific diocese. A diocesan priest does not take the vows of poverty, chastity, and obedience but instead makes "promises" of celibacy and obedience to his bishop.

As for obedience, it does not mean simply following Church teaching, but also making a public vow of obedience to the Church and to the consecrated person's lawful religious superiors.

Who are consecrated people? Well, in addition to religious order priests, sisters, and brothers who make up the majority of consecrated people, we have hermits, who are men who withdraw from society and live in silence and prayer and solitude, as well as "consecrated virgins" and "consecrated widows." These consecrated women, who remain out in the world, choose to live a life of chastity and celibacy in order to follow Jesus more closely. (923)

Religious Vocations

Those who choose a religious vocation profess the same three evangelical counsels as those in consecrated life, but their vocation goes a step further. These religious men (brothers) and women (sisters) become a part of communities of other like-minded religious, who often live together, worship together, and serve others based on the specific character of the community or order they have entered.

Religious life was founded during the earliest centuries of the Church. Sisters and brothers have been a critical part of the Church throughout history, operating ministries ranging from large colleges and hospitals to neighborhood soup kitchens, elementary schools, or hospices.

In addition to religious communities, the Church also has "secular institutes," which enable the Christian faithful living in the world to strive for the perfection of charity and to work for the sanctification of the world in a more structured way.

There are also societies of "apostolic life" whose members, sometimes with religious vows and sometimes without, pursue the particular purposes of their society and lead a life as brothers and sisters in common.

Lay men and women have an opportunity to more closely align themselves with religious communities by becoming "associates." These lay associates may live consecrated lives out in the world while remaining closely connected to a specific religious community through prayer, service, and a commitment to the society or institute's mission and goals.

The Least You Need to Know

◆ The Church does not exist for its own sake but rather as a reflection of Jesus Christ and to further his mission on earth.

◆ The People of God make up the Church and are called to imitate Jesus and to proclaim and defend the faith.

- Those who know Jesus and reject him cannot achieve salvation, but those who do not know Jesus or his Gospel message can still be saved if they are living lives of integrity.

- The Church originated with the triune God, was begun by Jesus and founded on the work of the apostles, and continues to this day through the pope and the college of bishops, who are successors to the apostles.

- Lay men and women have their own vocations and are called to seek the kingdom of God in their everyday lives.

- Some men and women choose to live consecrated lives, where they publicly profess vows of poverty, chastity, and obedience in order to commit their lives to God in a permanent and profound way.

Chapter 10

A Potpourri of Piety

In This Chapter

- ◆ What is the communion of saints?
- ◆ Devotion to the Virgin Mary
- ◆ The forgiveness of sins
- ◆ Resurrection of the body and the end of time
- ◆ Heaven, hell, and purgatory

We are now moving into the final section of the creed. As you run through the last sentences of either creed, it would be easy to think this is the catchall at the end, as if the Church fathers figured they'd better throw in everything. But that's not how this works.

The final part of the creed, every word and phrase, grows out of the earlier sections and spells out a significant Catholic belief. In the earlier parts of the creed, the focus is on the three persons of the Trinity. In the latter part of the creed, the focus shifts to the *works* of the Trinity. We've already covered the Church, which is one of those works. Now we'll take a look at the rest.

In this chapter, we will go from the saints and Mary, to death and resurrection, to hell and final judgment. In one fell swoop in the last section of the creed, the Church gives us some of its most critical beliefs and doctrines.

Communion of Saints

In the final lines of the Apostles' Creed, right after professing a belief in the Church itself, the prayer moves on to the *communion of saints*. The Catechism explains that this is a natural progression because the Church is, in a real sense, an "assembly of saints." So the communion of saints is the Church itself. (946)

Church Speak

The Latin term for **communion of saints** is *communio sanctorum*, which refers to the souls in purgatory, all of us here on earth, and the saints in heaven.

The Church teaches that the communion of saints, or the People of God, hold everything in common, meaning every Christian should be ready and willing to come to the aid of a neighbor, especially the poorest of the poor.

We see this in Scripture when the communal life of the early Christian community is discussed:

They devoted themselves to the teaching of the apostles and to the communal life, to the breaking of the bread and to the prayers. Awe came upon everyone, and many wonders and signs were done through the apostles. All who believed were together and had all things in common; they would sell their property and possessions and divide them among all according to each one's need. (Acts 2:42)

Now, the entire Catholic population cannot all live together at this point and share everything in common because there are simply too many Catholics spread throughout the world to make that physically possible. But they do share everything spiritually, and those smaller communities of Catholics—dioceses or individual parishes—do hold many things in common and support one another both spiritually, through prayer, and physically, through charity and service.

When many people hear the phrase "communion of saints," they probably assume the Church is referring to actual saints in heaven, and this line does include them, but not only them. The Catechism explains there are "three states of the Church": those Catholics living on earth right now, those Catholics who have died and are still undergoing purification, and those who have reached God himself in heaven. The saints fall into that last category. (954)

The Church teaches that the saints, who are closely united to Christ, can intercede on behalf of the faithful still on earth. In other words, Catholics can pray to the saints, asking them to go to the Father as a mediator.

You're Absolved If ...

You may think Catholics worship saints and pray to them in the same way they pray to God, but they do not. Catholics, like Christians of many other denominations, can and do pray directly to God. Catholics acknowledge that their prayers are always to be made through Jesus. However, the Catholic Church teaches that the saints, who are already with God and who are also in union with us, can join their prayer with ours. It's like asking a friend to help you with something. The saints listen to our prayers and then join us in putting those prayers before God on our behalf. Think of saints as connections in heaven.

How Does Mary Help?

Even though neither of the creeds specifically mentions the Virgin Mary at this point, she does have a logical connection to this part of the creed. We have to remember that Mary is "Saint Mary," meaning that she is part of the communion of saints we just discussed.

Earlier in the creed we talked about Mary's role in the Incarnation. Now, the Catechism explains, we need to talk about Mary's role in the "mystery of the Church." (963)

Through her "yes" to bear the Son of God, Mary became a collaborator with God's plan. So wherever Jesus is Savior, Mary is mother. The

Catechism explains that Mary's role in the life of the Church is "inseparable from her union with Christ and flows directly from it." (964)

As if those credentials aren't impressive enough, Mary is also known as the "Mother of God," which is pretty radical stuff. Mary, a completely mortal woman, is called God's mother because Jesus and God are one. So if Mary is the mother of Jesus Christ, and she is, then she is the Mother of God.

In the Gospel of John, when Jesus was dying on the cross, he turned to his mother and to the "beloved disciple" and said, "Woman, behold your son." (John 19:26) With those words, the Church teaches, Jesus did not give his mother to just one person but to all those disciples who follow him.

Church Speak

The **Assumption** refers to Church teaching that Mary, as a result of her preservation from original sin and by virtue of her role as the mother of God's Son, was taken up to heaven body and soul at the end of her earthly life. Through this she uniquely participates in the resurrection of her son and serves as an icon of hope for all Christians. The feast of the Assumption is August 15. (966)

The Church's devotion to Mary can be confusing to some non-Catholics. Mary is not worshipped and she is not adored as the Holy Trinity is worshipped and adored. However, the Church teaches and the Catechism explains that devotion to Mary is "intrinsic to Christian worship" and that she has been honored as the Mother of God since ancient times. (971)

Devotion to Mary is expressed through special feasts dedicated to her name and through "Marian" prayers, such as the *Rosary*, which the Catechism explains embodies all the teachings of the Gospel. (971)

Teachable Moment

The **Rosary** is both a prayer devoted to Mary and a string of beads consisting of five sets of ten small beads. The sets of ten are called "decades," with a larger bead between each set. On the larger beads, you pray the Our Father, also known as the Lord's Prayer, and on each of the smaller beads, a Hail Mary, which is the central prayer to Mary in the Catholic Church. To say a complete Rosary, you go around all the beads four times. For each of the decades, you reflect on an aspect of the Lord's life, known as "mysteries." There are four sets of mysteries: joyful, luminous, sorrowful, and glorious. So even though you are saying prayers devoted to Mary, you are focusing on the most significant moments in the life of Christ. (For more information on how to pray the Rosary, see the appendix on prayer at the back of this book.)

The Power to Forgive Sins

The Apostles' Creed next addresses the "forgiveness of sins," which it links to faith in the Holy Spirit as well as faith in the Church and the communion of saints. (976) The Church teaches that Jesus himself instituted the ability of the Church to forgive sins in his name, when, after his Resurrection, he gave his apostles the power to do so.

"Receive the Holy Spirit. Whose sins you forgive are forgiven them, and whose sins you retain are retained," Jesus said. (John 20:22-23)

The Catechism explains that sins are first forgiven during the sacrament of baptism. When sins are committed after baptism, the faithful can turn to the sacrament of reconciliation (also known as confession or penance), which we will discuss at length in Chapter 13. "It is through the sacrament of penance that the baptized can be reconciled with God and with the Church," the Catechism explains. (980)

Life Everlasting

The Apostles' Creed concludes with a belief in "the resurrection of the body and life everlasting," which we will look at individually, but which, of course, are intricately intertwined.

Resurrection of the Body

What does the "resurrection of the body" mean in the Catholic faith? It means not only that our souls will live after our death but also at the end of all time our bodies will be reunited with our souls and will live for all eternity.

The term "body" can also be translated as "flesh," which, the Catechism explains, refers to humanity's "weakness and mortality." Through the resurrection of the flesh, the creed professes that even the mortal body will come to life again one day. (990)

So how do the dead rise up? Well, let's begin with Jesus. He died on a cross, and he was buried in a tomb, but three days later that tomb was empty and a community of disciples were a witness to the resurrected Lord. Catholics believe just as Jesus Christ rose from the dead so shall all believers rise from the dead at the end of time. (995)

The Church teaches that after we die our souls live on but our bodies decay. At the last judgment, which we will discuss momentarily, God will raise up our mortal bodies and transform them into "glorious" or "spiritual" bodies. (999) How this will actually happen no one can really know because, as the Catechism explains, it "exceeds our imagination and understanding" and yet is based on the belief in Christ's Resurrection and Ascension. (1000)

Church Speak

Parousia refers to Jesus Christ's "second coming," which will coincide with "last days" or the end of the world as we know it. References to the Second Coming appear throughout the New Testament. At that time, Christ will judge the living and the dead.

In the Catholic faith, and the Christian faith in general, death is not a negative thing but rather an opportunity to live with God for all eternity. The Church teaches that through the sacrament of baptism believers die with Christ in order to live a new life, and that in physical death we complete the act and are united with him. (1010) Of course, in order for this to happen, we must die in "Christ's grace," which means we should be preparing for it all along through prayer and living out the Gospel and seeking forgiveness for our sins.

Heaven, Hell, and Purgatory

When we die, we enter into "eternal life" or "life everlasting," which starts at the moment of our death and has no end. But before we get to our eventual eternal destination, we have to make an important stop along the way: judgment.

Yes, that's right. We're not going to waltz right into heaven without paying a cover charge. The Church teaches that Jesus is going to take a look at what we've done—or haven't done—and make a decision based on that.

So what are our options? Well, the most sought-after destination is heaven, of course, but all is not lost if you don't make it to heaven straight off the bat. There are opportunities for "purification" if you haven't been living up to the Golden Rule. The last option, which no one wants to think about, is hell. Let's take a closer look at each.

Heaven is the goal. This is where, if we die in God's grace and are already purified, we get to meet Jesus Christ face to face and remain there forever. (1023) So when we talk about heaven, we're not talking about walking on clouds and eating chocolate all day; we're talking about achieving the "fulfillment of the deepest human longings, the state of supreme, definitive happiness." (1024)

In heaven we will not only be united with the triune God but also with Mary, the angels, and all those who have died before us and have made it to heaven as well, the Church teaches.

Now, if you're not quite up to heaven's standards, there is the possibility of purgatory. This is not so much a place as it is a "final purification." It means when you died, you were not quite perfect but you certainly weren't so bad off that you should be damned for all eternity. (1030)

Going to purgatory means eventually you are going to achieve eternal salvation and perfect union with God and with everyone else in heaven—you just might have to spend a few days or years or centuries working out the kinks.

The Church teaches that those souls who are doing time in purgatory can be helped on their path by the rest of us still doing time down here. By praying for them, offering Masses for them, and offering alms or doing penance on their behalf, we can get them the equivalent of time served.

Teachable Moment

Purgatory is based in Scripture. In St. Paul's First Letter to the Corinthians, he uses the metaphor of a building to discuss God's judgment after death, "… if someone's work is burned up, that one will suffer loss; the person will be saved, but only as through fire." (1 Cor 3:15) The fire is the purification of purgatory, as opposed to the pains of hell, through which no one can ever be saved, according to the Church.

So now we get to hell—well, not literally, thank goodness. The Church teaches once you go to hell you cannot come back. It's a one-way ticket. Do not pass Go; do not collect $200. There's no way to put this gently: Hell is eternal damnation, and it is reserved for anyone who dies in a state of "mortal sin without repenting." The Catechism says hell is a "state of definitive self-exclusion from communion with God and with the blessed." (1033)

Hell means you never, ever get to see God and all the others in heaven for all eternity. Jesus talked about *Gehenna* and its unquenchable fires, and he didn't mince words:

Just as weeds are collected and burned with fire, so it will be at the end of the age. The Son of Man will send his angels, and they will collect out of his kingdom all who cause others to sin and all evildoers. They will throw them into the fiery furnace, where there will be wailing and grinding of teeth. (Matthew 13:40–42)

That pretty much says it all, but take heart. The Church teaches that no one is predestined to go to hell. We each get to make a choice, but the main way to get there is by willfully choosing to reject God without ever accepting his mercy before death. (1037)

The Final Judgment

We talked about the resurrection of the dead, when our mortal bodies will be joined with our souls at the end of time. So when this happens, it means Christ has come again and the world has ended. Therefore, this is it, no more chances.

At this point, which is known as the "last judgment," the presence of Jesus Christ will bare the truth of each person's relationship with God. Based on what is revealed, Jesus will disclose a final judgment about where you will spend all eternity. (1039)

Because only God knows the date and time of this world-ending event, the Church continually urges its members to be ready: "Stay awake, for you know neither the day nor the hour." (Matthew 25:13)

New Hope

As desperate as all of this can start to sound, the Church—based on Scripture again—reminds us the "righteous" will get to reign forever in heaven with Jesus Christ. (1042)

Quoting from the Book of Revelation, the Catechism says in this "heavenly Jerusalem" every tear will be wiped away and death will be no more. There will be no suffering or mourning or pain.

So if you can get to heaven, you can look forward to an eternity of joy and happiness, beyond anything we can imagine here on earth.

The Least You Need to Know

◆ The saints are those people whose souls are now in heaven, and who, through their closeness to Christ, are able to intercede on our behalf.

◆ Devotion to the Virgin Mary, which dates to ancient times, is an integral part of the Catholic faith. Mary is the first disciple, a model for all Christians, and the Mother of God.

◆ Jesus instituted the sacrament of penance when he told the apostles that what they forgave on earth would be forgiven in heaven and what they held bound on earth would be held bound in heaven.

◆ The resurrection of the body means at the end of the world our mortal bodies will be reunited with our souls.

◆ After death, souls can go to heaven, hell, or purgatory, which is a place of purification for those who were not yet perfect when they died.

◆ At the last judgment, Jesus will reveal the truths about our lives on earth and will disclose our final and eternal resting place accordingly.

Part 3

A Mystery Not Meant to Be Solved

The seven sacraments of the Catholic Church are considered signs and instruments of grace that strengthen faith and move a believer ever closer to God and true holiness. For Catholics, they provide the pathway to divine life, which is communicated by the Holy Spirit in each of the sacraments.

In the previous section of this book, we looked at the basic beliefs of Catholics. Now we will look at the basic rituals and practices that take those beliefs and make them a part of Catholic life. In the coming chapters, we will explore each of the seven sacraments in detail, looking at scriptural references as well as practical applications.

GOD MUST REALLY LOVE PARADES. HE HAS ONE EVERY WEEK!

Chapter **11**

Mass: It's Not Just for Sundays

In This Chapter

- ◆ The liturgy and why it is so important
- ◆ Signs and symbols in liturgical celebrations
- ◆ Statues, stained glass, and sacred elements
- ◆ Breaking down the Church year

For Catholics, there is nothing quite like the Mass. It is considered a celebration commemorating, above all, the "paschal mystery," which is Jesus' Passion, death, Resurrection, and Ascension. Catholics attending Mass receive grace and strength of spirit while at the same time bearing witness to their faith.

While many people think of Mass as a Sundays-only obligation, it is actually celebrated daily—in fact, many times daily. Sunday may be a special day for worship in the Church, but it is by far not the only day for worship. The one day of the year when Mass is not celebrated in Catholic churches around the world is on Good Friday, the day that commemorates when Jesus was crucified and died.

The Mass consists of two parts, called the Liturgy of the Word and the Liturgy of the Eucharist, and is fundamentally the same no matter where you go. The language may vary from country to country, but the Mass itself remains the same.

In this chapter, we will take a closer look at liturgy, what it is, and why it's so important. We will also look at some of the elements most people so closely associate with Catholic liturgies, from holy water and incense to music and stained-glass windows.

What Is Liturgy?

The *liturgy* is where the People of God "participate in the work of God" and where Jesus Christ "continues the work of our redemption." (1069) The Catechism calls the liturgy the "summit" of all Church activity and a "privileged place" for proclaiming the Gospel of Jesus Christ. But the liturgy is not only the summit of Church life, it is also the "source" of Church life. All of the Church's "power" flows from it. (1074)

Church Speak

Liturgy at one time referred to a public work or duty. In the Christian faith, however, liturgy refers to official public worship, separating it from private prayer. When you attend Catholic Mass, for example, you are attending a liturgy.

Through the liturgy, believers are able to move from the visible to the invisible, from the "sign to the thing signified." (1074–1075) In other words, it is through the physical manifestations of faith—liturgy, sacraments, prayer—that Catholics are able to access the spiritual dimensions of faith in a deeper and more personal way. (1074)

The liturgy is intimately connected to the Holy Trinity. So the Father, Son, and Spirit have a role in every Mass. The Father blesses the faithful through his Word made Incarnate, Jesus, and pours into the hearts of believers the gift of all gifts, the Holy Spirit. (1082)

During the liturgy, Jesus Christ makes his own death and Resurrection present once again. The Catechism explains because Jesus destroyed death through his Resurrection, his paschal mystery does not remain in the past but "participates in divine eternity," meaning it is present in its fullness at every liturgy. (1085)

The Holy Spirit is front and center during the liturgy. In every celebration of the liturgy, the Holy Spirit is sent to bring believers into communion with Jesus Christ, and to form his "Body" on earth.

The Catechism calls the Spirit the "artisan" of the sacraments (1091) and says that he prepares the Church to encounter Christ in the liturgy. The Spirit, through his transforming power, makes the work of Christ present at every liturgy. (1112)

Teachable Moment

The Catholic liturgy blends worship elements from the Old Covenant, or Jewish tradition, while adding elements of the New Covenant. During liturgies, the faithful typically hear a reading from the Old Testament in addition to one of the Psalms, followed by a reading from the Epistles or Letters in the New Testament, and then a separate reading from one of the four Gospels. These Scriptures are read in a rotating cycle so that in a three-year period Catholics review much of Scripture.

On Earth as It Is in Heaven

The Church teaches that the liturgy is an "action" of the "whole Christ," meaning that as head of the Church, Jesus is the "high priest" who offers himself over and over again without end to his Father, together with his Church, both on earth and in heaven. That means that the liturgy celebrated by living Catholics is linked to a heavenly liturgy. (1136)

The teaching of a "heavenly liturgy" is found in the Book of Revelation, where John speaks of seeing a vision of heaven and what will happen in the next life. He sees a throne surrounded by 24 elders also on thrones, which refer to the "servants of the Old and New Covenants," the Catechism explains. (1138) He sees angels and the apostles, as well as the souls of those "slaughtered because of the witness they bore to the word of God," which refers to the Church's martyrs. He sees the "bride, the wife of the Lamb, which refers to Mary the Mother of God, and he sees "a great multitude, which no one could count, from every nation, race, people, and tongue." (Rev 7:9)

John is telling us that the liturgy Catholics enact here on earth is a participation in the very liturgy celebrated in heaven.

Liturgy brings Catholics together in a public devotion, which is a critical aspect of the faith. It is not enough to pray alone; community is an important aspect of being Catholic. That's not because Catholics are better as a group than they are as individuals but because Catholics are called to be the Body of Christ with one another.

That is why Catholics are referred to as a "priestly people," with each person acting according to his or her vocation and role but unified in the Holy Spirit. In other words, ordained clergy are present to preside at the Mass, and lay men and women are present and participating through ministries within the Church and as the assembly. (1144)

Signs and Symbols

The liturgy is a celebration that brings together signs and symbols designed to help human beings make a connection to their heavenly Father. In the Church, these signs and symbols are important and necessary because they allow humans to communicate with God in a way that is more comfortable and familiar to earthly beings used to physical realities. (1146) In other words, we use things that are real and understandable to us.

The Church takes its sacramental signs and symbols from creation, from humanity's "social life," and from the Old Covenant.

Creation symbols include light and darkness, wind and fire, water and earth, trees and their fruit. For Catholics, those symbols are found in physical elements like holy water, candles, and flowers. (1147)

You're Absolved If ...

Do you wonder why Catholics bless themselves with holy water? Holy water is water that has been blessed by a priest or deacon. It is called a "sacramental" and is a reminder of the cleansing waters of baptism. Catholics typically dip the fingers of their right hand into holy water upon entering a church and make the Sign of the Cross. It is at once an act of reverence, recognizing that you are entering a sacred place, and a recommitment to the vows made at baptism.

The symbols of "social life" include washing and anointing, breaking bread, and sharing the cup. These activities, which closely relate to the everyday activities of human beings, are an important part of the Catholic liturgy because they are "a means of expressing the action of God who sanctifies men, and the action of men who offer worship to God." (1148)

Finally, the symbols taken from the Old Covenant include anointing and consecration, laying on of hands, sacrifices, and, most important, Passover. The Church uses these symbols because they "prefigure" the sacraments of the New Covenant. (1147)

During his lifetime, Jesus used many of these same signs and symbols when preaching and healing. He mixed a paste of mud and water to cure a blind man. He turned water into wine at Cana. He multiplied the loaves and fishes to feed the 5,000. He walked on water. He talked about the birds of the sky and the lilies of the field, of mustard seeds and mountains. His teachings were filled with the kind of symbolism that could help humans understand something greater than them, and the Church continues that use of signs and symbols today.

Words and Actions

The Liturgy of the Word is the portion of the Mass that focuses on the reading of Scripture. The Catechism explains the liturgy is "a meeting of God's children with their Father, in Christ and the Holy Spirit." The meeting is a "dialogue" of words and actions, and the words are no less important than the actions. (1153)

Through the Liturgy of the Word, the faithful are nourished, but it is more than just a simple reading of Scripture. If you attend a Catholic Mass, you will see the lectionary, or book of Scripture, carried in procession with candles, and sometimes venerated with incense. It is read from a lectern, or *ambo*, and then the priest or deacon uses his homily to further explain the readings or teach through them. The congregation participates in the Scripture through responses and singing.

Catholics believe when the word of God is proclaimed with authority and received with faith, it has the power to change our hearts, our minds, our very reality.

Teachable Moment

Incense is a fragrant gum or resin that gives off smoke when it is burned. The Church uses incense as a "sacramental" (which we will discuss in more detail later.) It is used at Mass to "venerate" or show reverence for, the book of Gospels, the altar, the assembly of the faithful, the Eucharist, and more.

Making Music

Sacred music is an important part of Catholic liturgy, especially Sunday liturgy, but any old music won't do. The songs sung at Mass must conform to Catholic doctrine and Scripture and must be appropriate for the liturgical season.

You're Absolved If ...

You might think contemporary Church music means singing *Kumbaya*, that popular folk group favorite from the 1970s. Today's contemporary music is, like choir music, rooted in Scripture and Church teaching, even if it does include an occasional tambourine or maraca accompaniment.

The Catechism explains singing and music at Mass is "closely linked to the liturgical celebrations of the Old Covenant" and that the combination of sacred music and words is a necessary part of liturgy. (1156)

In addition, music is not supposed to be reserved for those in the choir. The Church teaches that sacred music should be accessible to the faithful and that the assembly should be encouraged to participate.

St. Augustine once said, "He who sings prays twice."

Sacred Images

When most people think of Catholic churches, they envision stained-glass windows and statues, and these things do give specific churches their personality. But why are those images so important?

First of all, the Church teaches that when it comes to sacred images, nothing is more important than the image of Jesus Christ. Any other sacred images simply reflect how Jesus has glorified others and are not meant to replace the image of Christ.

The Catechism explains, "Christian iconography expresses in images the same Gospel message that Scripture communicates by words." (1160)

So statues and stained-glass windows of the Blessed Mother, saints, and angels are meant to draw the faithful closer to Christ as they contemplate his promise of salvation and how these holy men and women served as witnesses to it in their lifetimes and now are united to Christ in eternal life. (1161)

Church Speak

A **crucifix** is a cross bearing a figure of Christ on it. Catholic churches place a crucifix behind or over the altar. Many Catholics have a crucifix hanging in their homes.

A Church for All Seasons

Sunday is the epicenter of the Catholic liturgical calendar because it is what the Church considers the "Lord's Day," which is a day of Resurrection. The culmination of the sacred commemoration of Resurrection is the annual celebration of Easter.

Although Sunday is central, the entire liturgical year is meant to celebrate the "mystery of Christ," from his Incarnation until he comes again at the end of time. In doing so, the Church celebrates the liturgy not only on Sundays but every day, with special feast days set aside to honor Mary and the saints. The Catechism explains that since the time of Mosaic Law, special "observed feasts" have been celebrated to give thanks to God and to instill the faith in each new generation. (1164)

How did Sunday get to be the Lord's Day? The Church celebrates the paschal mystery every seventh day, recognizing Sunday as the day handed down through Tradition from the apostles as the Lord's Day. The Catechism explains that Jesus' Resurrection is both the first day of the week, which commemorates the first day of creation, and the "eighth day," which Jesus—after he rested on the Great Sabbath—instituted as the "day the Lord has made." (1166)

The Liturgical Year

The Catechism explains that Easter is the "feast of feasts" in the liturgical year, celebrated after what is known as the *Triduum*, which are the three days leading up to Easter—Holy Thursday, Good Friday, and Holy Saturday. (1168)

You may have noticed that Easter, unlike Christmas, does not have a set date and moves from year to year. That's because at the Council of Nicea in 325, the Church decided the Christian Passover, as Easter is known, would be celebrated on the Sunday following the first full moon after the vernal equinox (this is the date when night and day are nearly the same length marking the first day of spring). Because of different methods of calculating this according to the Jewish calendar, the date of Easter sometimes varies between the Roman Catholic and Eastern Orthodox Churches.

Teachable Moment

The Church year begins with the first Sunday of Advent, which falls in late November or early December each year. Advent is the 4-week season of preparation for Christmas and is followed by the Christmas season. Lent is the 40-day season of preparation for Easter and is followed by the Easter season. The rest of the Church year is known as "ordinary time."

Liturgy of the Hours

The apostles preached that Christians should "pray constantly." This is made real in something called the Liturgy of the Hours, or the "divine office," which is a public prayer that is prayed in common according to the rhythm of the hours of day and night.

Most closely associated with monastic life, the Liturgy of the Hours is meant to be prayed by all of the faithful as much as possible. It is referred to as an "extension of the Eucharistic celebration" in the Catechism. (1178)

The Liturgy of the Hours consists of prayers, Psalms, hymns, Scripture passages, and spiritual readings that are recited at certain hours of the day.

> **Church Speak**
>
> **Lectio Divina** means "sacred reading" and refers to a method of going deeper into Scripture or other spiritual readings as a way of prayer. It typically includes four steps: reading a passage, meditating on it, praying or responding to God, and then contemplating or listening for God's response back to you.

Location, Location, Location

In order to celebrate the liturgy, people need a place to worship, and so we have churches—lots of them. The Catechism explains that as the "whole earth is sacred" and entrusted to humanity, there is no one place that is right for worship. After all, we are each supposed to be a temple of the Holy Spirit. (1179)

That being said, the faithful are expected to come up with a place that is "in good taste and a worthy place for prayer and sacred ceremonial." A church is a place for the community to gather. It is a place where the Eucharist is "celebrated and reserved," and where signs and symbols converge to show Christ to be present there. (1181)

Within every church, there are certain basic sacred elements:

◆ The **altar** is the center of the church, where Jesus' sacrifice on the cross is made present through sacramental signs. It is also the table of the Lord, to which the People of God are invited. (1182)

◆ The **tabernacle** is a place of dignity where the Eucharist is reserved. When the Eucharist, the consecrated bread also known as the Blessed Sacrament, is present in a tabernacle, a candle burns near it at all times. (1183)

◆ The sacred **chrism** is oil blessed by the local bishop and used for anointings in certain sacraments. It is reserved in a secure place in the sanctuary, which is the part of the church containing the altar. (1183)

◆ The **chair** of the bishop (*cathedra*) or the priest shows his position in "presiding over the assembly and of directing prayer." (1184)

◆ The **lectern,** or *ambo*, is where the Scripture is proclaimed. (1184) It is the podium from which Scripture is read.

- The **baptismal font,** which contains holy water, is where the celebration of the sacrament of baptism occurs. It also may be used when the faithful renew their baptismal promises at certain liturgies. (1185)

- The **confessional** must be present so that the faithful may seek reconciliation through the sacrament of penance. (1185) It is typically thought of as an enclosed booth or room where believers confess their sins privately to a priest.

- The church must have a place where the faithful can sit in **silent prayer.**

The Catechism explains the visible church is a "symbol of the Father's house" toward which the faithful are journeying. When you cross the threshold of a church, you pass from a "world wounded by sin" and into the world of "new life." (1186)

Teachable Moment

Although most liturgies are offered in churches, a church is not necessary for the celebration of Mass. Jesus said, "For where two or three are gathered together in my name, there am I in the midst of them." (Matthew 18:20) Priests can celebrate Masses in hospitals, in homes, in hotels, and many other ordinary places.

The Least You Need to Know

- The liturgy is the source and summit of all the Church's activity.

- Signs and symbols, such as water and fire, are physical manifestations of spiritual life that help humans better understand the work of God.

- Liturgical music, which must follow Church doctrine and Scripture, is an integral part of liturgy. The faithful are encouraged to participate in the music.

- Sacred images always have Christ at their center. Even images of Mary and the angels and saints are designed to draw the faithful closer to Christ by reminding them of the promise of salvation.

◆ Sunday is the focal point of the Church year and is considered the day of resurrection, which culminates on Easter each year.

◆ Churches are visible signs on earth of the Father's house in heaven.

Chapter 12

Sacraments of Initiation

In This Chapter

- The sacrament of baptism
- How confirmation strengthens the faith
- The Eucharist and its importance
- How bread and wine become the body and blood of Jesus Christ

The three sacraments of Christian initiation are baptism, confirmation, and Eucharist. Together they provide the foundation for a life of Christian faith. Through baptism the faithful are reborn, through confirmation their Christianity is strengthened, and through the Eucharist they are nourished.

These three sacraments are mainstays of the faith. All Catholics, whether they start out Catholic as infants or enter the Catholic Church as adults, will receive these three sacraments as a matter of course over time. Baptism and confirmation are received only once, and Eucharist is received often and regularly throughout a Catholic's life.

In this chapter, we will look at these three sacraments in detail, exploring not only their spiritual dimensions but the rituals and practices that bring the sacraments to life for Catholics receiving them.

I Baptize Thee ...

For most Catholics, *baptism* is not a sacrament they remember receiving, as they were probably infants at the time. Yet baptism is a sacrament that is critical to a life of faith. It is the "basis" of Christian life and the door to all the other sacraments. Quoting the 1314 Council of Florence, the Catechism calls baptism the "gateway to life in the Spirit." (1213)

Church Speak

To **baptize,** which comes from the Greek word *baptizein,* means to "plunge" into or "immerse" in water. Baptism is named for the main rite used in the celebration of the sacrament—the pouring of water over the head of the person being baptized or the immersion of that person into a pool of water. In the Catholic Church, the former is more common. (1214)

Through baptism, Catholics are freed from sin (original and actual sin), reborn in Christ, and welcomed into the Church. The Church teaches that by being immersed in the waters of new life, the faithful join in Christ's death and rise up with him as new creations.

The Catechism explains that baptism brings about the birth of the Spirit, which is necessary for salvation. Through it, the faithful receive "enlightenment," or the light of faith and, in turn, become a light of faith to others. (1215–1216)

Water, Water, Everywhere

Baptism is prefigured in the Old Covenant through the many references to water and its role in God's plan of salvation. We have the water that covered the earth at the dawn of creation and again during the great flood, the parting of the Red Sea that allowed the Israelites to escape Egyptian slavery, and the crossing of the Jordan River that brought the Israelites to the Promised Land. (1219–1222)

Fast forward a bit and we have Jesus—the fulfillment of the Old Covenant—beginning his public ministry with baptism in the Jordan River and ending his earthly life with a pierced heart, out of which flowed water (a sign of baptism) and blood (a sign of Eucharist).

After his Resurrection, Jesus told his apostles to "make disciples of all nations, baptizing them in the name of the Father and of the Son and of the Holy Spirit." (Matthew 28:19)

From the first Pentecost on, the Church has baptized those who believe in Jesus as a way to forgive sins and impart the Holy Spirit. The Church teaches that through baptism Catholics "put on Christ." (1227)

Teachable Moment

Over the course of history, the process of Christian initiation has varied, with the earliest Christians going through a period of catechumenate, or instruction, to prepare for baptism. Infant baptism obviously cannot include formal instruction before the sacrament, so it must include instruction after the fact. Baptized non-Catholic adults who wish to enter the Catholic Church are known as "candidates." They do not need to be baptized again. Nonbaptized adults who wish to enter the Catholic Church through baptism are called "catechumens." Both must spend a period of time in study to prepare to receive the sacraments, which typically occurs during the Easter Vigil Mass.

Rite of Baptism

So how is a baptism performed and what do the signs and symbols mean? Well, the rite begins with the Sign of the Cross. During infant baptism, typically it is the minister, parents, and godparents who make the sign of the cross on the forehead of the baby. For adults, the person being baptized does this himself or herself. The Sign of the Cross figuratively tattoos the person to be baptized, marking him or her with the imprint of Christ.

This is followed by the proclamation of the word of God, meaning Scripture passages are read aloud to "enlighten with revealed truth" the catechumen (the adult being baptized)or the infant through those standing for the infant as well as all others gathered for the baptism. (1235–1236)

This is followed by prayers of exorcism, which have nothing to do with Hollywood's version and everything to do with prayers to protect the person being baptized from evil and keep him or her free from sin (there will be more on exorcism later.) The catechumen (or, in the case of an infant, those standing in for the infant) then explicitly renounces Satan, at which point he or she is ready to profess faith in the Church. (1237) Finally we come to the "essential rite" of baptism, which is the immersion of the catechumen or infant in water or the pouring of water over the head of the catechumen or infant while invoking the three persons of the Trinity. With each name—Father, Son, and Spirit—the catechumen or infant is immersed or water is poured over his or her head again. (1239) The latter method is most typical in any Catholic baptism but especially those involving infants.

> **Church Speak**
>
> **Chrism** is a blend of oil and balsam that is blessed by a bishop and used during sacramental rites such as baptism, confirmation, and holy orders.

The newly baptized next receives three gifts:

1. **Anointing** with sacred *chrism*, which is a perfumed oil symbolizing the gift of the Holy Spirit. Through this anointing the baptized becomes one who is anointed by the Spirit into Christ.

2. A **white garment,** which symbolizes that the newly baptized person has "put on Christ."

3. A **candle** lit from the Easter candle, which symbolizes Christ as the light of the world and the light of the baptized person's faith. (1241–1243)

The rite of baptism concludes with a solemn blessing, and for the baptism of an infant, a special blessing for the parents of the baby. (1245)

Teachable Moment _____

If you've been to an infant baptism, then you've probably noticed the white dresses or outfits that are worn. The white garment is an important part of the baptismal rite and signifies that the person has "put on Christ" and has risen with him. Another important symbol is the lighting of a smaller candle from the larger "Easter candle," usually done by a godparent. This light signifies that Jesus Christ has enlightened the newly baptized person, who is now "the light of the world" to others. (1243)

Anyone, Any Time

Most people associate baptism in the Catholic Church with babies, but the truth is that anyone, at any age, can be baptized. Adult baptism was the norm in the early Church when the apostles baptized Jews and non-Jews who believed in Jesus Christ and wanted to be part of his growing Church.

Today, as in the earliest days of Christianity, adults seeking baptism are known as catechumens. In order to be initiated into the Catholic faith, they must prepare through formal instruction known as RCIA (Rite of Christian Initiation for Adults).

So why does the Catholic Church baptize babies if they cannot be formally instructed in the faith? Well, because the Church teaches we all enter this world with original sin, it offers baptism as a way to free children from the power of darkness and give them new life in Christ. (1250)

Teachable Moment _____

Calling infant baptism an "immemorial tradition of the Church," the Catechism cites Scripture references showing that young children in the early Church would have been baptized alongside their parents. "He took them in at that hour of the night and bathed their wounds; then he and all his family were baptized at once." (Acts 16:33) According to the Holy See's Congregation for the Doctrine of the Faith, infant baptism was common at least as far back as the second century, but may have been common from the beginning of the Church when entire households were baptized in one fell swoop. (1252)

When Catholics are baptized, they are asked what they seek of the Church, and they, or the baby's godparents and parents, answer, "faith." Baptism does not perfect faith but offers the newly baptized a starting point. The Catechism explains that baptism leads the baptized to the "threshold of new life." There is much more to be done after baptism, especially for infants who must rely on their parents and godparents to be examples of faith and to encourage them on their faith journey as they grow. (1235)

Baptism is ordinarily performed by the clergy: bishops, priests, and deacons. (We will discuss deacons in detail in Chapter 14). However, when a member of the clergy is absent, a person who has been legitimately designated can perform baptisms. In fact, any person—even a non-Christian—can baptize someone "in case of necessity," such as if death is imminent. This is possible as long as the person intends to do in the ritual what the Church wants done and as long as he or she uses the same formula as the Church—either immersing the person to be baptized or pouring water on the person's head and baptizing him or her in the name of the Father and of the Son and of the Holy Spirit. (1256)

True Confessions

There once was a theory popular in Church circles that babies who died without the benefit of baptism went to a place called *limbo*, where they would never be united with God, as the people in heaven are united with him, but would also never suffer. In 2007, however, members of the papally-appointed International Theological Commission took limbo off the theological map. Reflecting a 1980 Instruction on Infant Baptism from the Congregation for the Doctrine of the Faith, the Catechism specifically says that the Church entrusts unbaptized babies who have died "to the mercy of God as she does in her funeral rites for them." (1261)

Baptismal Benefits

The Church teaches that Jesus made it clear that baptism is the necessary way to salvation for those who believe, saying that you cannot enter the kingdom of God without being born of "water and Spirit." (1257)

Through baptism, Catholics receive forgiveness not only for original sin but also for all of their personal sins and the punishments that might come with them. They become adopted children of God and get to share in his "divine nature" through the graces they receive from the Holy Spirit. Baptism "incorporates Catholics into the Church" and gives them a role in Christ's mission.

The Catechism explains that through baptism, a person no longer belongs to himself but to Christ. (1265–1269) The sacrament also unites all Christians, even those who are not yet "in full communion" with the Catholic Church are united through their baptism into Christianity. (1271)

Finally, baptism is a sacrament received only one time. The Church teaches that baptism leaves an "indelible spiritual mark" or "seal" on the baptized person that lasts forever. No sin, no later choice of the baptized person can ever erase this seal. No matter what happens afterward, the effect of baptism is everlasting. (1272)

Teachable Moment

When you are baptized, you typically receive a baptismal name, which is the name of a Christian virtue, such Faith or Hope, or the name of a saint who will serve as a model of faith and patron, such as Anne or Joseph. Many parents today, however, don't give their children such baptismal names, and the Church is okay with that. However, the Catechism, quoting the Code of Canon Law, says that parents *cannot* give their children names that would be "foreign to Christian sentiment," say, something like Lucifer or Voldemort. (2156)

Sacrament of Confirmation

Confirmation is not an afterthought in the Catholic Church, even though in the Latin rite it typically comes many years after infant baptism. The Church teaches that confirmation is necessary to complete the grace received in baptism. It is through confirmation that Catholics are more perfectly bound to the Church and receive the strength of the Holy Spirit to aid them in their spiritual journey. (1285)

Sealed with the Spirit

Through confirmation, a Catholic becomes fully engaged in the life of the faith and the Church. The Catechism explains that the anointing of confirmation is a "sign of consecration" that allows the anointed person to "share more completely in the mission of Jesus Christ and the fullness of the Holy Spirit." (1294)

The person being confirmed receives the mark or "seal" of the Spirit, just as Jesus was marked with the seal of his Father. The seal of the Spirit in confirmation signifies a "total belonging" to Christ. (1295–1296)

As with baptism, confirmation leaves an indelible mark on a Catholic, and so this sacrament is received only once.

The essential rite of confirmation occurs when the person being confirmed, or "confirmand," is anointed on the forehead with sacred chrism while the following words are spoken: "Be sealed with the Gift of the Holy Spirit." (1300)

From Pentecost On

Confirmation is the modern-day equivalent of what the apostles experienced on the first Pentecost, a pouring out of the Holy Spirit.

The Catechism explains that through confirmation, Catholics receive an increase of baptismal grace, become more deeply rooted as children of God, are more firmly united to Jesus Christ, receive an increase of the gifts of the Holy Spirit, make their bond with the Church more perfect, and receive special strength to defend and spread the faith. (1303)

Every baptized Catholic who is not confirmed should be confirmed at the "appropriate time." In the U.S. Church, in the Latin rite, the appropriate time falls somewhere between the "age of discretion," which is around 7 years of age, and the age of 16. (1307)

The Catechism explains that in order to be confirmed, Catholics must prepare through instruction designed to "awaken a sense of belonging to the Church of Jesus Christ, the universal Church as well as the parish community." Confirmands typically receive their instruction within their parish communities, either through lessons provided as part of their Catholic school curriculum or, if they attend public school, through classes provided after school or in the evenings (typically on a weekly basis.) Most children attend regular religious education classes throughout their school years, culminating in confirmation some time in high school.

The person going through confirmation chooses a sponsor, who is often a godparent or a family member or friend who will provide spiritual help and serve as a role model. The confirmand also chooses a saint's name, as in baptism, as a patron and model of faith. There seems to be an almost unlimited supply of saints' names, but some of the more common examples include Joseph, Anne, John, Teresa, Catherine and Francis. It can be the name of a well-known saint or someone obscure, as long as the Church recognizes the person as a saint.

Confirmation is typically administered by a bishop, although a bishop may give priests the faculty to do so if necessary. The Catechism explains the reason for the bishop as first choice has to do with his role as successor of the apostles. As minister of this sacrament, the bishop unites those being confirmed more closely to the Church and its "apostolic origins." (1313)

Like the sacrament of first Eucharist or Communion (which we will discuss further in a few minutes), confirmation is a very special day in the life of a Catholic. Typically all the children to be confirmed from a parish will gather in the parish church with their family and friends for a ceremony in which each child (often dressed in red or white robes) goes before the bishop with his or her sponsor and is anointed with chrism.

Eucharist: The Greatest Mystery

The third sacrament in this series is the central sacrament of the entire Catholic faith, the Eucharist. Everything in the life of the Church flows from the Eucharist and is directed toward it: "The Eucharist is the source and summit of the Christian life." (1324)

To some people, the Eucharist, which Catholics receive during Mass may appear to be simple bread and wine, but it is so much more than that. In fact, Catholics believe that during Mass the bread and wine become Jesus' body and blood, which is known as the "real presence," even though they retain the appearance of bread and wine.

The Eucharist or Communion, as it is commonly known, is the sacrifice of the body and blood of Jesus Christ, made available to humankind as a way to "perpetuate the sacrifice of the cross throughout the ages until he should come again," the Catechism explains. At the Last Supper, when Jesus celebrated Passover with his apostles, he gave them the Eucharist (bread and wine transformed into his body and blood) as a memorial of his death and resurrection. The Catechism calls the Eucharist a sacrament of love, a sign of unity, a bond of charity, and a paschal banquet, at which believers who consume Christ are filled with grace and receive a pledge of future glory. (1323)

So to be sure you are clear on the depth of the Eucharist, Catholics believe the bread and wine offered at Mass truly become the body and blood of Jesus Christ through *transubstantiation*. They do not believe it is a symbol of the body and blood but that through the prayer of consecration prayed by the priest-celebrant, the bread and wine *become* Jesus.

> **Church Speak**
>
> **Transubstantiation** is a term used to describe the change of bread and wine into the body and blood of Jesus during the eucharistic celebration. It means an entire change of substance occurs during the consecration even though it maintains the appearance of bread and wine.

The Eucharist, the Catechism explains, is the "culmination" both of God's sanctification of the world through his Son and of humanity's worship offered back to Jesus Christ and, through him, to the Father in the Holy Spirit. (1325)

The sacrament of Eucharist is known by many different names in the Church. The word "Eucharist" refers to an act of thanksgiving to God. Other names for the Eucharist include Lord's Supper, Breaking of Bread, Memorial of the Lord's Passion and Resurrection, Holy Sacrifice of the Mass, Most Blessed Sacrament, and Holy Communion, among others. (1328–1330)

In the Old Covenant, gifts of bread and wine were offered as a sign of thanksgiving to the creator. The unleavened bread of Passover, the bread that commemorates the Israelites' exodus from Egypt, is made new by Jesus, who takes the unleavened bread of Passover and transforms it into his body. The wine, offered as a "cup of blessing" at the end of the Jewish Passover, is given new meaning when Jesus transforms it into his blood, leaving a never-ending memorial of his suffering for his Church. (1334–1335)

Teachable Moment

When Jesus multiplied five loaves of bread to feed the crowd of 5,000 (John 6:1–15), it prefigured the "superabundance" of the eucharistic bread. Similarly, when he turned water into wine at the wedding feast at Cana (John 2:1–11), it prefigured the wedding feast in heaven where the faithful will "drink the new wine that has become the blood of Christ." (1335)

Last Supper, First Communion

Jesus wanted to leave his followers with something that would forever connect him to them. He did this through the Eucharist.

At the Last Supper, Jesus gathered his apostles around him, knowing the hour of his death was fast approaching. When they were seated at the Passover table, he broke the bread, gave it to the apostles, and said, "Take and eat; this is my body." Then he took the cup of wine and said, "Drink from it, all of you, for this is my blood of the covenant, which will be shed on behalf of many for the forgiveness of sins." (Matthew 26:26–28)

With that, Jesus "gave the Jewish Passover its definitive meaning," the Catechism explains. Jesus' "passing over" to his Father through his death and resurrection becomes the "new Passover" and anticipates the final Passover that will come at the end of time. (1340)

So Jesus gave his body and blood, but he did something more: He asked his disciples to "Do this in remembrance of me" (1 Cor 11:24). During Mass, at the prayer of consecration, the events of the Last Supper are remembered, and through Christ's words and the power of the Holy Spirit, the bread and wine become Jesus' body and blood.

At every Catholic Mass, the Liturgy of the Eucharist "unfolds according to a fundamental structure that has been preserved throughout the centuries," the Catechism says. The liturgy, as we discussed in the previous chapter, breaks down into two parts: the Liturgy of the Word, which includes Scripture readings; intercessory prayer and a homily; and the Liturgy of the Eucharist, which includes the presentation of bread and wine, the prayer of consecration, and Communion. This two-fold celebration mirrors Jesus' Passover meal, where he talked first to his disciples about Scripture and then gave them his body and blood under the "species" of bread and wine. (1347)

Teachable Moment

At the Mass, Christ is considered the "high priest" with an ordained Catholic priest or bishop representing him and "acting in the person of Christ." (1348) You cannot have a Catholic Mass without an ordained priest or bishop, although it is possible to have Communion services or other liturgical celebrations that do not include the prayer of consecration of the Eucharist but instead use Communion hosts consecrated at a previous Mass. In those cases, a deacon, religious sister or brother, or lay man or woman may officiate. **Extraordinary ministers** of the Eucharist are lay men and women who have been trained to distribute Communion at Mass or bring it to the homebound.

A Never-Ending Sacrifice

The Eucharist is not just a recollection of Jesus' last Passover meal, but is a memorial that makes Jesus' sacrifice on the cross "ever present" to believers. (1364) In other words, the sacrifice of Jesus' death on the cross and the sacrifice of the Eucharist at Mass are "one single sacrifice." (1367)

To help in this understanding, think of it as every time a Catholic Mass is celebrated, we remember that Jesus offered up his body and blood in order to redeem humankind. In the Eucharist, the whole Church is united with the sacrifice of Jesus Christ, from the pope and diocesan bishops to members of individual parishes to the communion of saints in heaven. (1371)

It is impossible to explain fully in logical, human terms what happens during the consecration of the Eucharist. Like the Trinity, the Eucharist is a matter of faith that is in many ways beyond our comprehension, but I'll give it a shot because it is so critical to understanding the Catholic faith.

True Confessions

The Church teaches that through the consecration of the Eucharist, the bread and wine become Jesus' real Body and Blood but the appearance of bread and wine remains. Will the consecrated bread and wine look any different? No. Will it taste any different? No. It is wholly changed in *substance* but not in appearance.

The "real, true, and substantial" presence of Christ in the Eucharist makes this sacrament more significant than any other and accounts for some of the other aspects of Catholic life that many people are familiar with. For example, when Catholics enter a Church they genuflect, or bend one knee, in reverence to the presence of the Eucharist. When the Eucharist is present in the tabernacle on or near the altar, a candle burns at all times. During the consecration at Mass, most Catholics will kneel.

The Church teaches that from the moment of consecration and for as long as the eucharistic "species" remain, Christ is present in them, and cannot be divided. In other words, when the priest breaks the Communion bread and distributes it, he does not divide Jesus, who is wholly present in any morsel of consecrated bread or sip of consecrated wine. (1378)

You're Absolved If ...

Although most Catholics in the Latin rite now receive Communion in the hand, you may still receive Communion directly on the tongue. For those who choose to receive in the hand, it is not simply a grab-and-go method. There is a particular way to receive: You cup your dominant hand under the opposite hand—for example, right cupped under left—and you let the priest, deacon, or extraordinary minister place the Communion host in the palm of your hand. Then, before leaving the presence of the eucharistic minister, you use your dominant hand to reverently place the host on your tongue.

Really, This *Is* My Body

When exploring the significance of the Eucharist and what is known as "the real presence," the Church refers back to the words Jesus spoke not only at the Last Supper but also during his preaching.

"Amen, Amen, I say to you, unless you eat the flesh of the Son of Man and drink his blood, you do not have life within you." (John 6:53) In response to this stark and direct mandate, the Church invites believers to receive Communion on Sundays and holy days, or, if possible, daily, as long as they have made a preparatory examination of conscience or, when necessary due to grave sin, have gone to the sacrament of reconciliation, which we will discuss at length in the next chapter.

Although it is recommended that Catholics receive Communion whenever they are at Mass, they are obliged to receive Communion at least once a year, during the Easter season. (1389) In the U.S. Church, the time for fulfilling that obligation runs from the first Sunday of Lent until Trinity Sunday, which is the first Sunday after Pentecost, or about eight weeks after Easter.

Teachable Moment

The Catholic Church allows children to receive the sacrament of first Communion when they reach the "use of reason," typically around age 7, or second grade.

The Church teaches just as Jesus cannot be divided when the Eucharist is broken or distributed at Mass, he is also fully present in both species of bread and wine, meaning that if you receive under only one "form," you receive the real, true, and substantial Christ, whole and entire. The Catechism explains, however, that by receiving under both species the sign of Communion is "more complete." (1390)

By receiving the Eucharist, or Holy Communion, Catholics are intimately united with Jesus. The Eucharist serves as a foundation for a life in Christ, with the spiritual nourishment of Communion doing for the spiritual life of the believer what material food does for human life. (1391–1392)

The Least You Need to Know

◆ There are three sacraments of initiation into the Catholic faith: baptism, confirmation, and Eucharist.

◆ Baptism washes away original sin, actual sins, and their punishments, and lays the foundation for a life in Christ.

◆ Confirmation completes the initiation started at baptism, binding the recipient more perfectly to the Church as a true witness of Christ.

◆ Eucharist, which is a memorial of Christ's death on the cross, is the central sacrament of the Catholic faith.

◆ Bread and wine are transformed into the body and blood of Jesus Christ during the eucharistic prayer at Mass.

◆ The Church recommends that Catholics receive Communion at Mass on Sundays and holy days but obliges them to receive Communion at least once during the Easter season.

Chapter **13**

Sacraments of Healing

In This Chapter

- ◆ The meaning of the sacrament of reconciliation
- ◆ Is a priest really necessary to forgive sins?
- ◆ How to make a "good" confession
- ◆ Anointing of the sick, and who can receive it

The sacrament of reconciliation, also known as the sacrament of penance (or sometimes simply called "confession"), and the sacrament of the anointing of the sick are the two sacraments of healing. They have been instituted by Christ and committed to the Church as ways to restore strength of spirit to those who are suffering due to sin or weakness, in the case of reconciliation, as well as illness or old age, in the case of anointing.

The Catechism calls Jesus the "physician of our souls and bodies" (1421) and explains that these two sacraments pick up where the previous three left off. The sacraments of initiation give Catholics a new life in Christ and in the Christian community. But we are human, and so we are likely to face either spiritual or physical sickness—or both. The sacraments of healing enable the Church to continue the healing and salvation that Jesus Christ brought to others, and they give believers a way to renew their faith within the Church.

In this chapter, we will put these two sacraments under the microscope. We will explore the finer points of reconciliation—from confession and penance to sin and forgiveness, and we will look at the ins and outs of anointing of the sick, which is *not* reserved only for those who are dying.

Understanding Confession

The sacrament of reconciliation often raises a lot of questions for Catholics and non-Catholics alike. Why do Catholics have to confess to a priest? How can another human forgive someone's sins? What's with all the secrecy? Does anybody even go to confession anymore?

This sacrament is about pardon, mercy, and second chances. This is the place where Catholics go when they want to wipe the slate clean and start over again with sinless souls, as they did the day they were baptized.

When Catholics are baptized, original sin and any other sins they might have committed are washed away. So why is reconciliation even necessary, then, if baptism takes care of everything? Well, while baptism offers forgiveness for all previous sins, it does not provide blanket protection from future sins committed over the course of a lifetime, and it does not remove the human inclination to sin.

Church Speak

To be **contrite** means to be repentant or sorry. In Catholic terms, it means to be sorry for your sins. When Catholics pray an Act of Contrition, they not only express sorrow for the sins they have committed but also promise to try to avoid sin in the future.

The Church teaches that Jesus' "call to conversion," which begins at baptism, is an ongoing part of the life of individual believers and the Church as a whole. Through confession and penance and renewal, a Catholic with a "*contrite* heart" can be purified and drawn closer to God and to the Church. (1428) So it's not enough to go to confession; you have to be truly sorry for what you've done, and you have to have every intention of avoiding the sin down the road.

Penance Is Not Punishment

Penance is not only a name for this sacrament, but is also the word used to describe an action performed to make reparation for a sin. Whenever you go to confession, you receive a penance, which is usually a few particular prayers or actions that must be completed as a way to aid the conversion process. Even more, penance, if it is more than an empty gesture, presupposes penitence, or repentance.

Penance is not about punishment. The Catechism explains that Jesus' calls for conversion were not about public displays of suffering and fasting but about an interior penance that would produce a "conversion of the heart." The Catechism refers to this interior penance as a "radical reorientation of our whole life." (1430–1431)

So the sacrament of reconciliation is not just about spilling your sins to a stranger behind a screen or sitting across from you, but is instead about reforming your life, turning away from sin, expressing sorrow, and vowing to try to live a life with God at its center.

That's not to say that concrete forms of penance don't have their place in a life bent on conversion. They do. In fact, interior penance leads to more visible signs of penance, such as fasting, prayer, and almsgiving. (1434)

This conversion, the Catechism explains, can be further carried out in a Catholic's daily activities, such as caring for the poor, receiving the Eucharist, going to confession, reading Scripture, giving things up as a means of self-denial, and providing for others through charitable works. (1434–1439)

Teachable Moment

In the Scripture story of the Prodigal Son, a father gives his two sons their share of his inheritance. One stays home and saves his money and continues to help his father. The other son spends the money on wild living until there's nothing left and he has to take a job feeding pigs. He realizes the error of his ways and returns to his father, begging for mercy. His father welcomes him and gives him a feast fit for a king. (Luke 15:11–32) So what's the moral of this story? The depth of God's love runs so deep that no matter what we do, we will be forgiven if we repent and return home to him.

How to Repent

Now we get down to the basics of the actual sacrament of reconciliation. It consists in its most "fundamental structure" of two "equally essential" actions: The sinner's conversion through "the action of the Holy Spirit," and God's action through the intervention of the Church, who, through its bishops and priests, forgives sins in the name of Jesus Christ. (1448)

Let's break that down into even simpler terms. The sacrament of reconciliation requires a person who, responding to God's grace, is truly sorry for what he or she has done wrong and now wants to make amends and be reconciled with God. It also requires a priest or bishop, who will pray for this person, give this person a penance, and absolve, or forgive, this person's sins in the name of Jesus Christ.

You're Absolved If ...

Your image of confession may be from movies that always portray Catholics kneeling inside pitch-black confessionals whispering to a priest behind a screen. Although Catholics can and do use confessionals, they are really the product of an earlier era. While they have a right to confess from behind a screen, these days, more often than not, Catholics go to confession face to face. They simply sit opposite the priest in a room or quiet corner of a church and talk just as they would to a friend.

Here's how an actual experience of this sacrament would unfold. If you wanted to make a confession, this is what you would do:

- ◆ Prior to going to confession, you would spend time making an "examination of conscience." This means you would reflect on what you've done since your last confession and would think about the mistakes you've made or the problems you are trying to overcome.

- ◆ After you have pulled up your sins on the screen of your conscience, you don't simply look at them; you need to be truly sorry for them.

- ◆ Next, you would either kneel down in a confessional or sit opposite a priest, make the Sign of the Cross, and say the following words: "Bless me, father, for I have sinned. It has been [however long] since my last confession. These are my sins."

◆ Here's the hard part. Now you have to tell the priest your sins. You're supposed to tell him *all* of your serious sins, not just the ones you don't feel too embarrassed about.

◆ Finally, the priest will give you a penance, which is also called "satisfaction." He may tell you to say three Our Fathers and three Hail Marys, or maybe to do something nice for your wife, or to spend some time in prayer each day. There is no set penance for particular sins or sinners.

◆ After this, the priest will usually offer some counsel. Then he will pray over you and give you *absolution*. He may ask you to recite the Act of Contrition out loud.

Church Speak

Absolution refers to the essential part of the sacrament of reconciliation or confession, when the priest or bishop, through the power entrusted to him by Jesus Christ, pardons the sins of the person confessing. At the end of the confession the priest or bishop will pray over the penitent, saying, "God, the Father of mercies, through the death and the resurrection of his Son has reconciled the world to himself and sent the Holy Spirit among us for the forgiveness of sins; through the ministry of the Church may God give you pardon and peace, and I absolve you from your sins in the name of the Father, and of the Son, and of the Holy Spirit."

Let's back up a minute and talk about sin. There are two basic kinds of sins: mortal and venial. We're going to get into the specifics of these sins in greater detail in Chapter 15, but we will cover some of the basics now.

A *mortal sin* is a "grave" sin, something big and bad, and something you knew full well was wrong when you decided to go ahead and do it anyway. Any major violation of one of the Ten Commandments, for instance, would qualify as a mortal sin. Cheating on a spouse, stealing all a person had to survive on, deliberately killing another person. Those are a few examples of mortal sins.

A *venial sin*, on the other hand, is a lesser sin, something that's not very nice but is probably an everyday kind of mistake or fault, say, yelling at the kids or fighting with your husband.

You must confess all mortal sins when you go to confession. You don't have to confess venial sins, but it's recommended. In fact, the Church teaches that by going to confession regularly, we end up with better-formed consciences and are more likely to be able to withstand the temptations of sin. (1456–1458)

The Church requires all Catholics who have reached the "age of discretion" to go to confession at least once a year, preferably during the Easter season. In addition, if you know you've committed a mortal sin, you cannot receive Communion without first going to the sacrament of reconciliation. (1457)

True Confessions

The Catechism's section on confession omits an important line that exists in the Code of Canon Law, which is the law of the Catholic Church. The Catechism says if you know you are in a state of mortal sin, you cannot receive Communion without confession first unless there is a "grave reason" *and* you have absolutely no chance of going to confession. The Code of Canon Law (Canon 916) says the same thing except that at the end of that instruction it adds that you must remember that you are required to make a perfect Act of Contrition, which includes the commitment of going to confession as soon as possible. Canon law trumps Catechism.

Of course, all of this confessing has to be done before a priest. Why? Well, the Church teaches that Jesus Christ entrusted the ministry of reconciliation to his apostles when he gave them the faculty to forgive sins in his name through the power of the Holy Spirit.

"Receive the Holy Spirit. Whose sins you forgive are forgiven them, and whose sins you retain are retained." (John 20:21–23)

Remember, the Twelve Apostles are the original "permanent assembly" that now has its successors in the Church's college of bishops. So the Church teaches that Jesus granted the power to forgive sins to the apostles and their direct successors. The bishops and their "collaborators," the Church's priests, continue the ministry of forgiving sins in the name of the Father and the Son and the Holy Spirit. (1461)

The Catechism explains priests "must encourage the faithful to come to the sacrament of penance," and must make themselves available to celebrate the sacrament when asked. (1463) The priest, when he administers the sacrament, is considered a "sign and instrument of God's merciful love for the sinner." (1465)

Teachable Moment

The sacramental seal of confession means that a priest is bound "under very severe penalties" to keep secret everything he hears in confession. There are no exceptions. (1467) What happens in confession, stays in confession.

Forgiveness Rules!

So what is the point of confession? Couldn't you just whisper a quiet, "I'm sorry," to God and get the same effect? Not exactly. The Church teaches that the sacrament of reconciliation, when the penitent is truly sorry, brings about a "spiritual resurrection" as well as a sense of "peace and serenity." (1468) But even more, it brings about reconciliation with the People of God, the Church, restoring a communion with fellow Christians that had been broken by sin. (1469)

Although confessional experiences may vary from priest to priest, the overall experience of confession should be one of serenity and joy, not shame and fear.

Church Speak

An **indulgence** is a release from "temporal punishment" for sins that have been forgiven. (1471) The sacrament of reconciliation forgives "eternal punishment" but that doesn't necessarily mean that you don't have to do a little time for the consequences of your sins. Through reconciliation or particular prayers or actions (indulgences), you can reduce the punishment due you. On top of that, if you're feeling generous, you can offer particular prayers or actions on behalf of someone else and reduce their punishment.

The sacrament of penance, as it is one of the seven sacraments of the Church, is always a community action. Despite the communal aspect of the sacrament, however, the Church requires that Catholics ordinarily confess their sins individually to a priest, after which the priest imparts absolution. Even at a "communal" celebration of the sacrament of reconciliation, individual confession and absolution are "inserted" into the community celebration. (1482) Only in cases of "grave necessity" is it possible to offer general absolution to a group without prior individual confession. Even in cases of "general absolution," those who receive it must intend to confess the absolved sins individually for absolution to stick. (1483)

There are "profound reasons" for individual confession, the Catechism explains, and chief among them is the fact that Jesus Christ "addresses every sinner" individually and "reintegrates them" into communion with the Church. "Personal confession is thus the form most expressive of reconciliation with God and with the Church." (1484)

Anointing of the Sick

Few of us escape serious illness over the course of our lifetimes. Whether we suffer from physical or mental sicknesses or the debilitating effects of old age, we all eventually have to deal with things that slow us down, crush our spirits, or make us wonder why suffering is a normal part of life.

The Church offers the second sacrament of healing, anointing of the sick, as a way to bring spiritual comfort and strength to those who have attained the "use of reason" and are in danger due to sickness or old age. This is not a sacrament restricted only to the dying, and it is not a sacrament that can be received only once. Anointing of the sick is designed to shore up those who are losing spiritual and physical strength.

Spiritual Care of the Suffering

The Church looks to Jesus Christ in his role as "physician" and healer of bodies and souls when discussing this sacrament. Jesus had a special closeness with the sick and suffering, offering them hope and a healing touch. When he says, "I was ill and you cared for me" (Matthew 25:36), he identifies himself with the sick and reminds Christians of their call to reach out to those who are suffering from illness. (1503)

This deep connection between Jesus Christ the healer and those in need of healing serves as the foundation for the sacrament of anointing of the sick. Although sometimes this sacrament may result in physical healing, that's not what it is all about. Jesus did not cure all illness or remove all suffering. Rather, he taught his disciples that, because of his bringing God's kingdom, sickness does not own us. "By his Passion and death on the cross Christ has given a new meaning to suffering: it can henceforth configure us to him and unite us with his redemptive Passion." (1505)

You're Absolved If ...

You may think of this sacrament as "last rites," which was never the name of a sacrament but a term that applied to three particular sacraments offered to a dying person: anointing of the sick, penance, and Communion. Although they are not known as last rites anymore, those three remain the "last sacraments" a dying person receives.

The Who and Why of Anointing

The specific rite for anointing can be traced back to the Letter of St. James:

Is anyone among you sick? He should summon the presbyters of the Church, and they should pray over him and anoint him with oil in the name of the Lord, and the prayer of faith will save the sick person, and the Lord will raise him up. If he has committed any sins, he will be forgiven. (James 5:14)

This gives us the starting point for talking about the details of anointing of the sick. First of all, as we discussed earlier, the sacrament of anointing of the sick is exactly that: it is for the sick, not just for the dying. It doesn't matter how old you are or how young you are (as long as you have attained the use of reason), or what your particular illness might be. If you are seriously ill, you can receive anointing. (1514)

And you are not limited to only one anointing in a lifetime. If you receive anointing of the sick and then recover, you may receive the sacrament again if you become gravely ill or close to death due to old age. Even if you aren't healed, you may receive the sacrament again if your condition worsens. You may receive it before surgery, for mental or physical suffering, or for any condition that weakens your body or spirit. (1515)

Only priests and bishops can be ministers of anointing of the sick, which can be administered in a church, a hospital, or a family home, for one person or a group of people. (1517)

Typically preceded by an "act of repentance" and the reading of Scripture, the essential rite of anointing of the sick includes the laying on of hands with the recitation of a prayer by the priest. The core action of the sacrament is the anointing of the sick person's forehead and hands with oil blessed by a bishop or blessed by a priest during the actual celebration of the sacrament. (1518–1519)

Through this anointing, the believer receives strength, peace, and courage "to overcome the difficulties that go with the condition of serious illness or the frailty of old age." (1520) This does not mean there will be physical healing, although that is possible. Rather, it's about healing the soul, including the forgiveness of sins. In addition, this sacrament is meant to help sick people link their suffering with the Passion of Jesus Christ. (1521)

> **Church Speak**
>
> **Viaticum** is the final Communion, or Eucharist, given to a dying person in conjunction with the sacraments of reconciliation and anointing. Given just prior to the moment of "passing over," the Eucharist takes on increased significance as it prepares the dying person for his or her journey into the next life. (1524)

Finally, anointing of the sick prepares the believer for the next life and completes the journey that began at baptism. The Catechism explains that just as baptism prepares us for new life and confirmation strengthens us for the "combat of this life," anointing "fortifies" us at the end of our journey. (1523)

The Least You Need to Know

◆ The sacrament of reconciliation and the sacrament of anointing of the sick are known as the sacraments of healing.

◆ The sacrament of reconciliation, also called the sacrament of penance or simply confession, is a way for Catholics to receive forgiveness for their post-baptismal sins.

◆ When you go to confession, you receive a penance, which is usually a series of prayers or actions to help make up for the things done wrong and to re-establish habits befitting a disciple of Christ.

◆ The sacrament of anointing of the sick is for those who are dying as well as those who are suffering either physically or mentally due to serious illness or old age.

◆ Anointing of the sick, which can be received more than once, provides forgiveness of sins, and, when received at the end of life with reconciliation and Eucharist, prepares a Catholic for the journey to the Father.

Chapter **14**

Sacraments of Commitment

In This Chapter

- ◆ Holy orders and the all-male priesthood
- ◆ Understanding marriage as a sacrament
- ◆ Sacred signs of grace in sacramentals and popular devotions
- ◆ Christian funerals in the Catholic faith

Finally we come to the last two of the seven sacraments: holy orders and matrimony, known as sacraments of commitment or sacraments of service. Unlike the other five sacraments, which focus on building up the person receiving them, these two sacraments focus on building up other people. Specifically, they are aimed at building up the People of God.

The Catechism explains that holy orders and matrimony are "directed toward the salvation of others." They may contribute to personal salvation as well, but only as a byproduct of service. (1534)

In this chapter, we will explore holy orders, which include the ordination of bishops, priests, and deacons, and we will look at marriage in the Catholic Church and how it rises to the level of a sacrament.

That's an Order

You may be asking what the sacrament of holy orders is. Is it the Catholic version of getting drafted to serve the Church? Nope. The sacrament of holy orders is about answering a call from God, and about continuing with uninterrupted succession the ministry of the original Twelve Apostles until the end of all time.

The term "holy orders" has its roots in ancient Rome, where an "order" referred to an "established civil body, especially a governing body." (1537) In the Catholic Church, holy orders "confers a gift of the Holy Spirit that permits the exercise of a 'sacred power,' which can come only from Christ himself through his Church." So the gift of the Spirit received during ordination doesn't come from the community or even the Church but from Christ *through* the Church. (1538)

The Priesthood

Before we get into the specifics of holy orders, let's check the history of this sacrament. Like so many aspects of the Catholic faith, the Catholic priesthood is foreshadowed in the priesthood of the Old Covenant. Among God's chosen people, the Levites were selected by God to be priests. The Catechism explains how the Church recognizes the priesthood of Aaron, the service of the Levites, and the "institution of the 70 elders" (Numbers 11:24) as prefiguring the ordained ministry of the New Covenant. (1541)

Jesus, then, is seen as fulfilling the Old Covenant. He is the high priest, the "one mediator between God and the human race" (1 Tim 2:5). In the New Covenant, there is only one priesthood, that of Jesus Christ. There is also only one Priest, namely Jesus Christ. So what about all those who are ordained as priests? The Catechism says these priests make present the one Priest. St. Thomas Aquinas, the Catechism tells us, says that "only Christ is the true priest; the others (are) only his ministers." Because of this, ordained priests today are said to be members of the "ministerial priesthood." (1545)

Teachable Moment _____

Just because bishops, priests, and deacons are representatives
of Christ on earth, it doesn't mean that they are free from human
weaknesses, mistakes, and sins. The Catechism explains that the
Holy Spirit "doesn't guarantee all acts of his ministers in the same way."
What the Church does say, however, is the sins of the minister do not
"impede" the grace received in the sacraments, even though the sins
may sometimes harm the Church. (1550) So if you are baptized or confirmed by a priest who commits an egregious sin, the sacrament is still
valid.

Ordination Explanation

The Church teaches there are three "degrees" of _ordination_: episcopate
(bishop), presbyterate (what we call priest), and diaconate (deacon).
The first two, bishops and priests, are considered "ministerial priests,"
meaning they participate in and manifest the one priesthood of Christ.
Deacons, on the other hand, are there to help and serve priests and
bishops. Let's talk about what each of these "degrees" really means.

Church Speak _____

Ordination refers to the essential rite of the sacrament of holy
orders through which a man becomes a deacon, priest, or bishop.
The actual moment of ordination occurs during the "imposition of
hands," when the bishop puts his hand on the head of the person being
ordained and says a prayer of consecration.

A bishop starts out by being ordained a deacon (more on deacons in
a moment), and then is ordained a presbyter or priest. He becomes a
bishop after his _Episcopal ordination_, after being appointed by the pope,
and he typically will serve in a specific geographic location (diocese)
or in a particular office of the Church, or both. A bishop can do all
the things a priest does and then some. In addition to saying Mass,
hearing confessions, baptizing babies, anointing the sick, and blessing marriages, a bishop can also confirm and ordain. So a bishop has
the capacity to celebrate all of the seven sacraments. A bishop is also
in a leadership role on a broader scale than a priest. A priest may be

the shepherd of his parish, but a bishop is the shepherd of many, many parishes and is considered a successor to the apostles. In that role, the bishop becomes a member of the college of bishops and, with the pope, shares in the teaching authority of the Church.

A priest starts out as a seminarian, which is someone studying to be a priest. After years of theology and time spent working in parishes and other ministries, a seminarian becomes a deacon. This kind of deacon is known as "transitional," meaning that he is a deacon only for a short time (usually a year or so) before being ordained a priest.

A priest can do all of the things mentioned previously: baptize, bless marriages, celebrate Mass, hear confessions, anoint the sick, and, in some instances when the bishop requests it, confirm. A priest can work in a parish or in other types of ministries—as a hospital or prison chaplain, counselor, teacher, and many other positions.

Church Speak

Episcopal ordination refers to the ordination of a bishop, which brings about the "fullness" of the sacrament of holy orders. Through episcopal ordination, a bishop takes his place as a successor to the apostles as a teacher, shepherd, and priest. (1557–1558)

So how does ordination actually occur? Well, the essential rite of this sacrament is the "imposition of hands" by the bishop on the head of the person being ordained. At that point, the bishop says a special prayer of consecration, asking the Holy Spirit to come upon the person and guide him in his particular ministry—bishop, priest, or deacon. (1573)

An ordination would normally take place within the context of a Mass, preferably on a Sunday in a cathedral, with as many of the faithful in attendance as possible. Ordination is seen as incredibly important for the life of the Church, and so it is equally important that the Church community be there to witness it and celebrate it. (1572) As with baptism and confirmation, this sacrament leaves an indelible mark called a "character" and can be received only once.

Because the Church teaches bishops are the successors of the apostles and Jesus Christ continues to act through them, and because the sacrament of holy orders is considered "the sacrament of the apostolic ministry," only bishops are allowed to ordain other bishops, priests, and deacons. (1576) So who is allowed to be ordained? The answer is baptized men only. Why not women? Well, the Church sees the college of bishops as the successors to the original Twelve Apostles, who were chosen by Jesus and who were all men. In order to make the original Twelve Apostles "ever present," the Church teaches that it is "bound" to the choices that Jesus Christ himself, so that the "ordination of women is not possible." (1577)

The Latin Church also does not allow its priests and bishops to be married. This is based on the conviction that they are called to give themselves with "undivided heart to the Lord," and so they must remain celibate their entire lives. The Catechism explains that celibacy is a sign of their "new life" in the Lord. (1579)

Celibacy is a "discipline," not a matter of Church doctrine. The Eastern Church follows a different discipline. Its priests and deacons are allowed to be married, although its bishops must be unmarried, celibate men. (1580) There are some instances in the Roman Catholic Church where married Anglican priests have been welcomed in the Catholic priesthood along with their wives and children. (1580) In both the Latin and Eastern Churches, the one common rule on celibacy is this: married men may be ordained, but ordained men cannot marry.

True Confessions

> Although women are not allowed to be priests, they have always held positions of power within the Church. Sisters have served as hospital and college presidents for more than 100 years. Increasingly, women are being appointed "chancellor," which is basically the chief recording officer, of dioceses. Many sisters and lay women and men are administrators of parishes, taking care of most of the nonsacramental work of a local church.

What Are Deacons?

As mentioned briefly in the beginning of the previous section, a deacon is a whole other breed of ordained clergy. A deacon does not have the same capacities as a priest and bishop.

Deacons are considered to be at a lower level of hierarchy. Although they receive the imposition of hands during ordination and it is an "indelible" mark that can never be removed, it is not the same as that received by priests and bishops. (1569)

Through ordination, deacons take a share in the mission of Jesus Christ the Servant and commit themselves to serving their bishop and priests. A deacon can baptize, bless marriages, distribute Communion, proclaim the Gospel, preach, preside at funerals, and serve through charitable ministries. Deacons cannot celebrate Mass, hear confession, or anoint the sick.

Unlike priests and bishops, a "permanent" deacon—not a seminarian on the road to priesthood but a man who will remain a deacon for the rest of his life—may be married, as long as he is married before he is ordained a deacon. If his wife dies after he is ordained, he must remain celibate thereafter.

I Now Pronounce You ...

Now we come to marriage, which you probably never thought of as a vocation the way a calling to the priesthood is a vocation. Most of us grow up and get married; it's just what we do. But the Church looks at marriage in a different light. It's not just a general stage of life, but is a specific vocation. Husbands and wives are called to married life the way other men and women are called to the priesthood, religious life, or single life.

The Church sees marriage as a "covenant" between a man and woman that establishes a lifelong partnership designed to benefit the partners as well as their offspring. This covenant, then, is not just some sort of civil agreement. When it is between baptized people, marriage is a sacrament. (1601)

Teachable Moment

Marriage, according to the Catholic Church, is not a "purely human institution." God is the author of marriage: it springs from God and finds its strength in God, and despite differences in cultures and social structures and spirituality, all marriages have "common and permanent characteristics." The stability and well-being of marriage impacts not only the couples involved but also the Church of Christ, as well as society as a whole. (1603)

Here's how it works: God created man and woman out of love and calls them to love others. The mutual love of a husband and wife becomes a mirror of God, who is love, and of God's love for humanity. In husband and wife, we see the love of God reflected. The Catechism explains that this belief in the specifically religious nature of marriage goes back to both the Old and New Testaments. (1604)

First, we have the Book of Genesis, where we hear about how God created the first man but didn't want man to be alone. So God created a woman, "flesh of his flesh," to be the man's equal, the man's helpmate, the man's partner. "That is why a man leaves his father and mother and clings to his wife, and the two of them become one body." (Gen 2:24)

Flip to the New Testament, and we have Jesus reiterating the teaching of Genesis on the creator's plan from the beginning: "So they are no longer two, but one flesh. Therefore, what God has joined together, no human being must separate." (Matthew 19:6)

Now, the Church may teach that marriage is a sacrament and marriage is forever, but that doesn't mean the Church doesn't recognize that marriage isn't always easy. Because of humanity's original fall, man and woman have this tension between them, this penchant for sinning, hurting each other, fighting, cheating, and more. Like Adam and Eve, modern men and women struggle with issues of jealousy, lust, hatred, and domination, but the Church teaches that God is always there, healing their wounds, giving them the grace they need to carry on and restore their love for one another. (1606–1608)

> **Church Speak**
>
> **Nuptial** is anything related to marriage or a wedding ceremony. If you get married at a nuptial Mass, it just means that the sacrament of matrimony—the vows, the blessing, the exchange of rings—will take place during a Mass.

What Makes Marriage Holy?

When it comes right down to it, no matter how close a believing man and woman are, no matter how many years they've known each other or loved each other, their relationship is not a sacred reality until they declare their love before God.

In the Latin Church, it is considered optimal for Catholics to have the celebration of marriage within a Mass, connecting matrimony to the sacrament of the Eucharist where Jesus Christ is recognized as the bridegroom with the Church as his bride. The Catechism explains that when they "seal their consent" at Mass, the husband and wife unite themselves with Christ's sacrifice, and by receiving the Eucharist they form "one body" in Jesus Christ. (1621)

The Latin Church teaches that the baptized spouses are "ministers of Christ's grace" and, as such, confer the sacrament of marriage on each other in a public ceremony before a bishop, priest, or deacon. In the Eastern Church, the minister of the sacrament of marriage is the priest or bishop who, after receiving the mutual consent of the spouses, crowns them bridegroom and bride. (1623)

Teachable Moment

Although celebrating marriage within Mass is the typical method, it is possible to say your "I do's" in a stand-alone Catholic ceremony. The ceremony should normally take place in a parish church or some other religious venue, such as a college chapel. There are some circumstances that could warrant permission to hold the ceremony in some other "suitable place," as specified by canon law (Canon 1118). You can probably forget about getting married on a beach, however. To preserve the dignity and sacred character of the celebration of marriage, permission is rarely given for outdoor weddings.

Unbreakable Vows

The Church expects a baptized man and woman who want to commit to marriage to be "free" to marry, meaning there must not be any constraints or impediments of natural or ecclesiastical law. For example, there can't be any legal reasons—such as being younger than legal age or being blood relations—that would prevent the marriage from being valid. (1625)

The spouses also need to consent fully and unconditionally to the marriage (no shotgun weddings allowed). There also must be no effort to coerce one of the partners through intimidation or force. (1626–1628)

Normally, you must have a bishop, priest, or deacon present; he asks you to express your vows and then accepts these vows in the name of the Church. As a rule, there must also be at least two witnesses, and, because the sacrament of marriage is a "liturgical act," the Catechism explains it is appropriate to celebrate it in the "public liturgy of the Church." (1631) In other words, because marriage is a sacred action, the Church doesn't want you getting married in a secular setting, but within a religious ceremony.

Now, what happens if you're a baptized Catholic, but your future spouse is not? Well, if you're marrying a baptized non-Catholic Christian, the Church calls it a mixed marriage, or a marriage of mixed religion, and special permission of Church authority is required. If you're marrying a nonbaptized person, the Church calls it a marriage with disparity of cult (worship). Sounds somewhat ominous, but it just means there are significant differences in what you believe—more so than the differences between a Catholic and a baptized non-Catholic Christian—and so the Church needs to be extra certain you are aware of the potential issues that could arise down the road. For a disparity of worship wedding, a dispensation by Church authority from an impediment or ecclesiastical law is needed. (1633)

"Differences about faith and the very notion of marriage, but also different religious mentalities, can become sources of tension in marriage, especially as regards the education of children," the Catechism explains, adding that in such cases "religious indifference" can be the end result. (1634) The Church requires the Catholic partner to take responsibility for educating their children in the faith. (1635)

Most people know at least one family raising one child in the Jewish faith and one child in the Catholic faith. What the Church is saying is that no matter how pleasant everything may look on the surface, this sort of watering down of both partners' faiths only leads to problems or to a complete removal of faith from the center of the family's life in order to keep anyone from being upset or hurt.

The bottom line is this: the Church, in advance of the marriage celebration, is looking to catch any potential problems that could lead to an invalid marriage or to a marriage headed for disaster almost right off the bat. That's why the Catholic Church requires engaged couples to attend something called Pre-Cana. Named after the wedding feast at

Cana—the one where Jesus turned water into wine—the classes attempt to help couples face their issues *before* they face their I do's.

True Confessions _____

Although the Church teaches that the marriage bond between two baptized people can be dissolved only by death, there is also something known as an annulment. This is not the Catholic version of divorce. If you are granted an annulment, it means that something prevented your marriage from becoming the covenant God intended marriage to be. For example, your spouse did not tell you that he never wanted to have children, or your wife professed her marriage vows all the while planning to keep up an adulterous affair with another man. In most English-speaking countries, a Church annulment has no civil implications.

Conjugal Love

The Church teaches that conjugal love is about the total commitment of one spouse to the other. It leads to a "deeply personal unity," the Catechism explains, one that goes beyond the union of flesh to the union of heart and soul. In that sense, it "demands indissolubility and faithfulness" and must be open to "fertility." (1643)

As we will discuss in further detail in Chapter 20, marriage requires complete fidelity between spouses. Adultery, polygamy, and a host of other sins are contrary to the sacrament of marriage because they divide the conjugal love that is inherent there. (1645)

Of course, not every marriage is the fairytale variety, and the Church recognizes there may be some circumstances that would require spouses to live separately, such as adultery or the threat of danger (abuse) to a spouse or children. This doesn't mean the Church allows such a couple to be ethically divorced, but only physically separated. (1649)

That being said, plenty of Catholics get legal separations and divorces. What does this mean for them as Catholics? Again, we will discuss this in more detail in Chapter 20, but for now you need to know that being separated or divorced does not prevent you from receiving the sacraments. However, if you remarry, the Church sees the new marriage as invalid because the Church continues to recognize the first marriage. In the case of remarriage, you cannot receive Communion or go to confession unless your new marriage is recognized by Church ceremony or Church law after your former spouse has died, or you have received a dissolution or annulment of your former marriage. (1650)

Teachable Moment

All of this talk of conjugal love leads to the question of children. If you're Catholic, do you have to have 10, 5, or even any children? The Church sees marriage as "ordered to the procreation and education of the offspring" (1652), so, yes, children are expected. But that's not all. The Church not only expects Catholic couples to be open to children but also to be the "first educators" of their children. That doesn't just mean teaching them to throw a baseball or play piano. It means teaching them about the faith. The fundamental "task of marriage," the Catechism explains, is to be "at the service of life." (1653)

Domestic Church

Every Catholic family is known as its own little self-contained "domestic church." The Catechism explains that from the beginning of the Christian faith, the "core of the Church" often consisted of people coming together in their households. When they became Christian, entire households or families often converted at the same time. "These families who became believers were islands of Christian life in an unbelieving world," the Catechism says. (1655)

The Church today sees a parallel in Catholic families who keep faith at the center of their lives despite living in a world that is "often alien and even hostile" to the Catholic faith. The Second Vatican Council declared the family *Ecclesia domestica*, domestic church, because that is where the faith is encouraged and fostered through word and example. This is where children and parents learn about generosity, forgiveness, prayer, endurance, and more. This is where the "priesthood" of the baptized is exercised by family members in a privileged way. (1656–1657)

Sacramentals and Devotions

Let's switch gears a little and discuss something called sacramentals, which are "sacred signs" of grace, not to be confused with "sacred instruments" of grace, as are the sacraments. Sacramentals are designed to help Catholics in various circumstances of life to get closer to true holiness. (1667) Sacramentals won't get you the kinds of grace you get from actual sacraments, but they will make you more open to that grace when the time comes.

What are some sacramentals you might know about or even use on a regular basis? Well, a sacramental always includes a prayer and often includes a specific sign, like the Sign of the Cross, or sprinkling with holy water, or a blessing, or *exorcism*. (1668)

Blessings, which are "first" among sacramentals, can include the consecration of people: an abbot of a monastery, a consecrated virgin, a religious-education teacher—or the consecration of things: an altar, holy oils, or vessels used at Mass. (1672)

In addition to sacramentals, there are "popular" devotions. These are forms of piety that include veneration of relics, pilgrimages, Stations of the Cross, the Rosary, and the wearing of religious medals, among other expressions of faith. These devotions are not in place of the sacramental life of the Church but in addition to it, extending it beyond the boundaries of the liturgy. (1674–1675)

Church Speak

An **exorcism** is a sacramental through which the Church, in the name of Jesus Christ, publicly asks that someone or something be protected against the power of the "Evil One," also known as Satan. A "simple" exorcism is performed as part of every baptism rite. A "solemn" exorcism or "major" exorcism is performed when a priest, with permission of a bishop, attempts to free a person from demonic possession. Exorcism is not about healing mental illness, which the Church leaves to the medical professionals; it is about expelling demons—the presence of Satan—from a human being. (1673)

Christian Funerals

We're going to wrap up this section on the sacraments with a brief discussion of Christian funerals. It may sound a little strange at first, but the Christian funeral is the "fulfillment" of all the other sacraments. In our never-say-die world, Christians believe the goal is death because only then do you get to the fullness of life in the kingdom. (1680)

The Christian funeral is known as the "last Passover." In death, the Christian is ushered into a new birth that began at baptism. For the faithful Christian, death, while not always welcome at the time, is not something to fear. (1682)

Although local churches may celebrate the funeral rites in different ways, there is always one common denominator: they express the "paschal character" of Christian death, meaning they reflect the connection to Jesus' Passion, death, and Resurrection. (1685)

Regardless of the style of the rite, every Catholic funeral includes four basic parts: greeting the community with a word of consolation, Liturgy of the Word, the sacrifice of the Eucharist, and the "farewell" to the deceased person, at which point the deceased is entrusted to God and the body is buried in anticipation of the final resurrection. (1686–1690)

Teachable Moment

The Catholic Church allows cremation, as long as it is not done as a denial of faith in resurrection. (2301) This topic will come up again in Chapter 19, where it is addressed as part of respecting the dead.

The Least You Need to Know

◆ Holy orders and matrimony are considered the two sacraments of commitment or service.

◆ The consecration of bishops, priests, and deacons in service to the Church is called holy orders.

♦ Only unmarried men may be ordained priests and bishops, although married men may become permanent deacons (however, they may not marry after becoming deacons).

♦ A sacramental marriage is a covenant between a husband and wife, establishing a lifelong partnership that benefits the couple, their children, and society.

♦ Sacramentals are prayers, blessings, and other sacred signs that open the faithful up to the graces received during the sacraments.

♦ Christian funerals are the fulfillment of the seven sacraments, and usher the deceased into a new life that began at baptism.

Part 4

Living the Good Life

In the Catholic Church, faith is not something you simply profess on Sundays and then put into a box until you come back
the next week. In the Catholic faith, upholding human dignity,
caring for others, and living a righteous life are all part of the
package. Faith is not meant to be lived only inside churches, but
is meant to be lived outside in the world.

In the coming chapters, we will first look at morality in
general—virtue and vice, free will, conscience, sin—and we will
look at our role in caring for others. Then we will tackle the Ten
Commandments, no small feat.

Chapter 15

Morality: The Root of All Dignity

In This Chapter

- ◆ The meaning and responsibility of free will
- ◆ Listening to that voice in your head
- ◆ Exploring virtue and vice
- ◆ The various types of sin

Earlier in this book, we talked about how men and women are created in God's image. Now we will return to this all-important point because it plays a major role in morality. Being made in God's image influences—or should influence—everything a Catholic says and does.

Let's review the basics: being made in God's image means humans have intellect and free will. The Church teaches that these characteristics combine to give every human being an inherent dignity, something that provides a framework for all the decisions and actions that are part of everyday life.

In this chapter, we will look at how all of this works. What does it mean to have free will? Why do some choose vice over virtue? How serious is sin? And what does all of this have to do with our journey toward God?

Exercising Free Will

Earlier when we looked at the first section of the creed, we talked about God allowing all of his creations to work in cooperation with him, meaning God gives us free will and the ability to make mistakes or bad choices.

The Catechism explains that freedom is the "power, rooted in reason and will, to act or not to act, to do this or that, and so to perform deliberate actions on one's own responsibility." (1731)

That means we can't always claim that someone else is pulling the strings. If we do something wrong, or right, it is usually because we chose to do it all of our own accord. For the most part, we shape our own lives, and when we mature in "truth and goodness," we get closer to the perfection of freedom, which is always directed toward God. (1731)

Church Speak

Beatitude means "happiness" or "blessedness." The Catechism explains that all humans are called to eternal beatitude, which is life with God in the kingdom. (1719) Catholics most commonly associate this word with the Beatitudes, which are a series of teachings Jesus gave during the Sermon on the Mount (Matthew 5:3–12). A complete list of the Beatitudes is included in the appendix of Catholic prayers at the end of this book.

If our freedom is not fully and definitively connected to God, we run the risk of getting caught up in a game of good versus evil, and we all know that when that happens, sometimes evil wins. So our goal is to choose good, which will make us "freer," and to avoid evil, which, in the end, will enslave us. (1732–1733)

Because we are free, we are also responsible. The two go hand in hand. The Catechism explains that being "responsible" means we are responsible not only for our direct actions—like cheating on a test or stealing from work—but also for indirect actions or omissions that cause other bad things to happen—like ignoring traffic laws. Now, if you're ignorant of some rule or law, or you do something inadvertently, or you do something out of fear or habit, you are a little less culpable when it comes to the blame game. (1734–1736)

The Church teaches that every human being has a "right" to be a free and responsible person, and that we all owe each other respect. In order to live in dignity, people must have the right to exercise freedom. This freedom must be respected in moral and religious matters and protected by civil authorities. (1738) In other words, no freedom, no dignity.

So if we're all so free, how is it possible there are so many things that are forbidden? Isn't freedom all about doing whatever we want, whenever we want, with no one telling us what we can and can't do? No. We're not talking about freedom from rules and laws and morality here. We're talking about the freedom to set the course of our lives, the freedom to choose right from wrong (and we are, of course, supposed to choose right), the freedom to take responsibility for our own actions, and, ultimately, the freedom to come into beatitude with God.

And where are we supposed to find the courage and strength to attain this kind of freedom? In Jesus Christ, of course, through the grace of the Holy Spirit. (1742)

Teachable Moment

Morality refers to the good and evil acts that humans commit. The Church teaches that there are three "sources" of morality: the "object," which is whatever course of action you choose to take; the "intention," which is the end-goal you had in mind when you acted; and the "circumstances," which include the consequences of your action. You can have the best of intentions, but if the act or the circumstances are intrinsically wrong, you're out of luck. All three things have to be morally good. Bottom line is, the end can never justify the means. (1750–1755)

The Voice in Your Head

Now we're going to talk about conscience—you know, that little voice that tells you not to do something you really want to do. In the cartoon world, conscience is depicted as a little angel and a little devil sitting atop your shoulders, alternately whispering into your ears. According to Church teaching, your conscience isn't sitting on your shoulder but is, instead, centered in your heart. It recognizes the difference between good and evil and pushes you toward good. The Catechism says that if you listen to your conscience, you "can hear God speaking." (1777)

If you have a well-formed conscience, it means that you not only will recognize evil but will take responsibility when you commit evil, and will allow that judgment to remain with you and influence future decisions for the good. (1781) Let's back up a minute. What's a well-formed conscience, and where can you get one? The Catechism says a well-formed conscience is "upright and truthful" and that it "formulates judgments according to reason." (1783)

Now, obviously we don't start out in this world with a well-formed conscience. Something or someone has to help shape it, a process that continues over the course of a lifetime. From the time we're very young until early adulthood, our parents—as well as teachers, extended family, and friends—help us form a truthful conscience, but that is not enough. We must also assimilate the word of God into our lives, something that happens through the gifts of the Holy Spirit, the teachings of the Church, and the assistance of other Catholics, who serve as witnesses. (1785)

Of course, even people with the best-formed consciences can make mistakes. It doesn't mean they purposely went against their conscience to do something bad. It may mean they were simply ignorant about something, so their conscience didn't know enough to be outraged. In those instances, they are usually free from guilt. (1790)

But don't think if you just don't bother to explore a subject you can go your merry way and avoid responsibility. The Catechism explains if you purposely avoid finding out the truth about something or if you are "blinded" by the habit of sin, you are still responsible for the evil you commit. What might blind you to the truth? The bad examples of others, being a slave to your passions, staying purposefully and blissfully ignorant of the truth, or rejecting Church teaching, to name a few. (1792–1793)

Teachable Moment

Although it's usually pretty easy to determine right from wrong, there can be times when it's hard to see the forest for the trees.

The Church offers a few easy rules to remember whenever you're faced with a tough decision: Follow the "Golden Rule" and treat others the way you want to be treated; avoid doing anything that would make someone else sin; remember that good results cannot justify evil actions. (1789)

Virtue over Vice

You hear a lot about how important it is to be virtuous, but what does that mean? That we have to be living saints? And what exactly is a virtue anyway? It's actually very simple. A virtue is "a habitual and firm disposition to do the good," the Catechism says. If you are a virtuous person, you will not only perform good acts but you will give the very best of yourself. (1803)

The Church teaches there are two kinds of virtues: human virtues and theological virtues. We *get* "human virtues" through education and perseverance. (Remember the old saying: If at first you don't succeed, try, try again.) What we do on our own doesn't get us very far or keep us on balance very long, however. Because we are all wounded by sin, we also need divine grace to enlighten us, to elevate us, to keep us on the right path. (1811) We also need divine grace to keep us rooted in God's life. So we are endowed with "theological virtues," in which our human virtues must be rooted. (1812) Let's look at each type of virtue in a little more detail.

Cardinal Virtues

Of the human virtues, there are four "cardinal virtues" that play a pivotal role in the moral life: prudence, justice, fortitude, and temperance. All the other human virtues hinge on these.

◆ **Prudence** is all about using practical reason to figure out what is really good in every circumstance, and to choose the right means to get to that good. It guides all other virtues "by setting rule and measure." If you are a prudent person, it doesn't mean you're afraid to act, but that you have thought about the action and have judged it to be a good to be pursued or an evil to be avoided. (1806)

◆ **Justice** is the virtue that puts the rights and claims of others into the limelight. With justice as your guide, you respect others and promote and seek "equity" for individuals and for the common good. (1807)

◆ **Fortitude** gives you the strength to say no to something bad when you really want to say yes. It is the virtue that helps you resist temptation and overcome obstacles. (1808)

◆ **Temperance** is not the virtue that prevents you from having a margarita at your favorite Mexican restaurant. It is, however, the virtue that should prevent you from having five or six margaritas. Temperance is just a less-hip way of saying "balance." This virtue is about moderation and gives us "mastery" over our instincts. (1809)

Theological Virtues

All of the human virtues are rooted in the theological virtues, which are directly related to God and are the "foundation of Christian moral activity." They enable humans to "live in a relationship with the Holy Trinity." There are three theological virtues: faith, hope, and charity. (1812–1813)

◆ **Faith** is the virtue that enables us to believe in God, in what he has revealed, and in what the Church has proposed as revealed, for our belief. The Church says that faith is dead unless it is put into action. (James 2:26) A Catholic is called not only to profess the faith but also to live the faith and spread the faith. (1814–1816)

◆ **Hope** is what makes us search for happiness in God and in the kingdom of heaven and eternal life, as we place our trust in Christ's promises and not our own capacities. We get our strength and hope through the graces we receive from the Holy Spirit, who opens our hearts and keeps us from discouragement. (1817–1818)

◆ **Charity** is the virtue that inspires us to love God more than anything else in this world and to "love our neighbors as ourselves" for the love of God. Charity is the DNA of the moral life. The Catechism says that charity is "superior" to the other virtues and calls it the "source and the goal" of Christian practice. (1822–1827)

True Confessions

The Catholic Church teaches that to be fully united to Jesus Christ a Christian must live his or her faith in love, as this is disclosed through good works. How faith and love are related is a matter of some dispute among Christians. Catholics say love is the "form" of faith; Lutherans and other Reformation Christians say love is the "flower" of faith. The Catholic Church's belief in Jesus' call to put faith into action has led it to establish and operate some of the largest charitable organizations in the world. On both a worldwide and local level, the Church and various religious communities provide education, health care, orphanages, immigration services, care for the poor, and an endless string of other programs that touch on everything from prison ministry and soup kitchens to AIDS ministry and hospices.

Gifts and Fruits

On top of all of these virtues, Christians are guided in their moral lives by the gifts and fruits of the Holy Spirit. There are seven *gifts*: wisdom, understanding, counsel, fortitude, knowledge, piety, and fear of the Lord. The Catechism says that these gifts "complete and perfect" the virtues. (1831)

The Church teaches there are 12 *fruits* of the Holy Spirit: charity, joy, peace, patience, kindness, goodness, generosity, gentleness, faithfulness, modesty, self-control, and chastity. These fruits are "perfections" the Spirit forms in Christians in preparation for life in the kingdom. (1832)

Sin: The Sequel

We've already talked in some detail about *sin* in Chapter 13. Remember, there is mortal sin, which is the really bad stuff, and venial sin, which is the everyday stuff. Think murdering your neighbor versus arguing with your spouse. We'll talk about each in just a few minutes.

Right now we need to talk about God's mercy, which, after all, is the only way we get right with God. The Catholic Church teaches that

God created us all on his own; we didn't do anything to warrant our own creation. However, we can't be saved if we don't get involved and take responsibility for the bad stuff we've done. (1847)

Church Speak

Sin is an "offense against God." When we sin, we let our passions and attachments pull us away from God. Like the original sin of Adam, our sins are an attempt to become God on our own terms, setting ourselves up as the be-all and end-all of life. In this, we find we are in opposition to the way of life of Jesus, who shows us that salvation comes not from pride but from humility, not from inordinate self-love but from loving God and others, not from autonomy but from obedience. (1850)

Okay, so let's get back to all the different kinds of sins we can commit. There are spiritual sins, sins against God, and there are sins against our neighbors and ourselves. We can sin in our thoughts, in our deeds, and in our omissions. (1853)

The Catechism explains that sins are judged by their "gravity," and that the "distinction between mortal and venial sin" is found in Scripture, is corroborated in experience, and has been passed on through the Tradition of the Church. (1854)

To commit a mortal sin, three conditions must be present: it must be a "grave matter" you had "full knowledge" of in advance and committed with "complete consent." A grave matter would be some of the really big stuff specified by the Ten Commandments. (1857–1858)

A mortal sin destroys our charity, and separates us from God. If it is not redeemed by our repentance and God's forgiveness, it will land us in hell for all eternity. (1861)

Now, a venial sin is less serious than a mortal sin. It may weaken charity or slow down our progress toward the kingdom, but it won't keep us out in the long run. If we continue to commit venial sins without repenting, however, we can get used to the behavior of minor sinning, and that paves the way for the big stuff. So even though venial sins don't prevent you from receiving Communion or getting into heaven on their own, they can lead you down the garden path to hell if you don't nip them in the bud. (1863)

The Catechism says that through repetition, sin "reinforces itself." This is where vices come in. Vices are defined by the virtues they oppose and they come in many shapes and flavors. There are seven sins called *capital* sins (also popularly known as the "Seven Deadly Sins"), and they are labeled as such because they stand at the top of the list, engendering other sins and vices. They are pride, avarice (greed), envy, wrath (anger), lust, gluttony, and sloth (laziness). (1866)

Before you start checking off which vices and sins you have to worry about, here's one more to consider: you are not only responsible for your own sins but for the sins of other people if you cooperate in them. In other words, you take on the burden of another person's sin if you participate in it directly, order or approve it, praise it, do nothing to prevent it from happening, or protect the sinner after the fact. (1868)

The Least You Need to Know

◆ God gives each of us free will, which makes us responsible for our own actions, good or bad.

◆ If we sincerely listen to our conscience, which is centered in our heart, we can hear God speaking.

◆ Virtues, which can be human or theological, are habits that lead us to do good things.

◆ Sin comes in two basic forms: mortal, which is grave, and venial, which is less serious.

◆ Sin leads to more sin and to vices, which are the opposite of the virtues they offend.

Chapter 16

Our Place in the World

In This Chapter

- ◆ Our duty as human beings
- ◆ How to work for the common good
- ◆ Understanding social justice and solidarity
- ◆ The meaning of law
- ◆ Exploring grace and the call to holiness

We've talked a lot about the fact that faith is not meant to be something left in church on Sundays or kept in a little compartment of life to be taken out only on special occasions. Faith is to be lived every day, which brings us to this chapter.

In the coming pages, we are going to look at our "vocation" as human beings—in other words, what we are called to do in the world. We're not talking about our careers, although that could come into play; instead we are talking about our duty as Christians to bring justice, love, charity, and equality to all people because of their inherent God-given dignity.

Here we are going to cover the common good and social justice, natural and moral law, grace and merit. This is the final preparation we need before working our way through the Ten Commandments.

The Human Vocation

The Catholic Church teaches that human beings need to live out in the world. Society is not a take-it-or-leave-it proposition; instead, it is a requirement. Society is where we live our faith by serving others, sharing with others, and loving others—meaning our "neighbors." This is where we become the Christians we are called to be.

We find "society" within our families and our local communities, but also in a larger sense through associations and institutions that involve us in economics, culture, sports, professional endeavors, and politics. Quoting *Gadium et Spes* (Pastoral Constitution of the Church in the Modern World), the Catechism explains that our involvement in social organizations "expresses a natural tendency for human beings to associate with one another for the sake of obtaining objectives that exceed individual capacities." In other words, we need each other in order to grow and to fulfill our potential as human beings. (1882)

Church Speak

The principle of **subsidiarity** in Church terms refers to the idea that larger associations and organizations should not usurp the authority of lower-level communities and organizations but should instead support it. That means, for example, that international or national organizations should not interfere with local organizations on issues that can and should be handled on a local level.

The Church teaches that God does not keep all the power to himself and that he gives every one of his creatures the capability to perform certain tasks according to its "nature." Remember here the concept of vocation, and that God gives everyone special capabilities for that purpose. The Catechism also teaches that as God governs his creatures, humans should govern one another, and society should not intervene in the lives of individuals in a way that would threaten "personal freedom and initiative." (1883–1884)

Once again, we have to go back to freedom and free will and understand that when the Church speaks of personal freedom as a right, it is not talking about freedom from laws or morals but the freedom of human beings to set the course for their own lives in a righteous way.

The Catechism explains that it is through "inner conversion," or spiritual conversion, that humans are able to bring about positive social change. This conversion of the human heart requires a person to work to change societal situations that cripple justice or induce others to sin. We foster positive change through charity, which challenges people to love one another and to care for one another, even at risk to their own comfort and safety. (1888–1889)

We've been talking so much about personal freedom and social justice that it could sound like an advertisement for anarchy or, at the very least, libertarianism. But Church teaching is anything but anti-authority. The Church supports the role of "legitimate authority"—that is, an authority that protects and promotes the good of all of the people. (1897)

With regard to political authority, the Catechism, quoting Vatican Council II, states that political regimes and rulers must be freely chosen by their citizens, and they must serve the "legitimate good" of their communities in order to be "morally acceptable." This means no despots. In addition, political authorities must govern by the "rule of law" and not by the whims of a small minority. Any laws that are unjust or are "contrary to moral order" are not "binding in conscience." For example, German citizens who refused to obey government-ordered persecution and round-up of Jews would fit into this category. It means that we do not have to uphold a law that goes against the moral law that is meant to govern all humanity. (1901–1904)

Working for the Common Good

You may be wondering what all of this talk of society, community, and authority has to do with faith. Well, the Church teaches that the good of every person is caught up in the *common good*. But what exactly *is* the common good? The Catechism quotes *Gadium et Spes* again when it explains that common good refers to the "sum total of social conditions" that enable individuals and groups to reach their "fulfillment" more fully and easily. (1906)

Church Speak

Universal **Common Good** refers to what the Catechism calls "human interdependence" or the "unity of the human family." The Church, as explained in *Gadium et Spes*, calls on all nations to work together to provide for the various needs of people around the world by providing food, shelter, and education or by alleviating the suffering of refugees and migrants. (1911)

The common good includes three "essential" elements (1907–1909):

1. Respect for every person and his or her fundamental rights

2. The development of the "social well-being" of the group, meaning the flourishing of members or at least access to the basics of human life

3. Peace and security for society and its members

All of that sounds like a very nice sentiment, but how do we translate that into activity in real life? The Church teaches that every person should voluntarily participate in promoting the common good, depending on position and vocation. We do this first and foremost by taking "personal responsibility," which includes caring for our family and dedicating ourselves to our work. Then we move our involvement outward so that we participate in "public life" as fully as possible. (1913–1915)

Social Justice and Solidarity

Social justice, according to the Church, comes about when society provides conditions that enable individuals or associations to obtain what is their due. In other words, society's structure and policies should make it possible for all people and groups to support themselves in a basic fashion, at the very minimum, and to be viable and productive members of that society. In addition, social justice must be linked to the common good and the "exercise of authority," or a society's governing body. (1928)

To work for social justice requires us to respect the dignity of others, look at everyone as our "neighbor," serve those who are disadvantaged, and love our enemies even if we hate the evil they do. (1930–1933)

The Church teaches that every human being, created in the image of God, is equal in dignity. Of course, it doesn't take much to look around and see that while we may all be equal in dignity, we are not all equal in wealth or ability. According to the Catechism, these differences "belong to God's plan." God is counting on us to take care of those who are young, infirm, poor, or disabled, and such disparities are meant to foster charity. (1936–1937) There are also sinful inequalities in our world, which afflict millions of people and are in open contradiction to the teachings of the Gospel. Christians must not be afraid to address these affronts to God's love. (1938)

In addition to social justice, the Church puts heavy emphasis on something called "human solidarity," which Pope John Paul II referred to as "friendship" and "social charity" in his encyclical *Sollicitudo Rei Socialis* (On Social Concern). It is considered a "direct demand" of being human and being Christian. (1939)

Teachable Moment

How is solidarity different from social justice? Solidarity is a Christian virtue that focuses on sharing not only material goods but the spiritual riches of the faith as well.

Solidarity is not only about working to change unjust situations, it's also about a kind of brotherhood between the rich and the poor, the poor and the poor, nations and people. (1941) This kind of solidarity grows out of our common bond as members of one human family. The Church teaches that when we identify with those who are oppressed, in need, or suffering injustice, we are better able to understand their situations and create changes to improve their lives in particular and the world as a whole.

Moral Law

Now we're going to discuss law, starting with moral law. But first, when you think of the concept of law, what comes to mind is probably the do's and don'ts we abide by to keep us out of court and jail, or what is known as "civil law." The actual laws enforced by police officers and courts are indeed one form of the law explained in the Catechism, yet it's important to understand that all law is a product of moral law. Understanding moral law and all its forms inches us closer to the

Ten Commandments, so this discussion will pave the way for a better understanding of what's ahead.

Moral law is defined by the Church as being the "work of divine Wisdom," meaning it is God's teaching. If we follow moral law, we move closer to our eternal beatitude and away from the evil that separates us from our creator. (1950) This kind of law is like a moral compass, the thing that guides you and keeps you from doing bad things and encourages you to do good things. Sometimes you may do something simply because it is the right thing to do, not because you want a reward or want to avoid punishment. Moral law is about doing what's right in God's sight, regardless of what you might gain or lose in the end because of your decision.

Church Speak

Pedagogy is a fancy word for teaching or education.

All other law finds its beginning and end in moral law, and moral law is expressed in a number of interrelated ways: eternal law, natural law, revealed law, civil law, and ecclesiastical (Church) law. (1952)

Natural Law

Natural law is the moral sense to know the difference between good and evil. It is in the heart of every person and is "established by reason." When people follow natural law, they recognize and respect the dignity and rights of other people. (1954–1956) We don't have to do anything to get natural law; it is a universal law that exists for all people across all time. The Catechism explains that natural law is "immutable," which means it is unchangeable, and it is permanent. Even if people reject natural law, meaning they go against what is good, it is not extinguished or destroyed in the heart of humankind as a whole. "It always rises again in the life of individuals and societies," the Catechism says. (1958)

Natural law serves as the foundation for written moral law and as the basis for civil law—the day-to-day laws we live by in society. Civil laws are the things that keep us in line. They work by spelling out the consequences and punishments we will incur if we behave in certain ways. Going 100 miles on the highway might get you a hefty speeding ticket if you're caught. Killing the guy next door, might get you 20 years to life in prison. Civil law doesn't count on us doing things for moral reasons only. It counts on us doing things because we don't want to end up in jail.

Unfortunately, because humans are sinful creatures, we don't always appreciate or recognize natural law right away. (1958) The bottom line is that natural law applies to every person across the board and is something we are able to grasp simply because of our common human nature. Natural law grows out of "eternal law," which has God as its source. Eternal law is essentially the rational order of the universe as God created it, and part of that rational order is our ability to understand and obey natural law. (1952)

Old Law

Next we come to what is called Old Law, and it is the Law of Moses, at whose core is the Ten Commandments or the *Decalogue*. The Old Law is the first stage of what the Church teaches is "revealed law." Revealed law tells human beings what is "contrary to the love of God and neighbor." The Catechism calls the Ten Commandments a "light offered to the conscience of every man." St. Augustine is quoted as saying that God "wrote on the tables of the Law what men did not read in their hearts." (1962)

So the Old Law expands natural law while remaining true to it. It gives humankind a list of do's and don'ts, including a few big ones— killing, stealing, adultery—that are natural laws clearly spelled out in case anyone wasn't paying close enough attention to what their hearts were telling them.

The Catechism explains that Christian tradition holds the Ten Commandments as "holy, spiritual, and good" but imperfect because they do not give people the strength and grace to fulfill what is expected of them. That is found only in the New Law.

Church Speak

Decalogue literally means "ten words," and it is another name for the Ten Commandments given by God to Moses on Mount Sinai. In the Catholic Church the Decalogue makes up the essence of the *Old Law,* which is fulfilled in the *New Law* of Jesus Christ, who taught us to love one another as he loves us and to love our neighbors as ourselves.

New Law

The New Law is the law of the Gospel, which is grounded in the teachings of Jesus Christ, specifically as he expressed them during the Sermon on the Mount (see the Beatitudes in Appendix C on prayer). New Law is the "perfection here on earth of divine law, natural and revealed." (1965)

The Catechism explains that the New Law does not abolish the truth of the precepts of the Old Law but instead "releases their hidden potential." (1968) The New Law is summed up in Jesus' "new commandment":

Love one another. As I have loved you, so you also should love one another. This is how all will know that you are my disciples, if you have love for one another. (John 13:34–35)

Church Speak

Ecclesiastical law is the law that governs a church. In the Catholic Church, ecclesiastical laws and regulations are compiled in a book called the *Code of Canon Law.* The Church's most recent version was issued in 1983.

The New Law is also known as a "law of love" because, through graces received from the Holy Spirit, we are called to act out of love rather than out of fear. It is called the "law of grace" because through it we receive the grace we need to act on it, and it is called a "law of freedom" because it frees us from the "ritual" of the Old Law and prompts us to act spontaneously out of charity for one another. (1972)

Learning to Be Grace-Full

The Church teaches that on the road to salvation there is something called *justification*, which is the "most excellent work of God's love." Through justification, God forgives all our sins and makes us whole and holy. (1994–1995)

Our justification, the Catechism explains, comes from the grace of God; grace is defined as the "free and undeserved help that God gives us." The grace that we receive at baptism is called *sanctifying* or *deifying grace*. The grace that enables us to act in ways that are in keeping with God's call is called *habitual grace* because it is a "permanent disposition." (1996–2000)

There are other kinds of graces as well. Remember, grace is a gift from God that enables us to associate with his work and collaborate in the salvation of others. *Sacramental graces* are gifts of the Holy Spirit received during reception of specific sacraments. *Special graces*, or "charisms," are graces people receive that help build up the Church. We build up the Church on earth whenever we do anything to spread the Good News, put the Gospel into practice, or promote the Catholic faith. Among the special graces are *graces of state*, which are the graces we receive depending on individual responsibilities and our ministries within the Church. (2003–2004)

Because grace is a supernatural gift, it's not something we can recognize within ourselves or fully understand, and so we can't gauge when we have been justified or saved. The Catechism explains that we can see grace at work when we reflect on God's blessings and on the lives of the saints. When we can comprehend that—as God's grace has worked in others—so it is at work in us. (2005)

All Christians are called to holiness. Even though some may receive special graces or signs, we are all called to progress toward an "ever more intimate union" with Jesus Christ. (2014) The Catechism explains that there can be no holiness without "renunciation and spiritual battle." This means we have to fight the good fight until we are living the Beatitudes in peace and joy. (2015)

Church as Mother, Teacher

Christians fulfill their baptismal call within the community of the Catholic Church. This is where Catholics hear the word of God, receive the grace of the sacraments, and witness examples of holiness in Mary and the saints. (2030) In other words, the Church provides spiritual nourishment to its community and *through* its community.

The Catechism says "The moral life is spiritual worship." For Catholics, the celebration of the Eucharist nourishes the moral life through its prayers and teachings. The Eucharist, as the "source and summit" of all Christian life, is the source of moral life as well. (2031)

The Church's magisterium (teaching authority) provides believers with the guidance they need on moral matters based on Scripture, Tradition, and, grounded in the creed, the Our Father and the Ten Commandments. (2033)

Teachable Moment

The Church teaches there are five *precepts* or Church laws that outline the indispensable minimum, in the spirit of prayer and moral effort, which we need in order to grow in love of God and neighbor. They are to attend Mass on Sundays and holy days of obligation, confess your serious sins at least once a year, receive the Eucharist at the very least during the Easter season, observe Church days of fasting and abstinence, and financially support the Church according to your means. (2041–2043)

The Least You Need to Know

◆ Christians reach their full potential by living out in the world and working for the common good.

◆ The common good includes essential elements due to all people: respect, dignity, prosperity, security, and peace.

◆ The Church teaches that all human beings, made in the image of God, are equal in dignity.

◆ Moral law is God's teaching and the basis of all other law.

- ◆ Old Law refers to the Law of Moses, epitomized in the Ten Commandments; New Law is the law based on the teachings of Jesus, specifically in the Sermon on the Mount.

- ◆ The Church is where Christians fulfill their baptismal call, receive grace through the sacraments, gather strength through the Eucharist, and witness the examples of Mary and the saints.

Chapter 17

The First Three Commandments

In This Chapter

- ◆ Exploring behaviors that uphold or break the first commandment
- ◆ Naming promises, blasphemy, and oaths in the second commandment
- ◆ Learning how to keep holy the Lord's Day
- ◆ Our relationship with and duty to God as expressed in the first three commandments

The Ten Commandments can be broken down into two sets: the first three commandments, which focus on God's place in our lives and the reverence due him, and the other seven commandments, which focus on our relationships with other people and the respect due them.

In this chapter, we will explore the first three commandments, the ones that focus specifically on God. Even if you don't know the exact wording and placement of these commandments in the

Decalogue, which we'll get to in a minute, you probably know what's at the heart of them: God, who is supposed to be first and foremost in our lives.

Jesus took these first three commandments and transformed them with his law of love, that is, the New Law we read about in the previous chapter. Quoting from Deuteronomy, he preached the rule of love as it is found in the Old Law (remember, that's the Law of Moses, also known as Mosaic law, whose core is the Ten Commandments): "You shall love the Lord your God with all your heart, and with all your soul, and with all your mind." (Matthew 22:37) At the Last Supper, Jesus proclaimed a new law: "Love one another as I have loved you." (John 15:12)

Jesus puts a new face on God for all believers. He is no longer a distant authority figure to be feared but is instead a beloved Father who deserves all of our devotion.

With these first three commandments and all the rest to follow, Jesus transforms the Old Law into a living law where love of God and neighbor is always the overarching principle.

#1: God First—No Matter What

I, the Lord, am your God, who brought you out of the land of Egypt, that place of slavery. You shall not have other gods besides me. You shall not carve idols for yourselves in the shape of anything in the sky above or on the earth below or in the waters beneath the earth; you shall not bow down before them or worship them. (Exodus 20:2–5)

This is the first commandment, which may sound complex but simply reminds us in true Old Testament style that we are to have one God and one God only. In the New Testament we hear Jesus, when he is tempted in the desert by Satan, repeat this commandment in an abridged and simpler version: "The Lord, your God, shall you worship and him alone shall you serve." (Matthew 4:10)

So this commandment seems pretty easy to follow, doesn't it? As long as we don't worship any other gods, we're safe. But wait a minute. What qualifies as a god in God's book? There are some more blatant examples such as the golden calf of Old Testament fame, the one the

Hebrews built when they thought Moses was never going to come down off Mount Sinai. But don't be surprised to learn there are sneaky versions of other gods hidden right under our noses in our everyday lives.

When this commandment refers to avoiding "other gods," it is referring to anything that becomes an idol to us; this includes money, power, beauty, work, or fame. The list is endless, really.

Teachable Moment

When a young man asked Jesus what he needed to do to have eternal life, Jesus told him to "keep the commandments." (Matthew 19:17) When the man says he is already obeying the commandments, Jesus issued the ultimate challenge: "If you wish to be perfect, go, sell what you have, and give to the poor, and you will have treasure in heaven. Then come, follow me." (Matthew 19:21) The Catechism explains that the evangelical counsels—poverty, chastity, and obedience—are "inseparable" from the Ten Commandments. (2053)

So if we are to have no other gods other than God, then we must understand what it means to *have* God, meaning we must understand how to live our lives in such a way that indeed puts him first. So let's explore what the Catechism says about that.

Faith, Hope, and Charity

The Catechism explains, "God's first call and just demand is that man accept him and worship him." (2084) This involves living out the theological virtues of faith, hope, and charity, which we discussed in Chapter 15.

We are called to make these virtues an active part of our lives in an effort to give due reverence to God—putting him first—and to avoid sins that weaken these virtues in us. Let's break each one of these down, to more fully understand their unique characteristics.

Faith is considered the "source" of moral life. Sins against faith include voluntary doubt about or outright rejection of the faith; disbelief; heresy; apostasy, which is the "total repudiation of the Christian faith"; and schism, which involves a break with the Roman Catholic Church.

(2087–2089) *Hope* is the expectation that we will receive divine blessings and will one day see God in the kingdom. Sins against hope include despair and something called "presumption," which is when we think we don't need God to save us or when we presume we will get into heaven through God's mercy even if we are unrepentant and undeserving. (2090–2092)

Charity beckons us to love God above everything else and to love all of his creation in him and because of him. Sins against charity include indifference toward God's charity; ingratitude; "acedia," which is spiritual laziness; "lukewarmness," which is "hesitation or negligence" with regard to God's love; and, finally, hatred of God, which is grounded in pride. (2093–2094)

In other words, lack of faith, hope, and charity in their various forms does not put God first, but instead puts opposing forces at the forefront. Therefore, living by these virtues is honoring the first commandment.

Virtue of Religion

Next we come to the concept of the "virtue of religion," which is an "attitude" that puts us in the frame of mind to revere God in ways befitting the Father, Son, and Spirit. (2095) By practicing the theological virtues of faith, hope, and charity, we are more likely to practice the virtue of religion. Let's look at some ways that the virtue of religion can be put into practice:

Adoration is "the first act of the virtue of religion," the Catechism says. This involves, first of all, acknowledging God as creator and Savior, as the infinite Lord of all, and as infinite and merciful love. By worshipping God alone, humanity steers clear of the "slavery of sin and the idolatry of the world." (2096–2097)

Prayer, the Catechism explains, is an "indispensable condition" for obeying the commandments. It helps us live out the virtues of faith, hope, and charity, and it enables us to praise God and seek his help. (2098)

Sacrifice is an outward sign of our inner gratitude. We are not talking about Old Testament–style sacrifices involving lambs or other animals.

We are talking about personal sacrifices, spiritual sacrifices that unite us to Christ's sacrifice on the cross. (2100)

Promises and vows are an integral part of a life of faith. We find them in many of the sacraments—baptism, marriage, confirmation, holy orders—and we make them in our personal prayers when we offer a particular action or sacrifice to God. (2101)

The Catechism, quoting the Vatican II document on religious freedom as well as the Code of Canon Law, says all people are "bound" to seek out the truth about God and the Church and to "embrace it." Christians have a "social duty" to awaken in others the "love of the true and the good" and to tell others about the Catholic and apostolic faith.

Church Speak

A **vow** is a "deliberate and free promise made to God." When we profess a vow, we promise something before God or dedicate ourselves to God in a special way. (2102)

However, no one should be forced to act against their conscience, and no one should be prevented from adhering to their faith in public or private. (2104–2106)

Superstition and Magic

When the first commandment talks about honoring God above all else, it also forbids anything that attributes events or powers to something other than God. This includes things like superstition, idolatry, divination, or magic, where hope for a particular outcome or event relies not on God but on some other source of power.

When you rely on *superstition*, for example, then rather than putting your trust in God, you put your trust in an omen, a sign, a good luck charm, or a particular activity you always do at a certain time in order to influence—at least in your own mind—a certain outcome. The Catechism makes an important point here: when we think that the mere external performance of prayers or sacramental signs are effective, apart from the interior dispositions that they demand, we fall into superstition. (2111)

Idolatry, while it may sound like an old term, has a stronghold in our modern-day society. The first commandment forbids polytheism, which is the belief that there are other divine beings in addition to the Triune God. You are guilty of idolatry not only when you put another being in God's place but also when you put another thing—again we go back to money, power, fame—ahead of God. The Catechism says that idolatry is "a perversion of man's innate religious sense." (2114)

Divination is when you look to something or someone outside of God to give you information about the future and to bestow on you some sort of power over time. This certainly involves practices such as recourse to Satan, but it may sometimes even include things as seemingly benign as horoscopes and Tarot cards or clairvoyants and mediums. The Catechism calls divination a contradiction of the "honor, respect, and loving fear that we owe to God alone." (2116)

Magic or *sorcery* is an effort to "tame occult powers" in order to use them to have power over other people or things. Even using magic for good purposes is not allowed because it is "contrary to the virtue of religion." (2117)

Rejecting God

The first commandment also forbids *irreligion*. This category of sin includes *tempting God*, which is when you put God to some sort of test; *sacrilege*, which is when you profane some aspect of faith, in particular the Eucharist; and *simony*, which is the buying and selling of spiritual goods, such as a bishop taking money for making a priest a pastor, or a lay person trying to "buy" a baptism, wedding, or other sacrament by paying off a priest to administer a sacrament that should not be administered. (2118–2121)

Also on the forbidden list, for obvious reasons, is *atheism*, which is a complete rejection or denial of the existence of God (2125), and *agnosticism*, which does not deny God's existence but says it is impossible to prove. While agnosticism can include a search for God, it is more often "equivalent to practical atheism," the Catechism says. (2128)

Teachable Moment

The first commandment forbids the worship of "graven images." In the Old Testament this referred to any man-made representation of God. However, the Catholic Church teaches that Jesus, the Incarnate Word, ushered in a new "economy of images," meaning that not only Christ but Mary and the saints could be portrayed and venerated as well. These images do not constitute "graven images" because they are not worshipped as you would worship God; instead they are given honor and devotion because of the way they witness God's love to us. (2129–2132)

#2: Taking the Lord's Name in Vain

You shall not take the name of the Lord, your God, in vain. For the Lord will not leave unpunished him who takes his name in vain. (Exodus 20:7)

The second commandment is pretty clear-cut. We are meant to respect and honor God's name, and all variations of God's name, including the name of Jesus Christ. We're also supposed to respect the names of Mary and the saints to boot. (2146)

The Catechism explains that we are not supposed to use God's name in our own speech unless it is expressly to "bless, praise, and glorify" God. By respecting his name, we respect the "mystery of God himself" and evoke the "sense of the sacred." (2143–2144)

Keeping the second commandment also means keeping any *promises* we have made in God's name. Breaking such a promise is a "misuse of God's name" and, according to the Catechism, makes God out to be a "liar." (2147)

Blasphemy is when we speak or act in a way that is directly opposed to God or anything sacred. Blasphemy includes hatred, disdain, or defiance expressed toward God, the Church, and the saints. Blasphemy also includes killing, torturing, or committing a crime in God's name. (2148)

It is also a grave sin against the second commandment to profess a false *oath* in God's name or to commit perjury, which is when you make a promise to tell the truth with no intention of keeping it. This calls on God to be witness to a lie. (2150–2152)

True Confessions

The Church teaches that Jesus' teaching on taking oaths does not exclude oaths made "for grave and right reasons (for example, in court)." Discretion should be exercised, however, in calling on God's name as witness to the truth of what we say. (2154)

Jesus further explained and expanded the second commandment:

Again you have heard that it was said to your ancestors, "Do not take a false oath, but make good to the Lord all that you vow." But I say to you, do not swear at all; not by heaven, for it is God's throne; nor by earth, for it is his footstool; nor by Jerusalem, for it is the city of the great King. Do not swear by your head, for you cannot make a single hair white or black. Let your "Yes" mean "Yes," and let your "No" mean "No." Anything more is from the evil one. (Matthew 5:33–37)

#3: Keeping Holy the Sabbath

Remember to keep holy the Sabbath day. Six days you may labor and do all your work, but the seventh day is the Sabbath of the Lord, your God. No work may be done then either by you, or your son or daughter, or your male or female slave, or your beast, or by the alien who lives with you. In six days the Lord made the heavens and the earth, the sea and all that is in them, but on the seventh day he rested. That is why the Lord has blessed the Sabbath day and made it holy. (Exodus 20:8–11)

Teachable Moment

For Christians, the Sabbath, or Lord's Day, is celebrated on Sunday because it is the day of Christ's Resurrection. It is the "first day," recalling God's first creation, and the "eighth day," symbolizing the "new creation" that begins with Christ's Resurrection. (2174)

The third commandment focuses on the holiness of the Sabbath, recalling how God rested on the seventh day after the creation of the universe and made it holy. The Catechism explains that Scripture also "reveals in the Lord's day a memorial of Israel's liberation from bondage in Egypt." God told the Israelites to keep the Sabbath day holy. For the Sabbath is a day of protest against the servitude of work and the worship of money. (2168–2171)

Now, Jesus takes the original premise of the Old Law and adds deeper meaning to it. "The Sabbath was made for man, not man for the Sabbath. The Son of Man is lord even of the Sabbath." (Mark 2:27–28) Jesus, in compassion, declares that the Sabbath is the day of the Lord of mercies, a day for doing good rather than harm. (2173) The meaning here is that the day created by God for rest from your work does not mean you can take a rest from your faith, and further, that it's a day in which you should do good.

Sunday Obligations

Keeping the Lord's Day holy translates into some pretty concrete things for Catholics. First of all, it means participating in Mass, either on Sunday or at the Saturday *vigil*, and on holy days of obligation. But the Sunday obligation is about more than simply getting your ticket punched. It is about celebrating the Eucharist on Sundays as was passed through apostolic tradition. (2177)

Deliberately missing Mass on a Sunday or holy day is considered a "grave sin" unless you have been excused for a serious reason (for example, you are sick or caring for an infant) or have been given a dispensation. (2181)

Church Speak

Vigil Mass is a Mass celebrated the evening before a feast day or a day of solemnity. If you participate at a vigil Mass on the evening before a day of obligation, you satisfy your obligation to participate at Mass the next day. For example, Catholics may attend a Saturday evening Mass at 5 P.M. to fulfill their Sunday obligation. The same holds true on holy days.

For God's Sake, Rest

Sundays aren't just about attending Mass. The Sabbath is meant to be a day of rest, so that means we are supposed to take a break from the usual grindstone.

You are not only obliged to go to Mass but to relax, which does not mean you have to sit quietly at home. Sundays are meant to be for family activities, and for cultural or social events as well as religious ones. (2184)

"Sunday is a time for reflection, silence, cultivation of the mind, and meditation, which furthers the growth of the Christian interior life," the Catechism says. (2186)

The Church recommends that it is important for Sundays and holy days to be recognized as civil holidays and for Christians to serve as public examples of prayer, respect, and joy. Christians should also "defend their tradition as a precious contribution to the spiritual life of society." Even if you have to work, you should still set the day apart from the rest of the week "and the day should nevertheless be lived as the day of our deliverance …." (2188) In other words, punching the clock on a Sunday should not prevent you from making time for God and time for Mass.

The Least You Need to Know

◆ The first commandment forbids the worship of any gods other than the one Triune God, as well as superstition, magic, divination, and idolatry.

◆ Love of money, power, beauty, or fame are examples of what can usurp God's place in our lives as forbidden by the first commandment.

◆ The second commandment commands respect and honor not only for God's name in all its variations, but also for the names of Jesus Christ, Mary, and the saints.

◆ Breaking a promise made in God's name, making a false oath, or committing perjury are offenses against the second commandment.

◆ The third commandment requires Catholics to keep the Lord's Day holy by participating in Mass on Sundays and holy days, and by setting aside time on Sunday to relax and participate in leisure activities.

Chapter 18

#4: Honor Thy Father and Mother

In This Chapter

◆ Understanding family and authority in the first of the people-focused commandments

◆ How the fourth commandment is lived out in Christian lives

◆ The duties of parents, children, and citizens

◆ Respect due to and from those in authority

As we begin the fourth commandment, we make a shift from God-centered commandments to neighbor-centered commandments. The next seven commandments focus on how we treat the people all around us, from the people we live with to the friends across the street to those around the world.

Jesus said, "You shall love your neighbor as yourself." (Mark 12:31) Our neighbor is not just the person who takes in the mail when we're on vacation. Our neighbor is anyone we meet along life's way, and even those we don't meet but with whom we share our common human dignity.

In this chapter, we will begin at home, where we build our earliest and often our closest relationships. We will look at how parents and children must treat each other and how together, as a domestic church, the family serves the greater good.

It's a Family Affair

Honor your father and your mother, that you may have a long life in the land which the Lord, your God, is giving you. (Exodus 20:12)

The fourth commandment—the first to follow the God-centered commandments and the only one to have a promise attached to it—focuses on parents. After God, we are called to honor our parents, who gave us life and knowledge, and who deserve our respect and honor. Moreover, the Catechism states, we are also obliged to honor and respect all those whom God, for our good, has vested with his authority. The Catechism explains that this commandment is one of "the foundations of social doctrine of the Church." The fourth commandment introduces the other commandments that address respect for life and marriage and material possessions. (2197–2198)

While this commandment appears to be aimed directly at children, it extends to other family members as well as to people in a host of other positions: teachers, employers, and leaders of countries. "It requires honor, affection, and gratitude toward elders and ancestors," the Catechism says. The Catechism makes clear that obligations proposed by the fourth commandment are not a one-way street: the commandment "includes and presupposes the duties of parents, instructors, teachers, leaders, magistrates, those who govern, all who exercise authority over others or over a community of persons." (2199)

To understand this commandment fully, we need to start with the structure and meaning of the family unit itself. Family begins with marriage, and marriage begins with the consent of two spouses. A man and a woman, joined in marriage, together with their children form a family. The Catechism says this structure of family should be "considered the normal reference point by which the different forms of family relationships are to be evaluated." (2202)

The Christian family is meant to be a "sign and image" of the communion that exists within the Holy Trinity. By procreating and educating children, parents mirror the work of the Father. By participating in prayer and Mass, the family shares in the sacrifice of Christ. The family has an "evangelizing and missionary task." (2205)

The Catechism says that relationships within a family bring with it a host of strong feelings, all of which should rise from the mutual respect members of the family have for one another. It calls the family a "privileged community." (2206)

The family is also known as "the original cell of social life." What does that mean? Well, the Catechism indicates the family is the "natural society" and explains that the authority, stability, and relationships found within a family form the foundations for the freedom, security, and common brotherhood within society as a whole. It is within our families that we first learn right from wrong and get the foundation of our morality and faith. "Family life is an initiation into life in society." (2207)

Being part of a family means more than just looking out for the people who sit across from you at the dinner table. It means looking beyond your front door to care for your extended family and also for the human family as a whole, particularly those who need some extra help—old people, sick people, poor people. And it means getting involved in promoting or defending "social measures" that influence society. (2208–2209)

True Confessions

While making no specific statements about civil protections for same-sex unions, the Catechism notes that the Catholic Church is opposed to so-called "same-sex marriages." This is because the Church regards the union of a man and a woman in marriage as the foundation of society that is grounded in natural law and moral law. The Church says, in *Gadium et Spes*, that civil authorities have a "grave duty" to acknowledge the "true nature of marriage and family and to "protect and foster" both. (2210)

Duties of Children and Parents

It's pretty obvious from the basic message of this commandment that children have certain duties toward their parents. First comes honor and respect. Children are to respect their parents, not out of fear but out of gratitude for the gift of life and for all their parents have done to help them grow "in stature, wisdom, and grace." (2215)

This respect is shown through obedience, of course. The Catechism says children living at home with their parents should obey their parents whenever they ask for something that would benefit either the child in particular or the family as a whole. The same holds true for the "reasonable directions" of teachers. However, children do not have to obey anything that is morally wrong. (2217)

Once children have grown up and moved out, they still have duties to their parents. They may not have to obey anymore, but they still have to respect them, and the Church teaches that children should help their parents with "material and moral support" when they are old, ill, or lonely. (2218)

Harmony in the family is not limited to parents and children but must exist between siblings. Respectful sibling interaction shows respect for the parents as well, which fosters the family unity. "Respect toward parents fills the home with light and warmth." (2219)

Also, children aren't the only ones with duties in this family relationship. The Church calls on parents to regard their offspring as "children of God" and to "respect them as human persons." (2222)

The right and responsibility of educating children belongs, first and foremost, to parents. This is done through a loving home environment where "tenderness, forgiveness, respect, fidelity, and disinterested service (meaning you care for and raise your children without worrying about what you might get out of it) are the rule." Home is where children learn the virtues that will ground their character and guide their judgment later on. It is where children will learn that material possessions are not as important as spiritual strength, and it is where children learn to stand up for what is right and to avoid things that degrade others or threaten society. (2223–2224)

Parents not only have the primary right and responsibility to care for the spiritual and physical needs of their children, but they also have the right to choose a school for them that reaffirms the Christian foundation they are providing. Also, parents should offer counsel, support, and advice to their older children when it is time for them to choose a profession, or state in life, or spouse, without exerting undue influence over them. (2229–2230)

The Catechism says while family ties are important, they are "not absolute," meaning that parents must respect and encourage whatever vocation God is calling their child to follow, even if that means she'll never become a lawyer or doctor. (2232)

Teachable Moment _____

Jesus said, "For whoever does the will of my heavenly Father is my brother, and sister, and mother." (Matthew 12:49) This means that all people are called to be members of God's family and to live according to his teaching, loving one another, serving one another, and, in this, doing the will of the Father of Jesus. (2233)

Citizens of the World

The honor outlined in the fourth commandment doesn't stop at immediate and extended family. It also covers respect due to civil authorities and their duties, as well as respect from authority figures for their position and citizens.

Authority Figures

The Catechism says those in authority should see themselves as servants, and it stresses that no authority figure can "command or establish" something that is in opposition to natural law or the inherent dignity of human beings. Those in authority should govern with the needs and interests of the community at heart, not their own personal needs or desires. (2235–2236)

Political authorities, in particular, are "obliged to respect the fundamental rights of the human person," paying careful attention to the rights of families and the "disadvantaged." (2237)

Therefore, the Catechism teaches that the fourth commandment provides a foundation by which public authorities are to be motivated and guided in their service.

For God and Country

So what are the duties of regular citizens? The Church teaches that citizens should "regard those in authority as representatives of God," while at the same time voicing "just criticisms" of anything that threatens human dignity and the good of the community. (2238)

Citizens are called on to collaborate with authority for the "good of society" and to love and serve their country. Sharing in a country's common good means paying taxes, exercising the right to vote, and defending the country. (2239–2240)

In this section, the Catechism also explains that "more prosperous nations" are "obliged" to welcome immigrants who are seeking security and a "means of livelihood" not available in their own countries. These "guests" should be respected and protected, and they, in turn, should respect the country that welcomes them and obey its laws. (2241)

True Confessions _____

The Church teaches that citizens are obliged *not* to follow civil authorities when demands are in opposition to moral order, fundamental individual rights, or the teachings of the Gospel. "Armed resistance" to political oppression, however, is justified only when certain conditions exist: there are "grave and prolonged" violations of human rights; all other efforts to rectify the situation have been exhausted; it will not "provoke worse disorders"; there is real hope for success; and there is no better solution in sight. (2242–2243)

The Least You Need to Know

◆ The fourth commandment requires us to respect and honor our parents (who hold second place after God) for the gift of life and the love and guidance they give us.

- Respect and honor are also owed to siblings and extended family members, as well as civil authorities acting on behalf of the common good.

- Authorities are servants who should respect the fundamental rights of the people they serve.

- Citizens are called to collaborate with authorities for the good of society, to love and serve their country, pay taxes, vote, and defend their country.

- No one is obliged to follow a civil authority that demands something in opposition to moral order.

Chapter 19

#5: You Shall Not Kill

In This Chapter

- ◆ Respect for and defense of all life as defined by this commandment
- ◆ Where abortion, euthanasia, and suicide fit in
- ◆ The bounds of scientific research
- ◆ The rules of war

The fifth commandment against killing is one of those commandments that seem pretty straightforward. But this commandment is not just about acts of homicide and murder; it's about respecting all human life.

The Catechism refers to the Vatican's Congregation for the Doctrine of the Faith to explain that the Church sees all life as "sacred" because all life begins with God's "creative action" and is forever connected to God. No one has the right to destroy an innocent human life. (2258)

In this chapter, we will explore this commandment and what theologians have called "the seamless garment" approach, meaning that all of life is woven into the fabric of this teaching. All human life, from conception until its end, is to be defended, protected, and cherished.

Crime and Punishment

You shall not kill. (Exodus 20:13)

The Lord said, "What have you done! Listen: Your brother's blood cries out to me from the soil! Therefore you shall be banned from the soil that opened its mouth to receive your brother's blood from your hand. If you till the soil, it shall no longer give you its produce. You shall become a restless wanderer on earth." (Genesis 4:10) In other words, Cain would forever live with the consequences of his actions and would no longer live in God's presence.

The Catechism explains that the law against killing is "universally valid," applied to every person for all time. The Old Testament commanded: "The innocent and the just you shall not put to death, nor shall you acquit the guilty." (Exodus 23:7) During the Sermon on the Mount, Jesus expands this commandment, telling his disciples to avoid anger and vengeance, to turn the other cheek, to love their enemies. (2261–2262)

True Confessions

When Pope John Paul II released his encyclical *Evangelium Vitae* (Gospel of Life) in 1995, the language against the death penalty was so strong that the future Pope Benedict XVI, who was head of the Vatican's Congregation for the Doctrine of the Faith at the time, said that the next edition of the Catechism must reflect the stronger teachings against capital punishment. Both the Latin edition published in 1997 and the second-edition English version published in 2000 reflect the stronger language.

The Church teaches that state or civil authorities have the right to "curb the spread of behavior" that has the potential to harm individuals or society as a whole. It also teaches that "legitimate public authority" has the right and duty to render the aggressor unable to inflict harm, as well as to dole out punishments according to the gravity of the crime committed. The primary effect of punishment is to "redress," or remedy, the disorder caused by the offense. In other words, punishment should be "medicinal" in that it must contribute "to the correction of the guilty party." (2266)

The death penalty is not completely out of bounds, according to Church teaching. However, its use in a morally acceptable way is severely limited. The death penalty is to be used when it is the only way to defend people from a particular aggressor. If "nonlethal means" are available and sufficient to protect people's safety, then authorities should avoid use of the death penalty in keeping with "the dignity of the human person." (2267)

Pope John Paul II in his encyclical *Evangelium Vitae* (Gospel of Life) said that in the modern age, instances when the state is unable to protect the public through nonlethal means "are very rare, if not practically nonexistent." (2267)

Teachable Moment

The fifth commandment does not prohibit you from defending yourself or others against an imminent threat. The Church teaches that "it is legitimate to insist on respect for one's own life" and that someone who kills another in self-defense is not guilty of murder even if he "is forced to deal his aggressor a lethal blow." The Catechism says that someone who is responsible for the life of others has not only the right but the "grave duty" to defend those in his protection against an "unjust aggressor." (2264–2265)

The fifth commandment considers any "direct or intentional killing" to be "gravely sinful," and makes special note of the "especially grave" sins of infanticide, killing of siblings or parents, and killing of a spouse. The commandment also forbids any intentional actions that will indirectly lead to the death of a person, up to and including "murderous famines." The Catechism notes that "unintentional killing" is not as imputable as "homicide," but you will not be exonerated from "grave offense" if you act in an irresponsible way that brings about someone else's death, even if the intention to kill was not there. (2268–2269)

Seamless Garment

Now we get to some matters of controversy where society is concerned, but not necessarily where the Church is concerned, surrounding the seamless-garment concept we mentioned earlier. As far as Church teaching goes, respect for life is a consistent and seamless teaching that is absolute, unchangeable, and universal.

Abortion

The Church teaches that human life begins at the moment of conception, and that there are absolutely no exceptions. This means every single conception is a life worth protecting, no matter how it came into being, under what conditions, or who is involved. The Catechism says it like this: "From the first moment of existence, a human being must be recognized as having the rights of a person." (2270)

From the first century, Church teaching has forbidden "direct abortion" (meaning an abortion that is procured to achieve a certain end or as a means to further an end) as gravely opposed to moral law. In addition, willingly cooperating in an abortion is also considered a "grave offense." If you get an abortion, perform an abortion, or willingly assist in abortion, you are in serious violation of moral law. This could be something as seemingly innocent as driving your friend to the abortion clinic and sitting in the waiting room with her, even though you are opposed to abortion and tried to talk her out of it. Canon 1329§2 of canon law calls this kind of person a "necessary cooperator." By assisting with an abortion in any way, you are automatically excommunicated from the Church by the act itself. If, however, you are truly remorseful and confess the sin in the sacrament of reconciliation, the sanction may be lifted. (2271–2272)

The Church teaches that every human being, from the moment of conception, has an "inalienable right to life" and, therefore, deserves the protection and respect of civil society. Referring to the Congregation for the Doctrine of the Faith's document *Donum Vitae* (Respect for Human Life), the Catechism explains that whenever the law deprives any category of human beings protection, the state "is denying the equality of all before the law." Without protection for all, including the unborn, the foundations of law are undermined. (2273)

The Catechism states: "Since it must be treated from conception as a person, the embryo must be defended in its integrity, cared for, and healed, as far as possible, like any other human being." This impacts not only the decision to abort, but also decisions surrounding prenatal diagnoses and efforts to genetically manipulate embryos. The Church teaches that prenatal diagnosis is acceptable if it respects the integrity of the embryo and is "directed toward safeguarding and healing as an individual." In other words, you should not be getting amniocentesis or other tests in order to determine whether you will abort your child due to a birth defect. (2274)

Teachable Moment

While the Church opposes all "direct abortions," there are rare instances when the Church does not condemn a procedure that indirectly results in the death of an unborn baby in order to save a mother's life. For example, a woman suffering from an ectopic pregnancy, which is fatal if not treated, may have her fallopian tube removed even though it will result in the death of her unborn baby through what is known as "secondary effect." In other words, this kind of procedure is acceptable only if the desired outcome is not the death of the baby; the death of the child is instead an unwilled secondary side effect of a necessary procedure.

Euthanasia

The fifth commandment strictly forbids the use of *euthanasia* or medically assisted suicide to unnaturally end the life of someone who is seriously ill, disabled, elderly, or dying.

The Catechism explains that euthanasia is "morally unacceptable" no matter what the motive or means. "Sick or handicapped people should be helped to lead lives as normal as possible," the Catechism says. Even when committed through an "error of judgment," this does not change the nature of this "murderous act," which must always be forbidden and excluded. (2276–2777)

Church Speak

Euthanasia is to end by choice and intent the life of a handicapped, sick, elderly, or dying person either through a direct action or through the omission of an action. It is a violation of the fifth commandment.

This does not mean, however, that a dying person must be kept alive through "over-zealous" treatment. The Church teaches that life is a journey, and death is not something that must be avoided at all costs.

Therefore, it is within moral bounds to refuse or remove treatment that is "burdensome, dangerous, extraordinary, or disproportionate to the expected outcome." Here you are not intending death or causing death by action or omission, but are simply allowing life and death to take their normal course. This does not allow for the removal of "ordinary care," which would include food and hydration, in most cases. (2278–2279)

Palliative care, or the use of painkillers to alleviate suffering, are not only allowed but are encouraged as long as they are not used specifically to end a life. Even if the use of painkillers risks shortening the life of a dying person, their use is allowed as a form of "disinterested charity" that is in line with protecting human dignity. (2279) Disinterested charity refers to a charitable action done without any self-serving purposes involved. In other words, you give palliative care to your terminally ill parent simply because you want your parent to be free from pain and not because you don't want to provide other forms of care or hope the medicine will hasten death.

Suicide

All people are required to "accept life gratefully and preserve it" for God's honor. The Church teaches that we are not the owners of our lives but the "stewards of our lives," meaning that we are simply caretakers for God, who holds the title papers. And like anything you borrow, rent, or take out on a loan, you are required to keep it in good condition and are not allowed to throw it away. (2280)

The Catechism explains that suicide "contradicts this natural inclination … to preserve and perpetuate one's life." Also, suicide is not only contrary to "just love of self" and the love due to God, but also is contrary to love of neighbor because it "breaks the ties of solidarity" with those in our families and the greater community. (2281) In other words, the consequences of suicide do not affect only the person who commits the act but that person's family and friends and larger community as well. Although suicide is an act done in isolation, its ramifications are far from isolated.

The presence of "grave psychological disturbances" lessens the culpability of someone who commits suicide. (2282) This means that if someone with severe mental illness commits suicide, he or she does not bear moral responsibility for the action.

You're Absolved If ...

You may think the Catholic Church refuses Christian burial to a person who commits suicide. But in a letter of May 29, 1973, to the bishops' conferences of the world, the Congregation for the Doctrine of the Faith decreed that persons not married in the Church or persons who have committed suicide are *not* to be denied Christian burial.

Human Dignity

The fifth commandment not only prohibits us from harming others, but it also directs us to preserve and promote our own well-being and the well-being of others. We are expected to take care of our physical health and support those societal measures that protect the health of all citizens. (2288)

Although we are required to respect our bodies, we are forbidden from promoting something the Church calls the *cult of the body*, which is an obsession with physical perfection and athletic success. We are also expected to practice temperance with regard to any kind of excess, whether it is food, alcohol, tobacco, or medicine. "Those incur grave guilt who, by drunkenness or a love of speed, endanger their own and others' safety on the road, at sea, or in the air," the Catechism says. (2289–2290)

The Church takes particular note of drug use and the damage it inflicts on human life. The use of drugs is a "grave offense," except when used therapeutically. Production and trafficking in drugs is considered "scandalous" and constitutes "direct cooperation in evil." (2291)

In the Name of Science

Many people probably think that faith and science are diametrically opposed, and yet the Church considers scientific research a "significant expression of man's dominion over creation" and says that science and technology are "precious resources" when they serve humanity and promote the development of all. Even scientific experimentation on humans can be acceptable when it contributes to the "healing of the sick and the advancement of public health." However, scientific research must always be "at the service of the human person, of his inalienable right." (2292–2294)

Any research or experimentation that is an offense against moral law or human dignity is forbidden, even if the outcome is expected to improve the dignity of another's life or even save it. (2295) The Nuremburg trials, which were the allies' trials of Nazi war criminals after World War II, revealed human experimentation and a host of offenses to human dignity done in the name of "advancing medical knowledge." For Catholics, a modern-day example of this kind of offense would be embryonic stem-cell research. It's goes back to what we discussed in the earlier chapter on moral law: the end can never justify the means.

Teachable Moment

Organ donation is considered "noble and meritorious" by the Church, which encourages it as "an expression of generous solidarity." Moral law is upheld as long as the good that is sought outweighs the risks to the donor. The donor or his or her proxy must give "explicit consent," and nothing may be done to end or hasten a donor's death in order to harvest organs. (2296)

Respecting the Body

Human dignity prohibits certain grave acts, which most people readily recognize as harmful and against moral law. They include kidnapping, hostage taking, terrorism, and torture. In addition, the Church also forbids—except for "strictly therapeutic medical reasons"—direct amputations, mutilations, and sterilizations performed on innocent people. (2297)

Respect for the dying is also of utmost importance. The Church teaches that dying people deserve the kind of attention and care that will give them "dignity and peace" in their final days or moments. This care includes prayers and access to the sacraments one last time. (2299)

The Catechism explains that the dead must be treated with "respect and charity" in anticipation of the resurrection. The Church considers the burial of the dead a "corporal work of mercy." (2300) Autopsies may be permitted for legal investigations or scientific research, and the "free" donation of organs can be "meritorious." Cremation is also allowed as long as this option is not chosen in an effort to deny belief in the resurrection of the body. (2301)

War and Peace

On the subject of war, before we get to the actual fighting part, we need to talk about the kinds of things that lead to war in the first place. The fifth commandment, as taught by Jesus, requires more than simply not killing another human being; it requires us to avoid anger and hatred and to work for peace.

Anger, the Catechism says, is "a desire for revenge" and hatred is "contrary to charity." Both are grave sins when they deteriorate into a desire for grave evil or harm to come to another person. (2303–2303)

Teachable Moment

Bullying is a hot topic these days. Schools offer special classes to prevent bullying and to teach children how to respond when they find themselves at the wrong end of a bully's rage. In the Church's view, bullying is not just something that occurs only on the playground or in the classroom. It can be found in the boardroom, the bedroom, and everywhere in between. Bullying is an equal-opportunity offender and must be avoided by all.

The Church teaches that peace is "not merely the absence of war" and "not limited to maintaining a balance of powers between adversaries." Peace requires safeguarding the goods (not things like belongings, but things like rights) of people, free communication between people, and respect for all people. The Catechism quotes St. Augustine as saying, "Peace is the tranquility of order." It is the work of justice and the effect of charity. (2304)

"All citizens and all governments are obliged to work for the avoidance of war," the Catechism says. (2308) However, "legitimate defense by military force" is justified when *all* of the following conditions are present, and is judged by those who have responsibility for the common good:

- Damage inflicted on a country or community by an aggressor is "lasting, grave, and certain."

- All peaceful efforts to end the aggression have been "impractical" or "ineffective."

- There are "serious prospects" of success.

- The use of arms, particularly arms of mass destruction, will not produce evil and disorder worse than the evil being eliminated. (2309)

The Catechism explains that public authorities have a right and duty to "impose on citizens the obligations necessary for national defense," and that those who serve in the armed forces contribute to the common good and the "maintenance of peace" if they do their duty honorably. (2310)

Teachable Moment

Moral law must be upheld even during wartime. The array of rules for conducting war justly is called *ius ad bellum*, which is Latin for "justice of war." This means that civilians, wounded soldiers, and prisoners must be treated humanely. The Catechism says that any actions that are "deliberately contrary to the law of nations and to universal principles" are crimes that should not be carried out through "blind obedience." The extermination of a people, a nation, or an ethnic minority is especially grievous and "must be condemned as a mortal sin." The Church teaches that people are "morally bound" to resist any commands to commit genocide. (2313)

So in reality, how do we avoid war? I guess if we could answer that question, we'd get the Nobel Peace Prize. The Church teaches that in order to avoid war, nations must avoid the "accumulation of arms." The Catechism explains that rather than eliminating causes of war, the arms race "risks aggravating them." (2315)

It recognizes that the production and sale of arms "affect the common good" of nations and communities worldwide, and therefore must be regulated by public authorities. Avoiding war requires this regulation but also requires a concerted effort to wipe out injustices, excessive economic and social imbalances, envy, distrust, and pride. "Everything done to overcome these disorders contributes to building up peace and avoiding war," the Catechism explains. (2316–2317)

The Least You Need to Know

◆ The fifth commandment is about the absence of killing as much as it is about the presence of peace.

◆ All innocent life is to be protected from the moment of conception until its natural end.

◆ Abortion, euthanasia, suicide, and scientific research that exploits human life are forbidden.

◆ A series of specific conditions must be met to justify armed military action.

◆ Arms accumulation and severe economic disparity are among the causes of war that must be avoided.

Chapter 20

#6: You Shall Not Commit Adultery

In This Chapter

- ◆ A modern-day interpretation of the sixth commandment
- ◆ Chastity vs. adultery, lust, and a host of other offenses
- ◆ Church teaching on homosexuality
- ◆ The reasons behind bans on birth control and divorce

Chances are this is one of the first chapters you turned to when you started reading this book. Hey, this was the chapter I turned to first when I started writing this book. Maybe it has something to do with the fact that anything related to sex piques our natural curiosity. Or maybe it has more to do with the fact that this chapter covers some of the most controversial topics of our day.

The sixth commandment, as you might have guessed, is about much more than cheating on your spouse. The Church interprets this commandment as covering all aspects of human sexuality, and holds chastity up as the goal for all people, regardless of their state in life. It means whether you are single or married, straight or gay, chastity has a place in your relationship with others and your relationship with God.

In our overly sexualized society, the Church is very often viewed as being anti-sex. Its positions on everything from marriage to birth control are typically viewed as antiquated or oppressive. But the truth is, once you delve into this chapter, you will discover the Church's teaching on sexuality is really everything but oppressive, and is actually quite beautiful, as long as sex is part of a marriage that is open to the gift of life.

A Primer on Catholic Sexuality

"You shall not commit adultery." (Exodus 20:14)

The sixth commandment seems simple enough to understand, right? Don't cheat on your wife or husband. Yet *adultery*, in its basic definition, is actually a very narrow view of this commandment, so let's take a closer look to gain the full breadth of this law.

Church Speak

Adultery is voluntary sexual relations between a married person and somebody other than his or her spouse. The Church teaches the sixth commandment goes far beyond prohibiting only the behaviors that fit within those parameters and forbids many other related activities, from pornography to masturbation.

The Church isn't making this one up as she goes along when it comes to interpreting the sixth commandment. She looks directly toward Jesus and the words he spoke during the Sermon on the Mount: "You have heard that it was said, 'You shall not commit adultery.' But I say to you, everyone who looks at a woman with lust has already committed adultery with her in his heart." (Matthew 5:27–28)

Wow, that's big, isn't it? We're talking about thoughts here, not just actions, and that's pretty much the starting point for this commandment. What it comes down to is looking at human sexuality as part of the bigger picture. The Church sees sexuality as affecting every aspect of the human person, from the obvious—love and procreation—to the esoteric—our bonds with other people.

Every man and woman is seen as created in the image of God, with equal dignity that is lived out in different ways. When it comes to sexuality, the Church sees the union of a man and woman in marriage as a way of "imitating in the flesh the Creator's generosity and *fecundity*." (2335)

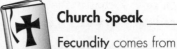

Church Speak

Fecundity comes from the Latin word *fecundus*, meaning the ability to produce offspring in abundance.

Chastity Is Not a Dirty Word

When the Catechism talks about chastity, it is not referring to an absence of sexuality but rather a correct balance of living out an individual's sexuality. The Catechism refers to chastity as the "successful integration of sexuality within the person and thus the inner unity of man in his bodily and spiritual being." (2337)

For the record, there is a big difference between sexual activity and sexuality—the two are not synonymous in the Catechism. Sexual activity is exactly what it sounds like: the physical acts. Sexuality, on the other hand, is that aspect of your being that includes not only your sexual desires but also your sexual identity, which are all of the innate qualities that make you a man or woman, including physical, moral, spiritual similarities and complementary differences. For example, a woman's sexuality would include her maternal instincts and femininity. (2333)

The bottom line is that living out the virtue of chastity means different things for different people, but the end result should be the same—integrity and unity.

A married couple lives out chastity by remaining committed to *conjugal chastity*, which can be hampered by a whole lot of offenses we'll get into in more detail in a little bit. We probably don't think of marriage and chastity as complementary, but the Church views chastity within marriage as a basic foundation that gives strength to the bond between husband and wife.

Church Speak

Conjugal fidelity is when spouses give themselves totally to each other in an irrevocable partnership established under God by their irrevocable personal consent. (2364) This grows out of that famous statement by Jesus: "Therefore what God has joined together, no human being must separate." (Mark 10:9)

A single person lives out chastity by refraining from any sexual activity; an engaged person lives out chastity by refraining from sexual intercourse until he or she enters into marriage. (2350) That may not be very popular these days, but the Church doesn't worry too much about popularity, making no exceptions for those almost-married folks who figure that having sex a few weeks or months before the wedding doesn't count. It does count.

Those who have taken vows of chastity or celibacy as priests or religious sisters and brothers live out that vow by refraining from all sexual activity in order to give themselves to God alone with an "undivided heart." (2349)

Although it doesn't seem so on the surface, it turns out that chastity, while always about sexuality, is often not about sex. In fact, the Catechism talks about the fact that chastity can be expressed in friendship as well, whether between members of the same sex or the opposite sex.

How can chastity have anything to do with friendship? Well, if we are living according to our individual and true sexuality, then we will bring certain elements of that sexuality to any relationship, but especially to a close friendship. Perhaps we bring a female sense of nurturing or a male sense of protectiveness. If we are living truly chaste lives, lives that put purity, God, and love of neighbor ahead of selfishness, then what starts out as a simple friendship can grow into a spiritually intimate yet platonic relationship. (2347)

The Catechism says that when chastity is lived correctly within a friendship, it can lead to a "spiritual communion" that benefits all parties involved. (2347)

Teachable Moment

Learning to live a chaste life must include an "apprenticeship in self-mastery" (2339). We do this by learning how to use our freedom in positive ways and by conquering the passions that threaten to control or even to enslave us. Self-mastery is never fully achieved in a permanent way. Throughout our lives, as we grow and change, we must continually rediscover our inner selves and re-master those passions that get in our way.

Offenses Against Chastity

So we've talked a lot about what chastity is. Now it's time to talk about what chastity is not. There is a long list of offenses against chastity in the Catechism. It covers all of the things you probably expect and a few that might surprise you.

Let's run through the list and see what jumps out at us. Here are the offenses: lust, masturbation, fornication, pornography, prostitution, and rape.

Well, I don't think we really need to get into why prostitution and rape are offenses against chastity. The Catechism notes them as "gravely sinful" and "intrinsically evil," respectively, but for the average Joe it is probably one or more of the other items on that list that are cause for concern on a regular basis. (2355–2356)

Let's start with lust. What's so bad about it? It goes back to what we talked about at the very beginning of this chapter. Human sexuality is supposed to be part of the whole person. We can't separate our desire for sexual activity from the other parts of our being—our spirits, our bodies, our minds. Lust, however, is not about this big picture; it's about sexual desire for desire's sake alone. It's not about the unity of a man and woman or about creating children. Lust is, for instance, when a guy tells a girl, "I love you," but what he really means is, "I love me, and I want you to satisfy me." So lust is really all about sex, sex, sex, and that's wrong, wrong, wrong. (2351)

The Catechism understands masturbation to be "the deliberate stimulation of the genital organs in order to derive sexual pleasure." Suffice it to say, the Church has a big problem with masturbation and considers it "gravely disordered," because it separates genital activity for the purpose of pleasure from the sexual relationship of marriage that results in unitive and procreative love. (2352) Alone or in collaboration with someone else, for Catholics, masturbation is strictly out of bounds.

So how is fornication any different? Fornication is the "carnal union" of an unmarried man and woman, which once again separates a sexual relationship from a marriage relationship, thereby turning it into something lustful and contrary to the dignity of the people involved. (2353)

Lastly there is pornography. It's hard to know where to begin with this one, given how our culture is saturated with sexual imagery, from magazine stands to TV sit-coms to the big screen. In this instance, the Church is talking about the deliberate display of nudity or real or simulated sexual acts for a third party. Pornography is forbidden not only because it "perverts the conjugal act" between a husband and wife but also because it injures the dignity of the people involved in producing it. (2354) The Catechism considers pornography a "grave offense" that should be prevented by civil authorities.

Teaching on Homosexuality

When the Catechism talks about homosexuality, it is referring to sexual relations between two people of the same sex, something the Church considers "contrary to the natural law," closed to the gift of life, and therefore unacceptable in any circumstances. (2357)

At the same time, the Church recognizes that there are many men and women with "deep-seated homosexual tendencies" and these men and women must be accepted with "respect, compassion, and sensitivity" and must be free from "unjust discrimination." (2358)

What the Church says about homosexuality is consistent with what it says about any sexual relations outside the confines of a sacramental marriage. Homosexuals are expected to live chaste lives, just as married and unmarried heterosexuals are expected to live chaste lives. They are called to self-mastery, just as all Catholics are called to self-mastery. (2359)

True Confessions _____

The Church has taken a lot of heat for its position on homosexuality. "Grave depravity" and "intrinsically disordered" are the words used in the Catechism to describe homosexual acts. While this can sound incredibly harsh to our often-progressive ears, those classifications follow the same strict set of rules that the Church applies to any sexual behavior—homosexual or heterosexual—that falls into the "morally disordered" category, including lust and masturbation. The Catechism is not referring to homosexual *people* as "intrinsically disordered" but to homosexual *acts*. If there is one thing to be learned from a reading of this section of the Catechism, it is the importance of keeping things in proper context. (2357)

Sex in Marriage

The age-old jokes about Catholic guilt and sexual pleasure—or the lack of it—can finally be put to rest thanks to this section of Catechism. This is where we discover that the Church believes sex is just fine. In fact, the Church thinks sex, when it is not disordered, is more than fine. It goes so far as to refer to it as "noble and honorable" and a "source of joy and pleasure." (2362)

So if the Church does indeed approve of sex, how did it get such a bad rap in the public eye? Ah, well, there's the rub. The Church says sex can only be true and good when it is part of a loving and marital relationship.

Check out this line from the Catechism's opening paragraph on marital love: "In marriage, the physical intimacy of the spouses becomes a sign and pledge of spiritual communion." (2360) This is the Church's view of an ideal marriage, a physical union that is taken to a spiritual level through intimacy. Who'd have thought we would find such romance in the Catechism? And yet there it is, in black and white.

Marriage rises to the level of religious reality and spiritual good in the Catholic Church because a man and a woman, living in fidelity to each other and to God, serve as witnesses to the same kind of fidelity God has for his people and Jesus Christ has for his Church. Over and over, the Catechism puts married love and procreation in close partnership with the divine.

To better explain this type of union, the Catechism relies on the words of St. John Chrysostom, a fourth-century bishop and doctor of the Church who is quoted as saying that young husbands should tell their wives: "I have taken you in my arms, and I love you, and I prefer you to my life itself. For the present life is nothing, and my most ardent dream is to spend it with you in such a way that we may be assured of not being separated in the life reserved for us." (2365) Talk about a marriage proposal!

Birth Control

In this section we have to go back to good old "fecundity" and the ability and willingness of married couples to procreate in a generous and loving way. So many people have a problem with this concept that it's doubtful it can get a fair shake even after thorough explanation, but we'll give it our best shot.

When the Catechism talks about marriage and sexual activity within marriage, it views their purposes as twofold: unitive and procreative. This means that the relationship draws the husband and wife into oneness, or unity, and at the same time is open to new life, or procreation. (2366)

Actually, the Catechism puts it in a much more poetic way, saying that married couples are called to share in the "creative power and fatherhood of God." That gives it a pretty hefty spin, doesn't it? We're not just talking about having a brood of kids. We're talking about sharing in God's creative power. (2367)

Teachable Moment _____

In *Gaudium et Spes* (Joy and Hope), a document of Vatican Council II, married couples are told to "regard it as their mission to transmit human life and to educate their children," realizing that in doing so they are "cooperating with the love of God the Creator and are, in a certain sense, its interpreters." (2367) That's a pretty extraordinary job description for moms and dads.

Children result from the "mutual giving" of one spouse to the other, making procreation an integral part of the relationship as a whole. Procreation therefore cannot be separated from the marriage act any more than unity can be separated from it. This means that in the performance of marital intercourse, you cannot build a wall between love-making and baby-making. (2366)

This brings us to the topic of contraception. And before we get into the issue of artificial birth control, we need to first look at what the Church says in general about having children. The Catechism talks about spacing children from the point of view of responsible parenthood. The reason for spacing children must not be based on the desire to have more material goods, more time, or more of anything else. Parenthood has to be about selflessness as opposed to selfishness. (2368)

So if the Church is saying there is a responsible way to space children, how can the Church also say that you cannot use birth control to manage that spacing? Well, it doesn't say that entirely. It says you are allowed to regulate having children using methods that rely on periodic abstinence and monitoring of the woman's fertile and infertile days of the month. The Catechism says such methods not only respect the bodies of spouses but also "encourage tenderness" between them. (2370)

Quoting the papal encyclical *Humanae Vitae*, the Catechism goes on to say any action that attempts to prevent procreation—either before, during, or after the sexual act—is "intrinsically evil." (2370) That means sterilization or any other contraceptive device or pill is out.

You're Absolved If ...

You may have thought the Catholic Church sanctions only the "rhythm method" as an acceptable method of spacing children. In fact, the Church promotes and teaches Natural Family Planning, a method that relies on couples charting fertile and infertile periods through basal body temperature readings and other signs of ovulation, and then abstaining from sex on fertile days. When followed accurately, this method can be 99 percent effective.

The Gift of Children

The Church considers children a blessing and a gift, not a right or a piece of property. Every child has a right to know his or her parents, the Catechism says, and every child should be respected from the moment of conception on.

In keeping with this view, the Church says that scientific efforts to reduce sterility in infertile couples should be "encouraged." However, the Church forbids any efforts that disassociate the husband and wife from each other and the unitive and procreative aspects of their marriage in order to conceive. (2376)

This means artificial insemination techniques that replace nature rather than assist it—in vitro fertilization, surrogate mothers, and donated sperm or ova—are all considered gravely immoral and unacceptable. Even nature-replacing techniques that involve only the sperm and ova of the married couple with no outside donors, while less offensive than other methods, are nonetheless morally unacceptable in the Church's eyes. (2376–2377)

So what is an infertile couple to do? Shouldn't they, too, get to share in the great blessing of parenthood? The Church says yes; and the Catechism suggests this might be through the adoption of an orphaned or abandoned child. (2379)

On the Offense

Although we previously ran through a whole series of offenses against chastity in general, the Catechism now gets down to the work of spelling out offenses specific to the "dignity of marriage." Obviously, based on the subject of the commandment at hand, the first and foremost offense listed in the Catechism is adultery.

Adultery

Adultery is marital infidelity, more commonly known as "cheating." Whenever two people, one of whom is married, have sexual relations outside the marriage relationship, we have adultery. It's pretty clear.

If you have sex with someone other than your spouse, or you have sex with someone else's spouse, you commit adultery. Remember, Jesus said even thinking about someone lustfully is adultery of the heart.

Adultery is considered an "injustice," something that not only damages the marriage bond and tramples on the rights of the injured spouse but also damages society and the children who "depend on their parents' stable union." (2381)

The bottom line is, don't sleep with anyone but your spouse. In fact, don't even *think* about sleeping with anyone but your spouse.

Divorce Decrees

Here we come to another hot-button topic: divorce. The U.S. Census Bureau says that approximately 50 percent of all first marriages end in divorce, so that leaves us with a lot of divorced Catholics out there. But what does divorce mean for Catholics who can't stay married but want to remain true to the Church?

Well, according to the Church, those who have been baptized and have entered into a sacramental and consummated marriage cannot undo their "I do's" for any reason until death them do part. That's pretty hardcore in this day and age, no?

You're Absolved If ...

You thought being divorced meant you are unable to receive the sacraments or are permanently separated from the Church in any way. Divorce itself does not bar you from receiving Communion or participating fully in the life of the Church. It is remarriage outside the Church that turns the tragedy of divorce into an obstacle to receiving the sacraments.

The Catechism says divorce is "a grave offense against natural law" and attempts to break a contract that cannot be broken. (2384) Remarriage, even when recognized by civil authorities, does more harm than good, creating "public and permanent adultery."

Divorce is also considered immoral because of the way it disrupts a family and traumatizes children. The Catechism goes so far as to call divorce a "plague on society." (2385)

The Catechism does have compassion for what it refers to as the "innocent victim" of civil divorce, saying that there is a big difference between the person who chooses to leave the marriage and the one who is left behind. It also says that sometimes marriages end not because either spouse is right or wrong or good or bad, but simply because the marriage cannot work. (2386)

Teachable Moment

When a seemingly valid marriage is flawed by some sort of defect in a spouse or in the consent to marry, the Church can sometimes declare the marriage null, meaning that the union was unable to rise to the level of what marriage was intended to be. This requires a formal process known as "annulment," which is explained in more detail in Chapter 14.

Other Serious Offenses

The Catechism throws together a grab bag of other offenses against marriage that include polygamy, incest, and "free union." While the first two offenses are pretty straightforward, that last one can slide by almost unnoticed, but it's a big one.

"Free union" would apply to anyone who is sexually intimate with someone on a long-term basis without the social fact of marriage. In other words, "free union" includes everyone who lives together before marriage or who chooses to live together with no intention of marriage. (2390)

The Catechism states that these types of situations "destroy the very idea of the family" and weaken fidelity. (2390) The Church specifically objects to what it calls "trial marriages," saying that the sexual union of a man and woman can only exist within a marriage, whereby the spouses give themselves completely to each other. (2391) In other words, living together is not an option, no matter how much money you'll save on rent in the process.

The Least You Need to Know

◆ Cheating on a spouse is considered adultery and is at the heart of this commandment.

◆ Every person—whether married or single, straight or gay—is called to live out chastity.

◆ The physical intimacy of marriage is a sign of spiritual communion between spouses.

◆ Spacing children through natural methods that include periodic abstinence is acceptable, but artificial contraception is forbidden.

◆ Divorce is often immoral because it destroys the family, traumatizes children, and attempts to break a contract that is breakable only by death.

◆ Living together before marriage or in place of marriage, known as "free union," is considered a grave sin.

Chapter 21

#7: You Shall Not Steal

In This Chapter

- ◆ Exploring everything from material stealing to economic justice
- ◆ How the care of creation fits into this commandment
- ◆ Working toward just wages for all
- ◆ Understanding commitment to the poor

Here we are at the seventh commandment, the one against stealing. As you will soon see in this chapter, the prohibitions spelled out in this commandment go way beyond stealing. This commandment isn't simply about not doing bad things, it's about actively doing good things, too.

In the coming pages, we are going to explore how the seventh commandment, while it does directly forbid taking material things that aren't yours, is just as much a call to justice and charity. (2401)

In the New Testament, we hear the story of Zacchaeus, the wealthy tax collector who seeks out Jesus. People are astounded when Jesus asks to stay at Zacchaeus' house. Remember, tax collectors were considered corrupt extortionists and collaborators with the Roman occupiers, and were therefore a universally hated group. But Zacchaeus, we are told, said to Jesus:

"Behold, half of my possessions, Lord, I shall give to the poor, and if I have extorted anything from anyone I shall repay it four times over. And Jesus said to him, 'Today salvation has come to this house because this man, too, is a descendant of Abraham. For the Son of Man has come to seek and to save what was lost.'" (Luke 19:8–10)

Here we see that not stealing is simply not enough. Amends must be made for wrongs committed, and generosity and justice must become the heart of this law.

Private Property, Public Promises

You shall not steal. (Exodus 20:15)

We begin our discussion of this commandment with a basic understanding of Church teaching on "common *stewardship*" of the earth. Remember, in the beginning, God created the earth and its resources for the good of humankind, and entrusted humans to care for his creation and to share it among themselves. After the fall from grace, the division of property and goods was seen as not only predictable but even necessary to ensure the freedom and dignity of all people. (2402)

> **Church Speak**
>
> **Stewardship** in the biblical or Church sense means to care for and preserve what you have been given. For Christians, that means caring for the earth's resources, for their neighbors, and for their communities, including their Church. In their parishes, Catholics often hear stewardship broken down into three methods of giving: time, talent, and treasure. This means they not only give monetary donations (treasure) but also serve the Church as a volunteer (time) and share their God-given gifts and abilities (talent).

People have a right to own private property as long as it has been "acquired or received in a just way." However, the rights of all people to have life's basic needs met—food, clothing, shelter, medical care—must always come first, sometimes trumping the right to private property. The Church teaches that God created the earth and its resources for all people, so all people must have access to the things that give life basic dignity. This principle is known as the "universal destination of goods." (2403)

The seventh commandment brings us back to a couple of key virtues explained in the Catechism. *Temperance* in economic matters is crucial in the quest for human dignity. This means you can't be too attached to your material possessions. *Justice* is necessary to ensure that your neighbor has his needs met and gets "his due," and *solidarity* needs to be practiced, because by treating others as we want to be treated, we come to understand, respect, and love those who have less than us and who need not only our material assistance but our spiritual companionship. (2407)

Okay, so we've been talking a lot about rights and justice and charity, but what about stealing? Isn't that what this commandment is about? The answer is yes. The seventh commandment absolutely says that you cannot take anything that does not belong to you. Not only that, but you can't keep things you've borrowed, pay unjust wages to your workers, defraud your place of business, or take advantage of another person who might be willing to drastically overpay for something out of ignorance or desperation. (2409)

The Catechism makes it clear that any promises you make, you must keep, and any contracts you sign, you must fulfill, as long as there's nothing immoral going on. If you take something that isn't yours, you need to make restitution. Remember Zacchaeus from earlier in this chapter? He said he would pay back fourfold anything he took unjustly. (2410–2412)

The seventh commandment isn't just about taking *things* unjustly but also about taking or using *people* unjustly. That means any action that leads to a kind of enslavement is "a sin against the dignity of persons." (2414)

Teachable Moment

The Church teaches that games of chance are not "contrary to justice" in and of themselves. Moral issues arise, however, when someone reaches a point where he starts using money needed for his basic needs or the needs of his family to pay for a gambling habit. The Catechism says that a "passion for gambling" can become "enslavement." (2413)

Care for Creation

It may come as a surprise that this commandment also covers environmental issues and caring for the natural world. It goes back to God's entrusting us as stewards of his creation. That means we are not only obliged to treat others and their belongings with respect, but we are also called to treat animals and all of creation with respect and dignity. "Use of the mineral, vegetable, and animal resources of the universe cannot be divorced from respect for moral imperatives," the Catechism explains. This means that while we are stewards of creation, we are not absolute masters—that's God's domain. It's our job to make sure we protect and preserve God's creation not only for ourselves and our neighbors but for our children and their children. (2415)

Animals are especially deserving of respect and kindness because they are "God's creatures" and are surrounded by his "providential care." The Catechism explains that because God gave animals to humankind, it is "legitimate" to use them for food, clothing, work, and as domesticated pets. It is even acceptable to use them for medical or scientific research if it "contributes to caring for or saving human lives." (2416–2417)

It is not acceptable, however, to cause animals to suffer or to "die needlessly." It's also not okay to spend exorbitant amounts of money on your animals when that money could be better spent to alleviate human suffering. "One can love animals; one should not direct to them the affection due only to persons," the Catechism says. (2418)

Teachable Moment

St. Francis of Assisi is well known for his love of animals and all of God's creation. Born into a wealthy family around 1181 in Assisi, Italy, Francis gave up all of his worldly belongings to follow Christ, preach the Gospel, and care for others. He founded the Franciscan Order and died in Assisi on Oct. 3, 1226. His feast day is celebrated on Oct. 4, a day on which many Catholic parishes hold a "blessing of the animals."

Economic Justice

The Church's "social doctrine," or its teaching on human dignity as it is affected by economic and social issues, is rooted in the Gospel. When the Church makes a statement about economic and social matters—such as in the papal encyclicals *Rerum Novarum* (Condition of Labour) and *Centesimus Annus* (marking the one hundredth anniversary of *Rerum Novarum*)—it does so based on its understanding of justice as it has been revealed in Jesus Christ. The Church does not cater to or base its teachings on whatever the most popular political philosophies of the day may be. For example, modern-day popes have been known to speak out against both the evils of communism and excesses of capitalism.

Any political system that puts economic factors above human beings is opposed to the Church's social doctrine. The Church rejects totalitarian and atheistic ideologies as well as the communist or socialist regimes that result from those ideologies. The Church also does not give blanket approval to capitalism, saying that "individualism and the absolute primacy of the law of the marketplace over human labor" puts profit before people and leaves many human needs unmet and not addressed by the "marketplace." (2425)

Right to Work

Although many of us look at work as something to avoid or, at the very least, tolerate, the Church tells us something else. For people called by God to be stewards of creation, work is a right and a "duty," something that enables us to contribute to the work of creation and to honor our creator.

"Everyone should be able to draw from work the means of providing for his life and that of his family, and of serving the human community," the Catechism explains. (2428)

All people also have the "right of economic initiative," meaning we have a right to earn a living and use our talents to contribute to the common good. The Church also teaches that all people must have "access to employment" without discrimination based on gender, race, or disabilities. Society, the Catechism says, should help people find employment. (2429–2433)

Teachable Moment

The Church teaches that the state has a responsibility to provide a secure environment with a stable currency and adequate public services so that workers can enjoy the "fruits of their labors." It is also up to the state—following the initiative of individuals and the groups and association that make up society—to ensure that human rights within the workplace are upheld.

Just Wage

According to Church teaching, it is a "grave injustice" to refuse a *just wage* to a worker. *Gadium et Spes* states that a just wage should enable a worker to provide a "dignified livelihood for herself and her family on the material, social, cultural, and spiritual level, taking into account the role and productivity of each, the state of the business, and the common good." Just because a worker agrees to accept a low wage does not make it morally justifiable. (2434)

Although management might not want to hear it, the Church teaches that the right of workers to *strike* is "morally legitimate" when it is absolutely necessary to achieve "proportionate benefit." Striking that includes violence or an effort to gain benefits unrelated to working conditions, however, is not acceptable. (2435)

Finally, the Church calls *unemployment* a condition that "wounds" the dignity of a person and "threatens the equilibrium of his life" and that of his family. (2436)

Worldwide Solidarity

Now we take this concept of economic justice to an international level, where it is obvious that tremendous gaps exist in the economic conditions of various populations. Remembering the spirit of the seventh commandment, the Church teaches that there "must be solidarity among nations" in an effort to bring resources to struggling nations and to help balance the global economic scales. (2437–2438)

"Rich nations have a grave moral responsibility toward those which are unable to ensure the means of their development by themselves or have been prevented from doing so by tragic historical events," the Catechism explains. (2439)

While it is "appropriate" for wealthy countries to provide "direct aid" in cases of natural disasters, epidemics, or other catastrophic events, that is not enough to "provide a lasting solution." Efforts to reform international economic policies and institutions are needed for long-term improvement in struggling nations. (2440)

As it turns out, money and reform are not enough. You've got to have God in order to have the "full development of human society," the Catechism explains. When people have an increased sense of God and an increased sense of themselves, they are more likely to help others, work to reduce poverty, and respect others, regardless of cultural background. (2441)

All lay Christians are called to work on "concrete" efforts to improve the common good, relying on the Gospel and Church teaching to animate life in this world with Christian commitment, and in this, to show themselves to be agents of peace and justice. (2442)

Loving the Poor

Jesus, who was born in poverty, preached about the need to love the poor and provide for the poor. Viewed in light of the Gospel, the seventh commandment challenges believers to care for those who are hungry, naked, and lonely in real and practical ways. The Church even goes so far as to say that one of the "motives" for the right and duty to work is so that those who work can give to those who are in need. (2443–2444)

The Church lays out the works of mercy to guide the faithful in caring for their suffering brothers and sisters. The *spiritual works of mercy* include instructing, advising, consoling, comforting, forgiving, and bearing wrongs patiently. The *corporal works of mercy* include feeding the hungry, sheltering the homeless, clothing the naked, visiting the sick and imprisoned, and burying the dead. Above all of these, however, the Church lists giving donations to the poor as one of the "chief witnesses" of charity and justice. (2447)

> **Church Speak**
>
> **Preferential love for the poor** (sometimes called preferential option for the poor) refers to the Church's unceasing efforts, "since her origin and in spite of the failings of many of her members," to serve the poor through various charitable programs. This work has its foundation in the teachings of Jesus Christ, who identified with the poorest of the poor. (2448)

The Least You Need to Know

- The seventh commandment prohibits stealing, cheating, fraud, enslavement of others, unjust business practices, and taking advantage of the hardships of others.

- Justice and charity—actively doing good—are also components of the seventh commandment.

- As stewards of God's earth, humans are called to show respect to all of creation, particularly animals.

- Every person has a right and duty to work and deserves access to employment with a just wage and without discrimination.

- Rich nations have an obligation to assist poorer nations with direct aid during catastrophic events and through international economic reforms for long-term improvement.

- Christians are called to love the poor as Jesus did, assisting them through the spiritual and corporal works of mercy, but above all, giving donations as a sign of charity and justice.

Chapter 22

The Last Three Commandments

In This Chapter

- ◆ Understanding lying and secrets in the eighth commandment: you shall not bear false witness against your neighbor

- ◆ Being pure of heart in the ninth commandment: you shall not covet your neighbor's wife

- ◆ Shunning greed and envy in the tenth commandment: you shall not covet your neighbor's goods

- ◆ Applying the last three commandments to modern-day life

At first glance, the last three commandments of the Decalogue may seem a little old-fashioned. Bearing false witness and coveting a neighbor's wife feel outdated on some level. So you may be wondering what these commandments have to do with life in the modern world.

Well, it turns out these commandments are more relevant to life today than you are likely to imagine. Once you take them out of the older, more vague—at least to our ears—language, you find that we are talking about lying and gossip, lust and immodesty, greed and envy. Sounds like the basis of any number of nighttime TV dramas.

In this chapter, we are going to discuss the real-life meaning of these commandments and what the Church teaches is the proper response to the neighbor who always seems to have the nicer car, the bigger house, the better job, the smarter kids ....

#8: To Tell the Truth

You shall not bear false witness against your neighbor. (Exodus 20:16)

The eighth commandment is all about truth and offenses against truth. The Catechism says that "misrepresenting the truth," whether through our words or actions, is a sin against God, "who is truth and wills the truth." (2464)

Also, Jesus said, "I am the way, the truth, and the life." (John 14:6) If believers follow Jesus, they live in the "spirit of truth." (2466)

The Catechism explains that humans lean "by nature toward the truth" and that they are impelled, because of their God-given dignity, to seek out the truth and to live according to the truth once they know it. (2467)

Church Speak

Truthfulness is the virtue that makes us want to tell the truth and show ourselves true to others in deeds and words, as well as guarding against hypocrisy. It is about honesty in all things, but also about "discretion" when appropriate. Yes, we must always tell the truth, but we must also know when to keep a secret in good faith. (2468–2469)

This commandment is about more than *not* bearing false witness against a neighbor; it is about "bearing witness to the truth." For Christians, that means standing up and being a witness to the faith through words and the example of their lives. In extreme cases, bearing witness to the truth has meant *martyrdom*, which is when being a witness to the faith costs someone his or her life. (2471–2473)

Beyond Lying

When it comes to bearing false witness, in addition to lying, there are a series of specific offenses against the truth spelled out in the Catechism. Starting off the list is *false witness* and *perjury*, both of which compromise justice and fairness in judicial decisions. "False witness" is a public statement contrary to the truth; perjury is a knowingly false statement made under oath. (2476)

Next we have *respect for reputation*, which means avoiding anything that would unjustly injure someone. These sins include *rash judgment*, which is when you assume something bad about someone to be true without any evidence; *detraction*, which is when you go around talking about other people's "faults and failings" for no good reason; and *calumny*, which is when you tell a lie that hurts another person's reputation and maybe causes other people to draw false conclusions about them. (2477)

Rounding out the list are *flattery* and *adulation*, which are especially bad when they are done to achieve some sort of goal that isn't particularly good or when they contribute to a vice or sin. *Boasting* is off limits, as is, surprisingly enough, *irony* when it is "aimed at disparaging someone" by caricaturing a certain behavior. (2480–2481)

And finally we have outright lying, which, of course, is a pretty obvious and direct offense against truth. The Catechism explains that if you lie, you are speaking or acting "against the truth in order to lead into error someone who has a right to know the truth." (2483)

The Church is pretty clear on the issue of lying, saying that it "does real violence to another" and that is it "destructive of society." (2486)

Teachable Moment

If you do tell a lie, you're going to have to make up for it in a pretty big way. The Church says liars must make reparations, public ones if at all possible, to rectify the situation and restore the reputation of the injured party. (2487)

Keeping Secrets

So if truth is a virtue and lying is a sin, what do we do when we know a secret truth? Are we obliged to reveal it as part of our duty to bear witness to the truth? No. The Catechism explains that there is no unconditional and universal "right to the communication of the truth." In other words, there may be times when it is not appropriate to reveal truthful but confidential information. (2488)

How do we know when it's okay to keep a secret and when it's a sin? "Charity and respect for the truth" must determine whether something should be kept secret. "No one is bound to reveal the truth to someone who does not have the right to know it," the Catechism says. (2489)

The secrecy of the sacrament of confession, which we discussed in Chapter 13, is absolute and can never be violated. In addition, "professional secrets," such as confidential information between doctors and patients or lawyers and clients, must be kept private unless "very grave harm" would result. (2490–2491)

Communications and Sacred Art

Modern media plays a pretty critical and influential role in our society, and so the Church gives a shout out to all communication media in this portion of the Catechism.

The Catechism explains that information provided by the media is "at the service of the common good" and that society has a right to expect that information to be based on "truth, freedom, justice, and solidarity." (2494) It specifically calls on journalists to take on two obligations: 1) to "serve the truth" and 2) not to "offend against charity in disseminating information." (2497)

Truth, the Catechism says, is "beautiful in itself," and as such, often inspires humans to express the truth through various art forms. When art is inspired by the truth, it "bears a certain likeness to God's activity in what he has created." Sacred art, which is any art that depicts sacred or religious subjects in order to give glory to God, in particular, can evoke the "transcendent mystery of God." The Catechism calls on bishops to promote sacred art and to remove from churches or liturgical celebrations anything that is not in conformity with the truth of faith and the "authentic beauty" that defines sacred art. (2500–2503)

#9: Not Lusting After Another

You shall not covet your neighbor's wife. (Exodus 20:17)

So what exactly are we talking about when we abide by this commandment? Is this about not pursuing the desperate housewife who lives across the street? And isn't this type of thing already covered in the sixth commandment about adultery? Not entirely. The ninth commandment challenges us to strive for purity and to avoid what the Church calls "carnal concupiscence," which is a very intimidating way of saying that you can't lust after another person. And, ladies, don't think the noninclusive language lets us off the hook here. Lust is a two-way street and is equally sinful whether the object is a woman or a man.

We talked a lot about this in Chapter 20, when we discussed adultery. But unlike adultery, which is a sinful action, breaking this commandment has to do mainly with sinful thoughts and desires. Jesus said, "Everyone who looks at a woman with lust has already committed adultery in his heart." (Matthew 5:28)

Those are some pretty strong words, so let's look at what it means for our day-to-day lives. This commandment is about purity of heart. "Blessed are the pure in heart, for they shall see God," Jesus said during the Sermon on the Mount. (Matthew 5:8)

The Catechism explains if we are "pure in heart," our minds and wills will be "attuned" to God's demands for holiness, especially in the areas of charity, chastity, love for the truth, and orthodoxy of faith. (2518) It is only with a pure heart that we can eventually see God and are able to see those around us as reflections of "divine beauty." (2519)

To achieve a pure heart requires some effort on our part. Baptism gives us a push in the right direction, but even the baptized are not free from disordered desires. We have to count on God's grace—through the virtue and gift of chastity—to give us what we need to prevail and make us want to seek to fulfill God's will in everything. (2520)

Church Speak

Modesty is an important part of purity and influences how we dress and how we act. The Catechism says modesty "protects the intimate center of the person" and is equivalent to "decency." (2521–2522)

That's a pretty lofty proposition, to get to the point where we can keep our hearts and minds so focused on God that we never allow any lustful or covetous thoughts in. But that is the long-term goal of this commandment. If you live the ninth commandment to the letter of the law, you will have a heart that is pure, centered on God, and able to withstand the kinds of temptations that typically trip folks up.

#10: Not Keeping Up with the Joneses

You shall not covet your neighbor's house ... nor anything else that belongs to him. (Exodus 20:17)

The tenth and final commandment "completes" the ninth, the Catechism explains. Where the ninth commandment is concerned with desires of the flesh, the tenth is concerned with the desire for material things that can lead to greed and envy at one end of the scale, and robbery and fraud at the other. (2534)

Banishing Greed and Envy

It's normal to desire things. We get hungry and desire food. We get cold and desire a coat. Those kinds of desires are okay. It's when we let our desires morph into *greed* for things we don't really need or into *avarice*, which is a vice focused on amassing money and power, that the problems begin. (2535–2536) These sins, along with the desire to commit injustice by harming our neighbor in her temporal goods, are strictly forbidden by the tenth commandment.

What about envy? At some time or another we all probably feel a twinge of envy over something someone else has. Seems normal enough in our world, right? Well, normal or not, the Catechism says envy can lead to the worst crimes and must be "banished from the human heart." (2538)

Envy, one of the seven deadly or *capital* sins, occurs when we feel bad over someone else's good fortune. You've probably experienced it once or twice. The neighbor gets a shiny new sports car or the guy in the cubicle next to you gets the promotion you thought was yours. That's envy at its finest. Now, when that bad feeling rises to the level of wishing something bad on the neighbor or the co-worker, it becomes a mortal sin. (2539)

Teachable Moment

Envy comes from everyday things that worm their way into our psyches and make us act in not-so-nice ways: pride is the big culprit here. To avoid envy, we must show goodwill toward others and "live in humility." That means taking pleasure in someone else's accomplishments. (2540)

Poverty of Spirit

As usual, it's not enough simply to avoid the bad stuff related to this commandment. We are challenged to work toward detachment from material things, to a spiritual place where we achieve the "poverty of heart" that Jesus preached about. "Every one of you who does not renounce all his possessions cannot be my disciple," Jesus said. (Luke 14:33) Hence, if you don't break that all-I-want-is-everything way of thinking, you can't get into the kingdom of heaven. (2544)

But what does that mean for those of us who live in the world and cannot give away *everything* we have to follow Jesus? It doesn't mean we cannot truly follow Jesus if we have money or belongings; what it means is those things cannot be more important to us than Jesus. We have to be poor in spirit and we have to be willing to turn our lives over to God without worrying about what will happen tomorrow. (2544, 2546–2547)

Jesus told his disciples, "Do not worry about tomorrow; tomorrow will take care of itself." (Matthew 6:34)

The Greatest Desire

If we keep our eyes on God and focus our desires on "true happiness," we can free ourselves from the worldly attachments that threaten to drag us down. This doesn't mean we won't struggle from time to time or take one step forward and two steps back. But with God's grace we can overcome those human weaknesses and reach a place where the "way of perfection" becomes more important to us than things, power, success, or glory. We can reach the point where the stuff we own doesn't own us. (2548–2550)

The Least You Need to Know

◆ Not bearing false witness, as proscribed by the eighth commandment, means not lying, gossiping, committing perjury, assassinating character, or revealing a secret that should be kept.

◆ In the ninth commandment, coveting your neighbor's spouse means you should avoid any deliberate cultivation of desires of the flesh, like lust, immodesty, or impurity of thoughts.

◆ The final commandment prohibits greed, envy, and the insatiable hunger for power or money.

◆ It's not enough to avoid coveting; you have to work toward being "poor in spirit" so that you are detached from material things.

Part 5

Turning Toward Heaven

Prayer is about our relationship with God. It is about the conversations we have with our Father, sometimes out loud and within our Church community, sometimes out loud in solitude, and sometimes without any words, sounds, or gestures. Prayer can be as individual as a fingerprint.

The next three chapters will look first at prayer in general—why we pray, how we pray, where Jesus and Mary fit in—and then at more specific types of prayer, including the Lord's Prayer, Christianity's "perfect" prayer.

Chapter 23

Why Do We Pray?

In This Chapter

- ◆ Understanding what prayer is
- ◆ Models of prayer through the ages
- ◆ Mary's role in Christian prayer
- ◆ Essential forms of prayer

Now let's turn to the subject of prayer, which can mean different things to different people. For some it is the quiet plea whispered in the darkness in the midst of a crisis or struggle. For others it is a daily, perhaps even ongoing, conversation with God. And for still others it is a ritual that precedes or follows specific devotions or traditions in an effort to reach the divine. The Catechism says that prayer is God's gift to us. Whether we pray through words or gestures, prayer is centered in our hearts. (2563) Regardless of what words we use or whether we sit, kneel, or walk when we do it, prayer is about a relationship with God. When we pray to God, whether we are praising him, petitioning him, thanking him, or asking his forgiveness, we are lifting our hearts toward heaven and opening ourselves up to the gracious love God wants us to receive from him.

In this chapter, we will look at prayer in the Old Covenant and then look at prayer as expressed by Jesus. We will also address the role of the Virgin Mary in Christian prayer, and talk about specific kinds of prayer.

The Old Masters of Prayer

The Catechism declares that all human beings are searching for God, as evidenced by the presence of so many religions throughout the world and its history. (2566) As significant as the human search for God may be, it is God, the Catechism states, who is the first to call out to humans. God is tireless in his call, even when we humans are running away with our hands over our ears. We may forget God or replace God with other things or accuse God of abandoning us, but God continues to call us back into relationship with him through the conversation, the drama of prayer. (2567)

There are several people in the Old Covenant who demonstrate for us the strength and meaning of prayer. Let's look at a few of them to see how prayer worked in their hearts, drawing them closer to God.

Abraham

Abraham, one of the heroes of the Book of Genesis, was an early model of prayer for us. He had an attentive heart and a willingness to submit to God's will no matter what—up to and including the requested sacrifice of the son God had given him. And while the sacrifice of his only son, Isaac, didn't come to pass in the end, Abraham proved that he was willing to do whatever God asked of him. (2572)

Abraham, a "man of silence," goes wherever God calls him. First Abraham expressed his prayer through actions: building an altar to the Lord at every stage of his journey. Later he puts words to his prayer, which turns out to be more of a complaint that God has not kept up his end of the bargain. But Abraham continued to believe. For his unwavering belief he was rewarded with a special relationship with God, which culminated in the "purification of his faith" when God asked him to sacrifice Isaac. (2570–2572)

At first blush it may be hard to view Abraham as a model for modern-day pray-ers, but what we need to focus on is not his willingness to sacrifice his son but his willingness to go where God called him and to keep faith with God no matter what.

Moses

Moses served as "the most striking example of intercessory prayer." (2574) God, first of all, spoke to Moses and asked him to be his messenger. In the conversation God had with him, Moses learned how to pray: "He balks, makes excuses, above all, questions." It is in response to Moses' question that God reveals his name. (2575)

Moses, accepting his call, continued to converse with God, and he interceded for his people, prefiguring the *intercession* of Jesus Christ who came to earth as the mediator between God and humanity.

> **Church Speak**
>
> **Intercession** is a prayer of petition said on behalf of someone else. Sunday liturgies always include a series of intercessions offered by the congregation for the needs of the Church and of the world, and for both the living and the dead.

The Catechism also talks about how Moses' prayer was a form of "contemplative prayer," which can seem a little confusing to those of us familiar with the wordless contemplative prayer that is the norm today. Moses' prayer is "contemplative" in that it is a complete surrendering to God. Moses experienced God in a deeper way than anyone ever had before him. (2576–2577)

David

David, king of Israel from whose lineage Jesus descended, was also a model of prayer. He faithfully followed what God told him to do and trusted in God's promises. (2579) Let's start with what we know about David. Born in Bethlehem, he was a shepherd. He defeated Goliath. He was a king. He is credited with writing the majority of the Book of Psalms in the Old Testament, making him the "first prophet" of Jewish and Christian prayer. (2579)

"His submission to the will of God, his praise, his repentance, will be a model for the prayer of the people," the Catechism states. (2579)

David is anointed by God, chosen by God, and he goes where God leads. When he sinned—and he did—he repented with such sincerity and accepted his punishment with such graciousness that he became a model for all penitents.

Elijah

Finally we have Elijah, the "father of the prophets." Elijah was a prophet during the reign of the Israelite king Ahab. Ahab "did evil in the sight of the Lord more than any of his predecessors" (1 Kings 16:30), his most grievous sin being that he converted, under the influence of his wife, Jezebel, to the worship of Baal. Elijah became the conscience of Israel during this time, most famously challenging 450 prophets of Baal to a contest on Mount Carmel: Elijah and the prophets would both set up an altar and sacrifice a bull and see which altar the Lord would set on fire. Nothing happens to the altar of Baal's prophets, but Elijah's sacrifice catches on fire and becomes a holocaust pleasing to the Lord. During this sacrifice, Elijah prays, "Answer me, O Lord, answer me" (1 Kings 18:37), asking the Lord to set his sacrifice on fire and to demonstrate that he is the true prophet of the Lord (18:37).

Elijah models hope and trust in the Lord that his prayer will be fulfilled, even when he is a lone voice, when the odds seemed stacked against him. In the prophets, we see how it is possible to draw strength from God through prayer, even when things are difficult. The Catechism reminds us that the prophets argued with or complained to God in their prayers at times, but their prayers were always intercessions offered in anticipation of the coming of the Savior. (2582–2584)

Teachable Moment

The Psalms are considered the "masterwork" of prayer in the Old Testament. This is where the word of God becomes humanity's own prayer. The Catechism explains that the Psalms are both personal and communal. Even when a particular Psalm reflects an event of the past, it still possesses a direct simplicity that allows it to be prayed in truth by people of all times and conditions. (2585–2589)

Jesus Teaches Us

Jesus, as we discussed at the beginning of this book, is both fully human and fully divine. So what did this mean for his prayer life? Did he have to learn to pray like the rest of us, or did he know how to pray from the get-go because he is the Son of God? The Catechism states that Jesus, in order to pray from his human heart, learned the formula and words of prayer from his mother and the traditions of the Jewish faith. However, Jesus also had a "secret source," which was first revealed when he, at age 12, remained at the temple in Jerusalem after his parents had gone. The "secret source" is his God-ness and his intimate connection to the Father. In the fullness of time, the prayer of Jesus is revealed as the prayer of a child to his Father, a prayer that the Father awaits from all his children, a prayer which, in the end, is going to be lived out by the only Son in his humanity, with and for all people. (2599)

Throughout the Gospels, we see Jesus praying before the decisive moments of his life, including his baptism and Passion, and before the important moments in his apostles' lives and mission. In Jesus we recognize the importance of prayer in our own lives, watching as he withdrew in solitude to pray in secret. In his prayer, Jesus included all people, for he took on humanity and offered all of us to the Father when he offered himself. (2600–2602)

Through Jesus we learn not only the words of prayer—such as the Our Father, which we will discuss at length in Chapter 25—but also the *attitude* of prayer. It is not just what we say but how we say it. (2607)

Jesus first expects a "conversion of heart" on the part of his disciples, which means we must forgive, love, and seek God above all else. That conversion then leads us to pray in such a way that we go to the Father fully expecting he will hear us. That doesn't mean we'll always get the outcome we desire, however. (2608–2610) It means that when we pray, even if we pray for something specific, we understand that God will answer it the way he sees fit, and we open ourselves up in prayer to cooperating with God's plan for us. (2611)

Jesus disclosed to his early disciples and to us that, once he had returned to his Father, we are to pray, asking "in his name." Faith in the Son results in the certainty that our prayer will be heard because it is founded on the prayer of Jesus. (2614)

Mary: The New Eve

Mary has a distinct role in teaching us the meaning of prayer, which is fully open to the will of the Father. Remember her fiat, which we discussed earlier in this book? That is when, during the Annunciation, the angel Gabriel told her that she would bear Jesus, son of David and Son of God, and she said, "Behold, I am the handmaid of the Lord. May it be done to me according to your word." (Luke 1:38) So in Mary, we see true cooperation with the Father, being wholly God's because he is wholly ours. (2618)

Later, during Jesus' ministry, we saw Mary at the scene of one of Jesus' first miracles, the changing of water into wine at the wedding feast at Cana. Scripture gives us this wonderful exchange between mother and son:

When the wine ran short, the mother of Jesus said to him, "They have no wine." And Jesus said to her, "Woman, how does your concern affect me? My hour has not yet come." His mother said to the servers, "Do whatever he tells you." (John 2:3–5)

Now, at first glance this could just seem like a mother telling her son what to do, but it's so much more than that. It was Mary doing exactly what Jesus told his disciples to do: ask for what you want in prayer and it will be given to you. She didn't doubt for one minute that Jesus would do what she had asked on behalf of someone else. And what she asked for at the Cana wedding feast looked forward to another feast: the Eucharist, the Wedding of the Lamb of God who gives his body and blood at the request of his Bride, the Church. (2618)

At the foot of the cross, when Jesus looked down on his mother and the beloved disciple, he said to his mother, "Woman, behold your son," and to the disciple he said, "Behold your mother." (John 19:26) In that moment, Jesus ushered Mary in as the "new Eve," proclaiming her to be mother of all the living. What this is saying is we can go to our mother, Mary, and ask her to intercede on our behalf, as she did at Cana. (2618)

Teachable Moment

The Magnificat, also known as the Canticle of Mary, is the prayer Mary said after greeting her cousin Elizabeth, who was pregnant with John the Baptist. "My soul proclaims the greatness of the Lord; my spirit rejoices in God my savior …," Mary said. (Luke 1:46–55) The Catechism explains that the Magnificat is not only the song of Mary but also that of the Church. The full text of the Magnificat is in the appendix on Catholic prayer at the back of this book. (2619)

Prayer Essentials

Before we get into the specific forms of prayer, we need to understand the role of the Holy Spirit in our prayer life. The Spirit, the Catechism explains, not only keeps the teachings of Jesus Christ alive in the Church, but also forms the prayer life of the Church, which is marked by the following characteristics: (a) it is founded on apostolic faith, (b) it is authenticated by charity, and (c) it is nourished in the Eucharist. (2623–2624)

Through Scripture and Tradition, the Church developed several forms of prayer: blessings, adoration, petition, intercession, thanksgiving, and praise.

Blessings and Adoration

The prayer of blessing expresses the basic movement of all Christian prayer—an upward movement and a downward movement. We send up our prayers, in the Holy Spirit through Christ, blessing the Father for blessing us. The prayer of blessing also implores the downward movement of the grace of the Holy Spirit that descends from the Father through Christ, by which the Father blesses us. (2626–2627) When we ask God to bless someone, for instance, it is as if we are dedicating that person to God's service or putting that person in God's care. It means we want good things to be with that person.

Adoration "exalts" the Lord, recognizing that he is our creator and savior. Through adoration we humbly pay homage to the Triune God. (2628) The Church offers adoration of the cross on Good Friday, when

Catholics commemorate the day that Jesus was crucified and humanity was redeemed through his sacrifice. Many Catholics regularly attend Adoration of the Blessed Sacrament, which is when the Eucharist is exposed on the altar so that people may pray before Jesus Christ and adore him.

Petitions and Intercessions

Prayers of *petition* are just what you'd expect. They are the prayers we send up when we are in need, whether we are begging for something in particular that we would like, or pleading for forgiveness and mercy due to something we regret. In our prayer of petition we pray first for the Kingdom, and then for what is necessary to welcome it and cooperate with its coming. (2629–2632)

Intercessions are prayers of petition on behalf of someone else. We are supposed to offer prayers of intercession not only for our friends but for our enemies as well. Intercessory prayer helps us to pray as Jesus did. (2634–2635)

Thanksgiving and Praise

Prayers of *thanksgiving* are how we thank God for all that he has given us, either in general or in particular. The celebration of the Eucharist is a prayer of thanksgiving. The Catechism explains that every event and need in the life of a Christian is cause for thanksgiving. (2638)

Prayers of *praise* are about giving glory to God not for what God does, but simply because God *is*. When we offer true prayers of praise, we have no ulterior motives or hopes to gain anything for ourselves. We're just praying because God deserves praise. (2639)

The Least You Need to Know

◆ Prayer is centered in our hearts and is God's gift to us.

◆ Jesus teaches us to pray not only through his words but by the way he prays, in faith, and with complete confidence in God's goodness and trust in his will.

◆ Mary gives us examples of prayer in her fiat and the Magnificat, both of which demonstrate her complete abandonment to the will of the Father.

◆ Forms of prayer include blessings and adoration, petition and intercession, thanksgiving and praise.

Chapter 24

The Way of Prayer

In This Chapter

- ◆ Praying to Jesus to reach God
- ◆ Understanding Marian prayer
- ◆ The guides for our prayer life
- ◆ Getting past obstacles to prayer

When we finally get down to the act of praying, sometimes it's hard to know exactly what to do. Do we have to say particular words for it to count? Do we have to be in a church? Do we have to close our eyes and clasp our hands together? Just what are the ground rules for a life of prayer? These are all legitimate questions, and we'll address them in this chapter.

The Church teaches that prayer should not be reduced to a laundry list of spontaneous thoughts. It should be formed by Scripture and Tradition and guided by the Holy Spirit. (2650–2651)

In this chapter, we will look at how to pray to the Father, Son, and Spirit, and how to pray *in communion* with Mary. We will also discuss prayer guides, different ways to pray, and habits and distractions that can prevent or disturb our prayers.

Sources of Prayer

For Catholics, prayer grows out of their experience with Scripture and liturgy, and is strengthened and deepened by the virtues of faith, hope, and charity. Prayer should be a part of everyday life. (2653–2660)

Teachable Moment

God has given us a name to use in prayer: "Jesus." Jesus is the name that "contains everything," the Catechism says. By becoming human, Jesus, the Word Incarnate, gave us a name that we could invoke and speak, a name that at once contains God and humanity and all of our salvation. (2666)

The Church teaches that the only way to reach the Father in prayer is through Christ. That is why Catholic prayers often end with the words: "We ask this through Christ, our Lord." That is why the Eucharistic prayer at Mass ends with "Through him, with him, in him, in the unity of the Holy Spirit, all glory and honor is yours, almighty Father, forever and ever."

Spirit of Prayer

The Holy Spirit is considered the "Master" of prayer. It is through the Spirit that we learn to pray to Jesus, and it is the Spirit who teaches us to pray. As we discussed in Chapter 8, the Holy Spirit is God as he remains on earth among us. We cannot see the Spirit. We cannot touch the Spirit. Most of the time we cannot even understand the Spirit, but we know it when we feel it. The Spirit pulls us toward God, gives us that feeling of peace that rests in our hearts when we are focused on our creator, and helps us to walk in the way of Christ.

When Jesus ascended to his father, he sent the Spirit, the Advocate, to his disciples so they would never be alone. It makes sense, then, that when we—Jesus' modern-day disciples—turn to God in prayer, it is the Spirit that leads the way, just as he did in the earliest days of the Church.

The Church says we should call on the Spirit daily and whenever we face important events or decisions in our lives because he is the guide God has given us while we are on earth. (2670–2672)

In Communion with Mary

Mary is an integral part of prayer life for Catholics. She is seen as the model pray-er. She said "Yes" to God, even when she was unsure of what that "Yes" would mean. She kept saying "Yes" to God, even at the foot of the cross. Even now she says "Yes" to God as she prays in the communion of the saints. The Church teaches that Jesus is the only mediator between God and humanity, the "way" of our prayers. Mary shows us the way to Jesus and is the sign of Jesus the way.

The Catechism explains that because of Mary's "unique cooperation" with the Holy Spirit, she has a special place in Christian prayer. *Marian prayers* do two things: They praise God for what he has done for us through Mary, and at the same time, Marian prayers give over to Mary our worries and needs so that she may intercede for us. (2675)

Church Speak

Marian prayers are prayers to and with Mary. The most common one is the *Hail Mary*.

The *Hail Mary* is the most common Marian prayer in the Catholic Church (see Appendix C for the full text of this prayer). The Hail Mary, or *Ave Maria*, which begins, "Hail Mary, full of grace, the Lord is with thee," reflects the greeting of the angel Gabriel to Mary at the annunciation: "Hail, favored one! The Lord is with you." (Luke 1:28)

Teachable Moment

The Rosary, which is a popular Catholic devotion to Mary, was developed in medieval times as a substitute for the Liturgy of the Hours. (An explanation of the Rosary is in Appendix C.) (2678)

In this prayer, which calls to mind that Mary is "blessed" among women, we ask Mary to "pray for us sinners," trusting that she will lead us closer to her Son.

The Rhythm of Prayer

When Catholics pray, they often look to the saints as guides. The lives and prayers of the saints serve as examples for those of us still working out the kinks on earth. Because Catholics believe that the saints are with God, they are viewed as having the ability to intercede in prayer for those on earth. In other words, they go to bat for you with God. (2683)

Okay, so we have the Spirit, Mary, and the saints as prayer guides, but how do we learn to pray in the first place? The answer is from our families, the "domestic church" we talked about earlier. If the domestic church is doing its job, the family is praying together daily. The rest of our background in prayer comes from bishops, priests, deacons, religious sisters and brothers, religious education programs at parishes, prayer groups, and spiritual direction—which is one-on-one spiritual guidance. (2685–2690)

Teachable Moment

Does prayer require a church? Although church is the proper place for liturgical prayer and a place most conducive to personal prayer, it's not the only place for prayer. At the same time, however, the Catechism insists that "a favorable place is not a matter of indifference for true prayer." The Catechism says that if you cannot get to a church, you can create a "prayer corner" in your home with sacred images to foster a spirit of prayer. You may also want to locate a nearby monastery where you can join in the Liturgy of the Hours or pray quietly alone. Finally, there is the option of a pilgrimage, which is when you visit a sacred place, such as a shrine, in an effort to deepen your prayer life. (2691)

Vocal Prayer

Expressing yourself in prayer can be a very personal thing. There are different ways to pray, one of the most obvious being *vocal prayer*. The Catechism explains that through words either spoken aloud or in our minds, our "prayer takes flesh." The most important thing to remember in vocal prayer is that it's not enough for your lips to move; your heart must be moved as well. Words are just words unless they are accompanied by an interior attitude that transforms the exterior and physical aspect of prayer into a spiritual endeavor. The Our Father is an example of vocal prayer. (2700–2702)

Meditation

The Catechism says that meditation is a "quest" that helps us to better understand the ins and outs of our lives as Christians. Meditation can focus on Scripture, liturgical texts, and other works of spirituality, or sacred icons. Although there are many ways to meditate, a Christian must always advance "with the Holy Spirit" toward Jesus Christ. (2705–2708)

Contemplation

Contemplation is about focusing on Jesus in silence with the "gaze of faith," the Catechism says. It is an inner prayer offered in silence. It should be frequent and grounded in the word of God with the aim of forging a union with the prayer of Jesus Christ. (2709–2719)

On the Battlefield of Prayer

Now, if you've ever tried to pray—whether it was vocal, meditative, or contemplative—you probably came up against some obstacles, those things that distracted you or pulled you away from your prayer. The Catechism explains that the "spiritual battle" we often encounter in our daily lives cannot be separated from the battle we experience when we try to pray.

The Enemy Within

Why is prayer so difficult? If we have the will to pray, why can't we just quiet our minds and get the job done? Well, that's part of the problem. We humans tend to look at everything—including prayer—as something that has to be "done." Maybe we think we don't have time in our busy lives, or maybe we don't really see it as anything more than a ritual. Maybe the mysterious nature of prayer goes against the prove-it-to-me attitude we get from our modern society. Or maybe we just think we could spend our time in more profitable ways. (2726–2727)

When it comes to prayer, we need to put aside our wounded pride and our human expectations and surrender to God. The Catechism reminds us that this requires "humility, trust, and perseverance." (2728)

More than anything, however, we have to remember that it's normal to experience difficulties when we try to pray. Even the Church's greatest saints experienced periods of dryness, or as St. John of the Cross put it, the "dark night of the soul." That's part of the journey of prayer and faith. So the key is to keep from getting thrown off course or disappointed. Anything we do to improve our prayer life is worth something, whether it's five minutes every morning, one Mass each week, or a retreat once a year.

Prayer Interferences

One of the most common interferences we encounter in prayer is plain old *distraction*. We may start out with our thoughts on Christ, but another thought easily meanders in, which actually "reveals to us what we are attached to." Rather than focus on the distraction, we must continue to turn our attention back to our centers. When distractions come up in prayer, they should make us aware of what's holding us back and strengthen our resolve to purify our hearts. (2729)

Dryness is one of the great obstacles to contemplative prayer, and it can be a disheartening experience for someone who is trying hard to connect with God. What the Catechism means by dryness is "when the heart is separated from God, with no taste for thoughts, memories, and feelings, even spiritual ones." This is when we try to pray but we feel no connection to God. We feel alone and cut off, as if we are wandering in a spiritual desert with no shelter in sight.

When this happens, the urge might be to give up on prayer, but instead the Church teaches that we should hang on to Jesus with all our hearts and know that he will guide us out of the desert. The Catechism refers back to John 12:24, which says that "unless a grain of wheat falls into the earth and dies, it remains alone; but if it dies, it bears much fruit." We have to traverse through the dryness and allow the spiritually withered parts of ourselves die and drop away so that we can reconnect with God in a much deeper and lasting way. (2731)

Hello? Is This Thing On?

Probably one of the most common prayer complaints is that God doesn't seem to be listening. We pray and we pray, and we beg and we beg, and nothing. Or so it seems. What this actually comes down to is our view of God. Is he our Father who knows what is good for us, or is he like a mail-order warehouse, receiving our requests and sending out shipments by overnight mail?

The Catechism notes that when we thank God or praise God, we don't necessarily expect any immediate answer. But when we petition God for something concrete, we often expect immediate results. Our prayer must be motivated not by what we can get from God but by our desire to be closer to God and to accept his will even when it is not *our* will. As the old saying goes, God answers all prayers, but sometimes he answers "No." (2735–2737)

Pray Without Ceasing

How can we possibly pray without ceasing? When would we get anything else done? The Church teaches that we can "pray constantly." That doesn't meant we are in church 24/7. It means that prayer is woven into the fabric of our days. Prayer is not something we seek out only during crises, but something that draws us closer to Christ whether we are standing in line at the grocery store, sitting in a meeting at the office, or kneeling at Mass in a cathedral.

The Catechism explains that prayer is a "vital necessity" and that Christian life is "inseparable" from prayer life. And so we are called to unite our prayer to our work life, our home life, all of our life. (2742–2745)

The Least You Need to Know

- ◆ To have access to God the Father in prayer, Christians must go through Jesus Christ with the help of the Holy Spirit.
- ◆ Catholics pray to and with the Virgin Mary because she can "show the way" to Jesus Christ, who is "the way," and because of her unique collaboration with the Spirit.

◆ There are three main ways to express prayer: through vocal prayer, meditation, and contemplation.

◆ It is common to battle with obstacles to and interferences during prayer.

◆ Christians are expected to accept God's will and are challenged to pray without ceasing.

Chapter 25

The Prayer of All Prayers: The Our Father

In This Chapter

- ◆ Understanding the Lord's Prayer as a whole
- ◆ What it means to call God "Father"
- ◆ Taking the *Our Father* one line at a time
- ◆ The perfect ending, the Final Doxology

Christians recognize the *Our Father*, also known as the Lord's Prayer, as the "perfect" prayer. When Jesus' disciples wanted to learn to pray, this is what he gave to them. To this day, the *Our Father* remains the central prayer of Christianity.

The Catechism explains that there are two different scriptural accounts of the Lord's Prayer. Luke's Gospel gives a text of the Our Father with five "petitions," and Matthew's Gospel includes seven petitions (which we'll explain in detail in a minute). The Catholic Church's liturgical practice uses Matthew's text.

In this chapter, we will look at the Lord's Prayer in general, and then we will dissect it one line at a time in an effort to understand more fully the significance of this single prayer.

The Sum of Its Parts

The exact wording of the Our Father can vary across the Christian faith, yet the meaning remains the same. Catholics say the Our Father prayer as follows:

> Our Father, who art in heaven,
>
> hallowed be thy name;
>
> thy kingdom come;
>
> thy will be done on earth as it is in heaven.
>
> Give us this day our daily bread,
>
> and forgive us our trespasses,
>
> as we forgive those who trespass against us;
>
> and lead us not into temptation,
>
> but deliver us from evil.
>
> Amen.

The Catechism, in beginning its discussion of the Our Father, quotes Tertullian, a second-century writer, who said the Our Father is a "summary of the whole Gospel." (2761) This prayer, which St. Thomas Aquinas called "the most perfect of prayers," is found in Scripture in the middle of the Sermon on the Mount and presents to believers the main teachings of the Gospel. (2763)

Church Speak

The Our Father is often called the Lord's Prayer, or *Oratio Dominica*, because it was taught by the Lord himself, Jesus Christ. (2765)

According to the Catechism (which refers to the first-century *Didache*), in the Church's earliest communities the Our Father was prayed three times each day as a substitute for the Jewish custom of "Eighteen Benedictions," which were prayers of praise and petition seeking wisdom,

assistance and forgiveness. (2767) The Lord's Prayer figures promi-
nently in the sacraments of baptism and confirmation and in every celebration of the Liturgy of the Eucharist. In other words, for Catholics,
praying the Our Father is an integral element in personal and communal prayer, specifically the sacraments, the Mass, and the Divine Office.
(2768–2769)

Daring to Call God "Father"

Before Jesus walked on earth, God of the Old Testament was supremely
holy, a rather distant figure—a God whose name should not even be
spoken, a Creator whose presence often invoked trembling awe. But
Jesus, in his humanity, brought divinity to us and has brought us into
the Father's presence. Jesus became the mediator between heaven and
earth, enabling us to go to God as an approachable Father, a beloved
protector whom we could call by name in our time of need. (2777)

When we lead off with the words "Our Father" at the start of this
prayer, we acknowledge that we have become part of God's new covenant. Even more, he is "our" God. If we pray the Lord's Prayer "sincerely," the love we get from this prayer will free us from the kind of
"individualism" that threatens to pull us away from God and our neighbors. (2786–2792)

The second line of the Our Father is: "Who art in heaven." So what
does that mean? It's not talking about God sitting on some sort of
heavenly throne. Instead it's talking about "a way of being," meaning
God is majestic. But God is not out of our realm or beyond us. Heaven
is the symbol for the dwelling place of God; it is also a symbol for the
perfection of love. Because God is close to us, in a real way we are
already seated with God. (2794–2796)

The Seven Petitions

Now we get into the fine print: the seven *petitions* that make up the rest
of this famous prayer. Maybe we never thought of them as petitions, but
the Catechism explains that the rest of this prayer includes three "theological" petitions or blessings that pull us toward God, followed by four
petitions that commend our "wretchedness" to his grace. (2803)

Hallowed Be Thy Name

When we say the next line of the Our Father, "Hallowed be thy name," we are saying we adore God and recognize him as holy. If we don't acknowledge that God's name is holy right off the bat, we're going to be kind of lost in this prayer and in this Christian life. God is holy, and that belief must shine its light on everything else in our lives. God's "name" is the statement of who God is. Even though God's name is holy, meaning totally other and essentially inaccessible, our prayer is framed by our belief that the holy God has chosen to reveal his name to his people most fully in Jesus. (2807–2815)

> **Church Speak**
>
> **Petition** is when we ask God for something in prayer. In the Our Father, we are asking God for specific things that will lead us ever closer to him.

Thy Kingdom Come

Although God's "kingdom," God's "rule," is all around us, we are reminded that we are working our way toward the fullness of the kingdom—our final destination—in the next line, "Thy kingdom come." This petition of the Our Father refers primarily to the final coming of the rule of God through Christ's return. It reminds us that Christ will come again. The kingdom has been coming since the Last Supper; it is present and effective in the Eucharist; it will come in glory when Christ, having come again, hands it over to his father. In the meantime, between Christ's first and second comings, however, this petition also reinforces for us that we must make the kingdom come to life in our own lives each day. (2816–2821)

Thy Will Be Done

Next we have "Thy will be done on earth as it is in heaven." This is a tough line if you give it more than a minute's thought. This is where we pray to accept God's will in our lives. Like Jesus in the garden at Gethsemane, we pray that we will be willing to put aside our own desires so that the Father's plan for us can come to fruition. Not an easy sell, but it is a critical part of this prayer. Although this petition is tough, it is consoling as well, since God's will, on earth and in heaven, is that all of us be saved and come to the knowledge of the truth. (2822–2827)

Give Us This Day

When we say the next line, "Give us this day our daily bread," we are asking not only for the physical nourishment and support we need to survive on earth but the spiritual nourishment we need to help us achieve blessedness. The Catechism stresses that by saying "our" bread and not "my" bread, we are expressing a love of neighbor that leads us to share our material and spiritual wealth with those who are poor. When we pray that the Lord give us bread "this day," the Catechism tells us, we petition not only for the todays in our mortal time, but also for the today of God, which has no beginning or end. When we pray for "daily" bread, we pray not only for what will get us through the next 24 hours, but for the bread of the Lord's eternal day, the bread of the kingdom. (2828–2837)

Forgive Us Our Trespasses

The next full line of the Our Father says, "and forgive us our trespasses as we forgive those who trespass against us." This is another difficult teaching. Yes, we want God's forgiveness for what we've done wrong, but when we say this prayer sincerely, we are linking God's forgiveness of our sins with our forgiveness of the wrongs committed against us. We have to forgive—even our enemies—if we expect God to forgive us. (2839–2845)

True Confessions _____

The text of Matthew's Gospel uses the form of the Our Father that says, "… and forgive us our *debts*, as we forgive our *debtors*." (Matthew 6:12) The Latin form of the Our Father uses the term "debts" and "debtors" as well (*debita nostra/debitoribus nostris*). Catholics, however, say, "… and forgive us our *trespasses*, as we forgive those who *trespass* against us." Although the Our Father passage in Matthew uses the term "debts," what Jesus says in the next passage of Matthew makes it clear that the debts to be cancelled are sins. "If you forgive others their transgressions, your heavenly Father will forgive you." (Matthew 6:14)

Lead Us Not into Temptation

For this next line, you may be wondering why would God lead us into temptation in the first place, because isn't it Satan who does that? This line, "and lead us not into temptation," appears as "and do not subject us to the final test," in Matthew 6:13. The Catechism explains that some of the confusion lies in the translation. The Greek words mean that we want God to keep us from "entering" into temptation and to keep us from "yielding" to temptation. So God isn't tempting anyone; we're asking for his help to keep us from ever even going there in the first place. Through this prayer, we ask God to keep us from the temptation that is bound to find us because we are human. (2846–2849)

Deliver Us from Evil

The last line of the Our Father, "… but deliver us from evil," is a reference specifically to Satan. We are not invoking God's help against any kind of generic evil here. Here we are talking about the Evil One and all of the inherent evil that comes with him. (2850–2854) This line, on the heels of asking for help against temptation, further solidifies the petition to God for his help and protection from the things that keep us from him and his kingdom.

> **Church Speak**
>
> **Amen** is a Hebrew word that means, "So be it." It is often used to end prayers, signifying affirmation: Yes! I believe. Truly.

The Final Doxology

For Catholics, the Our Father ends there, with the petition for protection against evil. During Mass, the priest will say a prayer that expands on "Deliver us from evil," which is then followed by what is called the "final doxology." It goes like this: "For the kingdom, the power, and the glory are yours, now and forever." For Protestants, this doxology is recited within the Our Father prayer at the end, and it is usually recited as: "For thine is the kingdom, and the power, and the glory, forever. Amen."

The Catechism explains that the final doxology reinforces the first three petitions of the Lord's Prayer: the glorification of God's name, the coming of God's reign, and the power of God's saving will. Only now these prayers are "proclaimed as adoration and thanksgiving." The "Amen" at the end affirms it all. (2855–2856)

True Confessions

The final doxology, recited as part of the Our Father by Protestants and as a separate prayer in the Catholic Liturgy of the Eucharist, is not part of the actual prayer in the earliest texts of the Gospel of Matthew. The doxology is found in some of the later manuscripts (like the one used in the King James translation of the Bible) and may also be found, in a variant form, in the first-century *Didache*, considered by some to be the first unofficial catechism.

The Least You Need to Know

◆ The Our Father is considered "the most perfect of prayers" central to Christianity.

◆ Taught by Jesus to his disciples during the Sermon on the Mount, the Our Father of Catholic liturgical tradition is considered a summary of the Gospel.

◆ By becoming human, Jesus gave believers a real and approachable vision of God, a savior to be known and loved rather than a creator who cannot be approached.

◆ The Our Father contains seven petitions, found in Matthew's Gospel, that draw us closer to God.

Appendix A

Glossary

absolution   The act by which a priest, through the power given to the Church by Jesus Christ, forgives a penitent's sins during the sacrament of reconciliation.

Advent   The four-week period devoted to preparing spiritually for Christmas, the day that celebrates the birth of Jesus Christ.

amen   A Hebrew word meaning, "So be it," said at the end of most prayers.

angel   A free spiritual and intellectual creature that never had a mortal body and serves as God's messenger and servant.

annulment   A declaration by the Church that a marriage is invalid or "null" because one or both of the parties did not have the ability to fulfill the obligations of marriage or because a particular impediment prevented it from being the true covenant relationship that God intends marriage to be.

Annunciation   The moment when the angel Gabriel appeared to the Blessed Virgin Mary and announced that she would bear the Christ child through the power of the Holy Spirit.

anointing of the sick   One of the seven sacraments, a sacrament of healing that provides spiritual comfort and strength to those who are seriously ill or in danger of death.

Apostles' Creed   A profession of faith or "symbol of faith," summarizing the beliefs of the Catholic Church in prayer form and recited during the sacrament of baptism and during the renewal of baptismal vows.

Ascension   The moment the risen Jesus ascended body and soul into heaven.

Assumption   A Church teaching that the Virgin Mary was taken up to heaven, body and soul, at the end of her earthly life. The feast day marking this event is August 15.

baptism   The first of the seven sacraments, baptism frees believers from original and actual sin, gives them new birth, joins them to Christ in a permanent way, and incorporates them into the Church.

Beatitudes   A series of teachings Jesus gave during the Sermon on the Mount (Matthew 5:3–12). The word *beatitude* means "happiness" or "blessedness."

bishop   A successor to the apostles and a member of the college of bishops who is typically head of a particular diocese, or local church, assigned by the pope.

Blessed Sacrament   Another name for Eucharist, which is the body and blood of Christ under the appearance of bread and wine. It often refers to the reserved Eucharist kept in the tabernacle for adoration by the faithful.

canon law   The official laws and rules of the Catholic Church, which includes the Code of Canon Law, decrees by the Holy See (Vatican), and laws and decrees by bishops and religious superiors.

catechism   A manual of doctrine used to teach the faith.

catholic   With a lowercase "c," this word means "universal." Eastern Orthodox Churches and some Protestant denominations use the word "catholic" in their creeds.

Communion   The body and blood of Jesus Christ received by Catholics at Mass and during sacramental celebrations.

confession   The part of the sacrament of reconciliation (sacrament of penance) when a penitent confesses his or her sins. Sometimes it is a term used to describe the sacrament of reconciliation through which any sins that have been committed since baptism are forgiven by the absolution of a priest.

confirmation   A sacrament by which the baptized continue on their path of Christian initiation, are enriched with the gifts of the Holy Spirit, and are more closely linked to the Church. As a result of this sacrament, marking them with an indelible seal of the Holy Spirit, those who are confirmed are made strong and more firmly committed to Christ by word and deed, and to spread and defend the faith.

creed   A statement of a community's belief, also known as a symbol of faith.

covenant   A solemn agreement that contains promises but also imposes obligations.

deacon   A member of the ordained clergy who has the capacities to baptize, officiate at weddings, distribute Communion, proclaim the word of God, preach the homily at liturgies, celebrate Benediction of the Blessed Sacrament, and preside at funerals. They may not celebrate Mass, hear confessions, confer holy orders, or administer the anointing of the sick. Transitional deacons are men working toward the priesthood; permanent deacons are men who will remain deacons for the rest of their lives. Unlike priests, permanent deacons may be married.

Decalogue   Another name for the Ten Commandments given to Moses on Mount Sinai.

diocese   A portion of the People of God in a particular geographic area, headed by a bishop.

disciple   A follower of Jesus Christ.

encyclical   A letter written by the pope and distributed to the universal Church and often to the world at large in order to convey Church teaching on a particular matter.

Eucharist   One of the seven sacraments, Eucharist is the memorial of the sacrifice of the cross, a meal in which the body and blood of Jesus Christ is present under the appearance of bread and wine. It is considered the "source and summit" of the Christian faith. It also refers to the form of blessed bread and wine in which the Lord Jesus is really, truly and substantially present.

evangelization   To proclaim the Gospel in order to bring others to Jesus Christ.

excommunication   A penalty that removes a Catholic from communion with the Church, excluding him or her from participating in the Eucharist and other sacraments due to a grave offense against the faith.

Good News   The root meaning of the word "gospel," it refers primarily to the story of the life, teachings, death, and resurrection of Jesus as they are found in the books of Matthew, Mark, Luke, and John in the New Testament. The term also refers to the reflection on the life and death of Jesus in the other books of the New Testament.

Gospel   The account of the life, teachings, death, and resurrection of Jesus Christ as revealed in the books of Matthew, Mark, Luke, and John in the New Testament.

grace   A supernatural gift that God bestows on men and women to allow them to participate in the divine life, to help them live as children of God, and to enable them to achieve eternal salvation.

holy orders   One of the sacraments of commitment or service, when a man is ordained a bishop, priest, or deacon.

Holy Spirit   The third person of the Holy Trinity. When Jesus ascends to his Father, he, together with the Father, sends the Spirit—also known as the Paraclete, the Advocate, and the Consoler—to dwell in the hearts of believers and in the Church.

Immaculate Conception   The term used for the Catholic dogma that states the Blessed Virgin Mary was, from the first moment of her conception, preserved from original sin in anticipation of the role she would play in bringing God's Son into the world. The feast day for this event is December 8. This doctrine, which concerns Mary's conception, is often confused with the way Jesus was conceived, virginally.

Incarnation   The doctrine that the second person of the Trinity assumed human flesh and, in Jesus Christ, was at once truly human and truly God.

Lent   The 40-day season of spiritual preparation before Easter, usually marked by prayer, fasting, and works of charity.

liturgy   The Church's official public worship, separating it from private prayer. The Catholic Mass and the sacraments are examples of liturgy.

magisterium   The Church's teaching authority, which is founded on the authority of the first apostles and which rests today with the pope and the college of bishops.

Mass   A liturgical action in which Catholics gather to pray, receive the word of God, and celebrate the Eucharist.

matrimony   One of the sacraments of commitment or service, also called marriage, referring to the covenant relationship established between a man and a woman. The marriage partnership serves the well-being of the spouses and the procreation and upbringing of children. To be a sacrament, a marriage must be between two baptized Christians.

Nicene Creed   A profession of faith that was begun by the Ecumenical Council of Nicea in 325 and is recited by the faithful during Mass.

original sin   Refers, first, to the sin of prideful disobedience by Adam and Eve, humanity's first parents, in the Garden of Eden, and secondly, to the consequence of that sin in us. All humans (except Jesus and the Virgin Mary) inherit this sin, which is washed away during baptism.

Passion   Refers to the suffering and death Jesus Christ endured, from the Last Supper to his Crucifixion.

penance   Another name for the sacrament of reconciliation. In this sacrament, the faithful who confess their sins to a priest, and who are sorry for those sins, receive from God, through the absolution given by the priest, forgiveness of any sins they have committed since baptism, and at the same time are reconciled to the Church. Penance is also the word used to describe either an interior disposition or exterior action that moves a person away from sin and its consequences and closer to God.

Pentecost   Commemorates the day described in the Book of Acts when the Holy Spirit descended upon the apostles. The solemnity of Pentecost is celebrated 50 days after Easter.

pope The bishop of Rome and head of the college of bishops and successor to St. Peter, the first pope, he is the vicar of Christ on Earth and pastor and head of the universal Church.

priest A man ordained by a bishop through the sacrament of holy orders to serve the Church. He shares in the bishop's tasks of teaching, leading, and making holy the People of God.

prophet Someone sent by God to proclaim God's word and to speak in God's name.

purgatory A place of purification for those who have died in God's grace and friendship but need to be purified further in order to enter heaven.

reconciliation Another term for the sacrament of penance or confession. (*See* penance.)

Resurrection With a capital "R," refers to the Resurrection of Jesus Christ from the dead three days after his Crucifixion. With a lower case "r," it refers to the resurrection of all people after death. Resurrection of the body means that our mortal bodies will become incorruptible and will be reunited with our souls through the power of Jesus' Resurrection.

Rosary A prayer to Mary composed of a series of Hail Marys and Our Fathers and other prayers recited in a repeated pattern. It also refers to the string of beads used to count the prayers.

sacraments The seven sacraments, instituted by Christ and entrusted to the Church, that are signs and means through which the faith is expressed and strengthened: baptism, confirmation, Eucharist, reconciliation or penance, anointing of the sick, holy orders, and matrimony.

saint A holy person who has lived an exemplary life of faith while on earth and now resides in heaven with God for all eternity. Saints serve as models of the Christian life and as intercessors with God for their fellow Christians. The pope can canonize a deceased person as a saint of the Church, but any deceased person who is in heaven is a saint, whether the Church officially declares it to be so or not.

Scripture The writings contained in both the Old and New Testaments.

Sign of the Cross A common Christian prayer that acknowledges and honors the Holy Trinity. A person forms a cross by marking forehead, heart, and each shoulder, first the left and then the right, with the right hand while saying the following words: "In the name of the Father and of the Son and of the Holy Spirit."

soul The spiritual part of human beings that lives on after the body dies.

Ten Commandments The essence of the "Old Law" given to Moses by God on Mount Sinai. Also known as the Decalogue.

Tradition With a capital "T," refers to the living faith that is not necessarily contained in Scripture but is handed down from generation to generation, first by the apostles and now by their successors, the bishops.

Transfiguration The moment when Jesus was transformed and appeared between Elijah and Moses in the presence of the disciples Peter, James, and John. A voice from heaven spoke, revealing not only Jesus' divinity and his role as the divine word of revelation but also his role as the suffering servant of God.

transubstantiation The term used to describe the change of bread and wine into the body and blood of Jesus Christ during the Eucharistic celebration.

Trinity The central Christian doctrine about God, affirming that there are three persons in one God: Father, Son, and Spirit. Each person of the Trinity has existed since before time began and each is fully divine and distinct from the other, and yet they are one.

Virgin Mary The Mother of Jesus Christ, who was chosen by God to bear his son through the power of the Holy Spirit. She is known by many names, including Saint Mary and Mother of God.

vocation A person's "calling," which has its origins in God. The Church teaches that every person has a vocation, which is part of God's plan.

Word of God All of God's revelations to humanity as expressed in human words in the Old Testament and New Testament. It is also a reference for Jesus.

Additional Resources

Reference Books

The Companion to the Catechism of the Catholic Church: A Compendium of Texts Referred to in the Catechism of the Catholic Church. San Francisco: Ignatius Press, 1994, 2002.

Hardon, John A. *Pocket Catholic Dictionary*, abridged edition of *Modern Catholic Dictionary*. New York: Doubleday, 1985.

Libreria Editrice Vaticana. *Compendium of the Catechism of the Catholic Church.* Washington, D.C.: USCCB Publishing, 2005.

Livingstone, E.A. *Concise Dictionary of the Christian Church.* New York: Oxford University Press, 2006.

The New American Bible for Catholics. New Jersey: World Catholic Press, 1990.

Spiritual Reading and Prayer Books

Bishops' Committee on the Liturgy. *Catholic Household Blessings & Prayers*. Washington, D.C.: USCCB Publishing, 1988.

Buckley, Michael (ed.) *The Catholic Prayer Book*. Ann Arbor, MI: Servant Publications, 1986.

Haase, Albert. *Swimming in the Sun: Discovering the Lord's Prayer with Francis of Assisi and Thomas Merton*. Cincinnati, OH: St. Anthony Messenger Press, 1993.

Martin, James. *My Life with the Saints*. Chicago: Loyola Press, 2006.

Pope John Paul II. *Crossing the Threshold of Hope*. New York: Alfred A. Knopf, 1995.

Ratzinger, Joseph (Pope Benedict XVI). *Jesus of Nazareth*. New York: Doubleday, 2007.

Scaperlanda, Maria Ruiz. *The Complete Idiot's Guide to Mary of Nazareth*. Indianapolis, IN: Alpha, 2006.

———. *The Seeker's Guide to Mary*. Chicago: Loyola Press, 2002.

Websites

Holy See

www.vatican.va

The Vatican's official site, available in six languages, provides links to everything from papal encyclicals and messages to news photos and archives.

United States Conference of Catholic Bishops

www.usccb.org

Statements of the U.S. bishops on public policy issues, links to American Catholic dioceses, the New American Bible, and numerous other resources.

Canadian Conference of Catholic Bishops

www.cccb.ca

Includes access to documents and statements by the bishops of Canada, as well as links to Canadian dioceses.

U.S. Catholic Bishops Office for the Catechism

www.usccb.org/catechism

An entire site dedicated to the Catechism of the Catholic Church, its history, Frequently Asked Questions, articles, and more.

Bible Search Engines

www.usccb.org/nab/bible

This site enables you to search the New American Bible translation of the Bible, including the deuterocanonical books of the Catholic Bible.

www.biblegateway.com

This site enables you to search the Bible by book, topic, verse, language, and Bible version. (The deuterocanoncial books of the Catholic Bible are not included here.)

Catholic Encyclopedia

www.newadvent.org/cathen

A useful tool for those seeking more in-depth information on people, subjects, and facts related to Catholic topics.

Catholic Online

www.catholic.org

This site is a clearinghouse for news and feature stories from a variety of Catholic periodicals around the country.

Daily Scripture Readings

www.usccb.org/nab

The Scripture readings for each day in the Catholic liturgical cycle are provided here in the New American Bible translation.

Mass Times for Travel

www.masstimes.org

Find Mass times at any parish across the United States or around the world by zip code, city, and/or country.

Sacred Space

www.sacredspace.ie

This site provides daily online guided prayer from the Jesuit Communication Centre in Ireland.

A Treasury of Catholic Prayers

Traditional Prayers

Sign of the Cross

In the name of the Father and of the Son and of the Holy Spirit.
Amen.

The Our Father (Lord's Prayer)

Our Father, who art in heaven,

hallowed be thy name;

thy kingdom come;

thy will be done on earth as it is in heaven.

Give us this day our daily bread,

and forgive us our trespasses,

as we forgive those who trespass against us;

and lead us not into temptation,

but deliver us from evil.

Amen.

The Hail Mary

Hail Mary, full of grace,

the Lord is with thee.

Blessed art thou among women,

and blessed is the fruit of thy womb, Jesus.

Holy Mary, Mother of God,

pray for us sinners,

now and at the hour of our death.

Amen.

Glory Be

Glory be to the Father

and to the Son

and to the Holy Spirit,

as it was in the beginning,

is now and ever shall be,

world without end.

Amen.

Apostles' Creed

I believe in God,

the Father Almighty,

creator of heaven and earth,

and in Jesus Christ, his only Son, our Lord,

who was conceived by the power

of the Holy Spirit,

and born of the Virgin Mary.

He suffered under Pontius Pilate,

was crucified, died, and was buried.

He descended into hell.

On the third day he rose again.

He ascended into heaven

and is seated at the

right hand of the Father.

He shall come again to judge

the living and the dead.

I believe in the Holy Spirit,

the holy Catholic Church,

the communion of saints,

the forgiveness of sins,

the resurrection of the body,

and life everlasting.

Amen.

Act of Contrition

O my God, I am heartily sorry

for having offended Thee,

and I detest all of my sins

because of thy just punishments,

but most of all because they offend Thee,

my God, who art all good

and deserving of all my love.

I firmly resolve with the help of Thy grace

to sin no more and

to avoid the near occasion of sin.

Amen.

Jesus Prayer

Lord Jesus Christ, Son of God, have mercy on me, a sinner.

Prayer to the Holy Spirit

Come, Holy Spirit,

fill the hearts of your faithful,

and enkindle in them the fire of your love.

Send forth your Spirit and they shall be created.

And you shall renew the face of the earth.

Let us pray.

O God, who has taught the hearts

of the faithful by the light of the Holy Spirit,

grant that by the gift of the same Spirit

we may be always truly wise and

ever rejoice in his consolation.

We ask this through Christ our Lord.

Amen.

Hail, Holy Queen

Hail, Holy Queen,

Mother of Mercy,

our life, our sweetness, and our hope.

To thee do we cry,

poor banished children of Eve.

To thee do we send up our sighs,

mourning and weeping in this valley of tears.

Turn then, most gracious advocate,

thine eyes of mercy toward us,

and after this our exile

show unto us the blessed fruit of thy womb, Jesus.

O clement, O loving, O sweet Virgin Mary.

Pray for us, O holy Mother of God.

That we may be made worthy of the promises of Christ.

Amen.

The Magnificat

My soul proclaims the greatness of the Lord,

my spirit rejoices in God my Savior,

for he has looked with favor on his lowly servant.

From this day all generations will call me blessed.

The Mighty One has done great things for me and holy is his name.

He has mercy on those who fear him in every generation.

He has shown might with his arm;

he has scattered the proud in their conceit.

He has cast down the mighty from their thrones,

and has lifted up the lowly.

He has filled the hungry with good things,

and the rich he has sent away empty.

He has come to the help of his servant Israel

for he has remembered his promise of mercy,

the promise he made to our fathers,

to Abraham and his children forever. (cf Luke 1:46–55)

The Memorare

Remember, O most loving Virgin Mary, that never was it known that anyone who fled to your protection,

implored your help, or sought your intercession

was left unaided.

Inspired by this confidence,

I fly unto you, O virgin of virgins, my mother.

To you I come, before you I stand,

sinful and sorrowful.

O Mother of the Word Incarnate, despise not my petitions,

but in your mercy hear and answer me.

— St. Bernard

Angel of God

Angel of God,

my guardian dear,

to whom God's love

commits me here,

ever this day be at my side,

to light and guard,

to rule and guide.

Amen.

Prayer for Peace (Prayer of St. Francis)

Make me an instrument of your peace.

Where there is hatred, let me sow love.

Where there is injury, pardon,

where there is doubt, faith,

where there is despair, hope,

where there is darkness, light,

and where there is sadness, joy.

O Divine Master, grant that I may not

so much seek to be consoled,

as to console;

to be understood, as to understand;

to be loved as to love.

For it is in giving that we receive;

it is in pardoning that we are pardoned,

and it is in dying that we are born

to eternal life.

Amen.

How to Pray the Rosary

1. Holding the cross on your Rosary beads, make the Sign of the Cross and recite the Apostles' Creed.

2. On the first separate bead, say the Our Father.

3. On each of the next three beads, say a Hail Mary.

4. On the next separate bead (or medal, depending on your Rosary beads), announce the first mystery and say an Our Father.

5. On the next 10 beads, say a Hail Mary on each bead. End the decade on the next bead with a Glory Be.

6. Repeat this process for the next four decades, or forty beads: announcing the mystery, then saying the Our Father, then the Hail Marys, then the Glory Be, until you go around the entire set of beads. While going through each decade and saying each prayer, reflect or meditate on the story of the principal mystery (fixing that story or image in your mind).

7. End with the Hail Holy Queen.

Joyful Mysteries (recited on Monday and Saturday)

The Annunciation

The Visitation

The Birth of Our Lord

The Presentation in the Temple

The Finding of the Child Jesus in the Temple

Luminous Mysteries (recited on Thursday)

The Baptism in the Jordan

The Wedding at Cana

The Proclamation of the Kingdom of God

The Transfiguration

The Institution of the Eucharist

Sorrowful Mysteries (recited on Tuesday and Friday)

The Agony in the Garden

The Scourging at the Pillar

The Crowing with Thorns

The Carrying of the Cross

The Crucifixion

Glorious Mysteries (recited on Wednesday and Sunday)

The Resurrection

The Ascension of our Lord

The Descent of the Holy Spirit

The Assumption of Our Lady into Heaven

The Coronation of the Blessed Virgin Mary

The Stations of the Cross

Stations of the Cross, or Way of the Cross, refers to a devotion that commemorates the Passion of Jesus Christ. Typically, one would pray in front of a series of 14 pictures or sculptures in a church, shrine, or garden depicting scenes from the final events of Jesus' life. Before each station one recites the following prayer:

We adore you, O Christ, and we praise you. Because by your holy cross you have redeemed the world.

First Station: Jesus is condemned to death.

Second Station: Jesus takes up his cross.

Third Station: Jesus falls the first time.

Fourth Station: Jesus is met by his mother.

Fifth Station: Simon of Cyrene helps Jesus carry his cross.

Sixth Station: Veronica wipes the face of Jesus.

Seventh Station: Jesus falls a second time.

Eighth Station: The women of Jerusalem mourn for our Lord.

Ninth Station: Jesus falls for the third time.

Tenth Station: Jesus is stripped of his garments.

Eleventh Station: Jesus is nailed to the cross.

Twelfth Station: Jesus dies on the cross.

Thirteenth Station: Jesus is taken down from the cross.

Fourteenth Station: Jesus is placed in the tomb.

Catholic Basics

The Ten Commandments

1. I am the Lord your God. I brought you out of the land of Egypt; you shall have no other gods before me.

2. Do not take the name of the Lord your God in vain.

3. Keep holy the Sabbath.

4. Honor thy father and mother.

5. You shall not kill.

6. You shall not commit adultery.

7. You shall not steal.

8. You shall not bear false witness against your neighbor.

9. You shall not covet your neighbor's wife.

10. You shall not covet your neighbor's goods.

Jesus' "New" Commandment

You shall love the Lord your God with all your heart, with all your soul, and with all your mind, and you shall love your neighbor as yourself.

The Beatitudes

Blessed are the poor in spirit,

for theirs in the kingdom of heaven.

Blessed are they who mourn,

for they will be comforted.

Blessed are the meek,

for they will inherit the land.

Blessed are they who hunger and thirst

for righteousness,

for they will be satisfied.

Blessed are the merciful,

for they will be shown mercy.

Blessed are the pure of heart,

for they will see God.

Blessed are the peacemakers,

for they shall be called children of God.

Blessed are those who are persecuted

for the sake of righteousness,

for theirs is the kingdom of heaven.

Blessed are you when they insult you

and persecute you and utter every kind of

evil against you falsely because of me.

Rejoice and be glad, for your reward

will be great in heaven. (Matthew 5:3–12)

The Corporal Works of Mercy

1. Feed the hungry.
2. Give drink to the thirsty.
3. Clothe the naked.
4. Shelter the homeless.
5. Visit the sick.
6. Visit the imprisoned.
7. Bury the dead.

The Spiritual Works of Mercy

1. Counsel the doubtful.

2. Instruct the ignorant.

3. Admonish sinners.

4. Comfort the afflicted.

5. Forgive offenses.

6. Bear wrongs patiently.

7. Pray for the living and the dead.

Index

D

M

T-U

"To their great credit, the authors sidestep all temptations to fly to either a liberal or conservative extreme."

Mitch Finley, author of *The Seeker's Guide to Being Catholic* in *St. Anthony Messenger*

"Kind of the autobiography of Catholicism—the story told... from the inside."

The Catholic New World

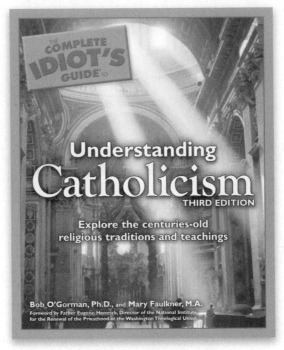

THE COMPLETE IDIOT'S GUIDE to

Understanding
Catholicism
THIRD EDITION

Explore the centuries-old
religious traditions and teachings

Bob O'Gorman, Ph.D., and Mary Faulkner, M.A.
Foreword by Father Eugene Hemrick, Director of the National Institute
for the Renewal of the Priesthood at the Washington Theological Union

978-1-59257-535-0

The Complete Idiot's Guide® to Understanding Catholicism, Third Edition, explores exactly what it means to be Catholic—from its ancient origins to its role in modern times.

ALPHA

idiotsguides.com